Creativity in Research

Creativity is at the heart of successful research, yet researchers are rarely taught how to manage their creative process and modern academic life is not structured to optimize creativity. *Creativity in Research* provides concrete guidance on developing creativity for anyone doing or mentoring research. Based on a curriculum developed at Stanford University's Hasso Plattner Institute of Design, this book presents key abilities that underlie creative research practice through a combination of scientific literature on creative confidence, experiential exercises, and guided reflection. By focusing attention on how research happens as well as its outputs, researchers increase their ability to address research challenges and produce the outputs they care about. Simultaneously, they may also transform their emotional relationship with their work, replacing stress and a harsh inner critic with a more open and emotionally empowered attitude.

NICOLA ULIBARRI is an assistant professor in Urban Planning and Public Policy at University of California, Irvine, USA. Her research investigates the environmental, social, and regulatory dimensions of infrastructure planning and management.

AMANDA E. CRAVENS is a research social scientist for a US federal agency. She cofounded the Research as Design project to adapt design thinking training for researchers with Nicola, Anja, and Adam when she realized how much her past experience as a web designer was influencing her scholarship.

ANJA SVETINA NABERGOJ is a lecturer at the Hasso Plattner Institute of Design at Stanford University, USA, where she teaches graduate classes and Executive Education programs. She also works with Fortune 500 companies on building their capacity for innovation.

SEBASTIAN KERNBACH is a lecturer, project manager, and researcher at the University of St Gallen, Switzerland and a visiting fellow at Stanford University, USA. He is the founder of the Visual Collaboration Lab (vicola.org) and the Life Design Lab (lifedesignlab.ch) in Switzerland.

ADAM ROYALTY is Lead Design Research Investigator at the Hasso Plattner Institute of Design at Stanford University, USA. He also founded the Columbia Entrepreneurship Design Studio, which amplifies peoples' problem-solving capacity through design.

Creativity in Research

Cultivate Clarity, Be Innovative, and Make Progress in Your Research Journey

NICOLA ULIBARRI AND
AMANDA E. CRAVENS WITH
ANJA SVETINA NABERGOJ,
SEBASTIAN KERNBACH,
ADAM ROYALTY

CAMBRIDGE
UNIVERSITY PRESS

CAMBRIDGE
UNIVERSITY PRESS

University Printing House, Cambridge CB2 8BS, United Kingdom

One Liberty Plaza, 20th Floor, New York, NY 10006, USA

477 Williamstown Road, Port Melbourne, VIC 3207, Australia

314–321, 3rd Floor, Plot 3, Splendor Forum, Jasola District Centre,
New Delhi – 110025, India

79 Anson Road, #06–04/06, Singapore 079906

Cambridge University Press is part of the University of Cambridge.

It furthers the University's mission by disseminating knowledge in the pursuit of
education, learning, and research at the highest international levels of excellence.

www.cambridge.org
Information on this title: www.cambridge.org/9781108484220
DOI: 10.1017/9781108594639

First published 2019

Printed in the United Kingdom by TJ International Ltd. Padstow Cornwall

A catalogue record for this publication is available from the British Library.

Library of Congress Cataloging-in-Publication Data
Names: Ulibarri, Nicola, 1987– author. | Cravens, Amanda E., 1982– author.
Title: Creativity in research : cultivate clarity, be innovative, and make
progress in your research journey / by Nicola Ulibarri and Amanda E. Cravens ;
with Anja Svetina Nabergoj, Sebastian Kernbach, and Adam Royalty.
Description: 1 Edition. | New York : Cambridge University Press, [2019] |
Includes bibliographical references and index.
Identifiers: LCCN 2019007843 | ISBN 9781108484220 (alk. paper)
Subjects: LCSH: Creative ability. | Research – Psychological aspects.
Classification: LCC BF408 .U437 2019 | DDC 153.3/5–dc23
LC record available at https://lccn.loc.gov/2019007843

ISBN 978-1-108-48422-0 Hardback
ISBN 978-1-108-70611-7 Paperback

Contents

v

Figures

Tables

Acknowledgments

This book is the result of a decade of learning, experimentation, and iteration. Along the way we have benefited from bountiful and generous feedback, support, and assistance, which we welcome the chance to acknowledge publicly.

The Hasso Plattner Institute of Design at Stanford University ("the d.school") nurtured and incubated our project, our curriculum, and the author team in our development as creativity educators. Each of us originally came to the d.school as a student of creativity and design; we are thankful for the guidance of our own teachers and mentors. We would like to share one story that illustrates this support. In September 2010, when we had just begun to think about the relationship between creativity and science, Amanda was taking a design immersion course and becoming increasingly convinced that there needed to be a course that tailored design thinking training for use specifically by researchers. As graduate students tend to do, Amanda assumed the best way to make this exciting new idea a reality was to convince one of her professors to sponsor it. Bernie Roth looked her in the eye and said, "That's a great idea. I think you should do something about it." Thank you, Bernie, for just the right challenge at the right moment. And thank you to the d.school for creating an educational environment that encourages students to take ownership of their own ideas. We are grateful to the many d.school staff and instructors who have provided input into our curriculum over the years, particularly Banny Banerjee, Thomas Booth, Charlotte Burgess-Auburn, Bill Burnett, Carissa Carter, Scott Doorley, Dave Evans, Kathryn Segovia, Sarah Stein Greenberg, Jeremy Utley, Terry Winograd, and Scott Witthoft.

Colleagues in other Stanford departments and offices have also provided invaluable intellectual, material, and logistical assistance, including the Emmett Interdisciplinary Program in Environment and Resources (Jen Mason, Deb Wojcik); Graduate School of Education (Nicole Ardoin); Vice Provost for Graduate Education (Helen Doyle, Chris Golde, Anika Green); School of Earth, Energy, and Environmental Sciences (Pamela Matson); and Woods Institute for the Environment (Meg Caldwell, Margaret Krebs).

At University of California, Irvine, Nicola would like to thank Scott Bollens, Martha Feldman, Nick Marantz, and Virginia Parks for guidance and support along the way. At University of Ljubljana, Anja would like to thank Marko Pahor and Mateja Drnovšek, heads of the Doctoral Program, for allowing her to prototype and test new content and learning experiences for doctoral students. Anja would also like to thank her mentor and friend at the d.school, Perry Klebahn, for helping her focus on things she cares deeply about. At University of St. Gallen, Sebastian would like to thank Martin J. Eppler for his feedback, insights, and guidance. Ashley Hooper provided research assistance, ably handling scientific literature on a wide array of topics. Malte Belau created the graphics that appear in the text, helping us coherently and playfully express our ideas.

Our curriculum development and the insights about creativity we had along the way simply would not have been possible without our incredible students. Through many iterations, they have experimented willingly with new ways of doing and thinking, shared bravely their triumphs and struggles, and collaborated enthusiastically across academic disciplines and types of challenges. They also participated willingly in our design-based research evaluations and gave candid feedback on exercises. Some have returned to our classes and workshops as coaches, providing an essential bridge between the student and teacher perspectives. We are particularly grateful to the students and colleagues who gave us permission to use their stories in the book. While we do not mention them by name here in order to preserve their anonymity, we reiterate our gratitude once again. We would also like to acknowledge Lindley Mease and Marilyn

Cornelius's significant contributions to the Research as Design project and curriculum.

We drew extensively on our own feedback network to write this book. Scott Bollens, Tom Hayden, Lauren Oakes, and Dan Stokols provided important feedback on our proposal and guidance on the process of finding a publisher. Profound thanks go to Kendra Brown, Scott Doorley, Mateja Drnovšek, Martin Eppler, Greg Marsden, Pamela Matson, Jamie McEvoy, Rebecca Nelson, Anne Siders, Julia von Thienen, Susie Wise, and Scott Witthoft for reviews of various versions of this manuscript. And thank you to our editor, David Repetto, and everyone at Cambridge University Press for supporting this project and shaping our final book.

Since the beginning, this project has been sustained by the collective passion of its authors. As a result, time and energy devoted to it have often had to be borrowed from precious family time. Thank you to Ryan McCarty; Andrej, Jun, and Zai Nabergoj; Kimberley Köttering; Cathy Chase, Romy, and Juno Chase Royalty; and of course Mighty Dog for their patience, continued support, and daily inspiration.

Finally, each of us would like to recognize our coauthors. We are grateful for our sustained partnership and the chance to work together to put these ideas out into the world.

1   The Creativity at the Heart of Your Research

Chloe was frustrated. She had spent the last week staring at a computer screen making absolutely no progress. At this point, her team had a contract with a publisher, chapter outlines, and were long past the brainstorming stage. The project was moving slower than expected. One coauthor was derailed by a family emergency, and the other was struggling to fit their work in between administrative duties and teaching, so Chloe was picking up the slack. But Chloe felt like an impostor writing about a field she didn't know as well as her coauthors, and she was entirely unsure how to get from the muck she and her team were stuck in to a finished book manuscript. She had solved many other problems through sheer force of will, and she desperately hoped she would be able to do the same with this one.

***

Alexander had spent the last few months alternating between being excited and overwhelmed. He was in the second semester of his PhD and had so many ideas for his dissertation work. Every time he attended a seminar or read a paper, it sparked a dozen new potential topics. While having all these new ideas was exhilarating, it was also exhausting. Whenever Alexander's advisor asked for his thoughts on research topics, he floundered – he really didn't know how to prioritize among his many ideas and thus would answer with a simple, "I'm not sure yet; I'm still exploring." For all his ideas, it felt like he was making no progress at all.

***

Paloma was a talented amateur painter who had even sold a few of her paintings in a local gallery. She had spent so many years experimenting with color on canvas that when she was painting, time seemed to disappear. She somehow simply knew what needed to happen next to create surprising new depictions of familiar locations in the city. When it came to her graduate work, however, she was a very analytical scholar, approaching her research on human–computer interaction methodically and afraid to do anything that had not been done before. Paloma kept bringing her advisor data she had analyzed, but she didn't know how to fix it when he looked at her attempts at analysis and kept pushing her to think bigger and break new ground as she considered how the variables might be related.

***

Eric had been hired into a tenure-track job based on his award-winning history dissertation. He loved the process of archival research: the pursuit of rare documents in the archives, the intellectual quest of telling a coherent story about the past based on often fragmented evidence, and the process of building an argument that took into account others' research and theories. The only trouble was, he was now responsible for teaching five courses a year, was traveling regularly for conferences, and was directing his department's undergraduate degree. All this, combined with a two-year-old daughter at home, meant that the amount of quiet time Eric had to think had essentially disappeared. He no longer felt like he had the space to produce quality history.

***

Each of these scholars faced a different challenge, but they actually needed the same tool: greater awareness of their creative research process. This book is a practical guide for researchers who want to apply creativity more effectively to the challenge of performing scholarly research.

Creative thinking provides a way to explore ambiguous, messy problems and find ways to resolve them. At its core, creativity is a problem-solving tool demonstrated countless times, from ancient humans creating early devices to harvest and hunt, to medieval artists expressing their artistic vision in cathedrals, to modern entrepreneurs developing groundbreaking technologies. In research, many times the big goal is clear: Earn the PhD, write a winning grant, finish the master's thesis, reach tenure, think up the next big thing in your field. But knowing which direction to go or how to move concretely toward that big goal is often not clear. This book is a distillation of methods you can use to build your creative competence and find effective paths toward your goals.

Each of the stories that led this chapter describes a real person sharing real concerns. All these people recognized the need for creativity in their research and sought out the classes and workshops that we've been leading for the last ten years. Our classes adapt design thinking and other approaches to building creativity to the specific needs and challenges of academic research.[1] Now, we offer the curriculum and exercises that we've developed in book form. Our students' experiences of learning to manage their creative process consciously compelled us to write this book. We provide practical guidance that combines the conversational tone of a workshop with the scholarly grounding to help you understand how these skills and techniques can be applied to your research. Whatever your background, discipline, or career stage, this book can give you concrete tools to gain clarity, be innovative, and make progress in your research journey.

THE CREATIVITY PARADOX OF MODERN RESEARCH

Creativity is the heart of research. No matter your field, scholarly work prizes novelty and innovation: identifying new problems worth solving, explaining unexplained phenomena, solving problems that haven't been solved before, producing new interpretations of important cultural or historical events, or developing new methods to study the world. While creativity is a nebulous construct (kind of a "you know it when you see it" thing), it is generally defined as the ability to produce new ideas or solutions.[2] This generation of novel ideas is the basis for innovation, so to be a truly innovative researcher, you need to be creative.[3]

In addition, scholarly research is messy, nonlinear, and ill-defined – not the clearly structured method you probably followed in high school science labs.[4] Doing research requires that you define a problem that is only partially known in advance, and you don't know whether an answer even exists until that answer is found. This means that researchers spend their days engaged in problem solving, by which we mean that they are taking a number of complex mental steps to reach solutions.[5] Every day you make small decisions, for instance whether to spend the next hour revising a manuscript, reading a paper, synthesizing a new lab sample, or getting a snack. And you make big decisions, like who to collaborate with or what topic to study for a research project. Each of these decisions forces your brain into problem-solving mode, and the same creativity skills used to generate new ideas can help you work through these decisions in a more innovative and effective way.

Unfortunately, though, modern research conditions don't support optimal creativity, so many scholars are not achieving their full creative potential.

First, many researchers are never explicitly taught how to be creative, which means that most learn about creativity by trial and error. Graduate students don't tend to receive instruction in creativity as part of their training. A lucky few PhD students might learn the skills to manage creativity from mentors; a few exceptional courses also cover these skills. Some scholars with hobbies or previous careers in "creative" fields like music, fiction writing, software design, or printmaking may bring those lessons to their research. But these are the exceptions, rather than the rule. The majority are self-taught creative scholars: Over multiple years and multiple projects, researchers develop an appreciation for creativity and tailor their own techniques. Most of the time, this learning is left to the learner to figure out, meaning it becomes more sporadic, difficult, and stressful than it has to be. Developing creative skills or strategies from scratch – under pressure because you need them – is about as fun and useful as reinventing a wheel because you are stuck somewhere without transportation. You get yourself wherever you need to go, which is the immediate goal, but perhaps you later realize that you could have done it with a bit less effort.

Second, academic life in the twenty-first century is not structured to foster creativity. Compare a day in your life to one of Charles Darwin's. When he wasn't sailing around the world in HMS *Beagle*, Darwin spent only a few hours in dedicated work. The bulk of his day was spent writing letters, going on walks, resting on the sofa, or eating with his family.[6] This is exactly the setup that people who study creativity would espouse: leaving plenty of downtime for reflection and an idle mind. Part of generating novel ideas is absorbing information and then coming up with new associations between things you have assimilated.[7] Activities where your mind isn't focused on a particular task, like going on a walk or daydreaming, help shift your mind into an idle state where generating and associating ideas is easier.[8] In fact, you can even distract your conscious mind with easy tasks like brushing your teeth – which probably explains why so many people say they have great ideas in the shower!

But if you're like most modern scholars, your daily reality is not creative idle time, but being busy. In an industry that was once considered relatively low-stress, surveys of academics point to increasing levels of stress, "identifying both mounting workload and an increasing pressure both to publish and acquire external research funding as significant contributory factors to academic distress."[9] It is increasingly hard to land a full-time job after completing the PhD, pressuring graduate students to come up with stellar research questions, publish a lot, and become well-known scholars just to land a job.[10] Successfully doing this requires significantly different abilities than succeeding in coursework (where a problem is handed to students).[11] The emotional investments are potentially greater, too, given the passions that lead many students to pursue a PhD in the first place. And once you do find that coveted job, if you are one of the lucky ones, surveys suggest that it's more difficult to obtain tenure now than it was ten years ago.[12] This leads to an unhealthy "publish or perish" mindset – especially among pre-tenure faculty.[13]

What this adds up to is a focus on productivity and outcomes. Open any publication or blog providing advice for academics and you'll find guidance on how to write regularly, manage your time better, or work more efficiently so you can produce more and/or maintain work–life balance. But rarely do you see advice telling academics to slow down and revisit how they are doing their research.[14]

The result is tragic but all too common: Just like Chloe and the others from the introduction, many researchers are frantically trying to produce as much innovative research as possible without doing the things that science suggests lead to optimal creativity. In other words, they are focusing on outputs without paying attention to the process by which their research happens or developing awareness of the conditions in which their creativity flourishes.

GUIDANCE FOR YOUR CREATIVE PROCESS

What if you could be more intentional about being creative? That's where this book comes in. Our team's goal is to save you and/or your students from the need to reinvent creative wheels.

By shifting from a focus purely on *content* and paying conscious attention to the creative *process* of research, you can create conditions that lead you toward the innovative outputs you ultimately desire. We want to highlight our use of the terms "content" and "process," as this is a key distinction we will make throughout the book. "Content" refers to the substance of research, such as finding a research question, figuring out which analytical technique to use, or deciding how to structure an argument in a manuscript. "Process" refers to the ways you move through your research, such as addressing writer's block, deciding when to ask a colleague for input on a draft paper, or deciding how to communicate a research idea in a way that excites your coauthor or PhD advisor. While content and process are closely intertwined, we'll encourage you to be conscious about the distinction and to practice designing creativity in both. Ultimately, a focus on creative process can yield more creative research content, making you more productive.

How do we do this? We give you tools and exercises to practice specific skills employed by creative scholars. There are plenty of books about how to be creative written by choreographers, writers, animators, designers, and other creative professionals.[15] But their examples and advice require translation to apply them to scholarly research. We as an author team have explored many of the mindsets, abilities, and tools that people in creative professions use and spent a decade applying, testing, and iterating them in the specific context of research.

First, this book explores four foundational abilities that reflect things that creative people do: being aware of your thoughts and behaviors, understanding and using emotions, making sure that you solve the right problem, and learning through iteration and experimentation. Second, we dive into three additional abilities that help create the conditions for creative thinking; we call these support structures. The support structures are using language and stories to generate the creative behaviors and identity you want to adopt, managing your energy to create motivation, and using input from other people to amplify your creativity. Together, these seven abilities (Figure 1.1) provide different cognitive, emotional, and behavioral lenses through which to operationalize creativity.

(Our framework is not the only one available for understanding the mental abilities that contribute to creativity and creative problem solving. We have focused on the abilities we believe to be most relevant in the research context. But if you'd like to explore how other scholars describe the mental attitudes underlying creativity, in the Appendix we have mapped the abilities we use to those that appear in other frameworks in the literature.)

For each ability, we provide guidance on what it is and how it works, as well as exercises for you to practice using it in your research. You might think of your research endeavors like a sport,

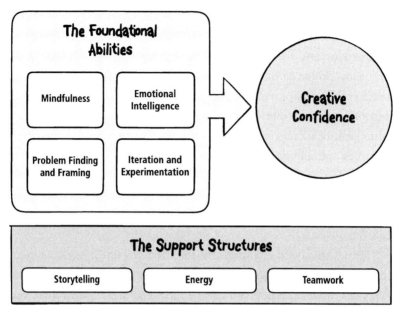

FIGURE 1.1 The creative abilities

where you need endurance, strength, flexibility, and balance to perform effectively. You do different exercises to develop these distinct skills, allowing you to combine them seamlessly when you perform during a competition. By practicing each of the creative abilities, you can increase your facility with generating novel ideas and solving problems – skills that will contribute to your overall creative research practice.

DEFINING CREATIVITY

What exactly do we mean when we say creativity? Is it about being imaginative? About being skilled at artistic endeavors? About generating new ideas or solutions?

A number of scholars who study creativity emphasize the final point – that creativity is about creating something new, whether that something is an idea or a product.[16] However, what counts as novel depends on whether you adopt what's called a "little-c" or "big-C" view of creativity.[17] According to big-C Creativity, the novel thing also has to be deemed "appropriate, useful, or valuable by a suitably knowledgeable social group."[18] In other words, a scientific idea or a work of art is deemed creative only if it is also judged to be creative by other people. In contrast, the little-c creativity also requires novelty, but not social recognition. In little-c creativity, a teacher figuring out a new way to encourage a shy student to engage in class would count as creativity, as would figuring out a way to repair a piece of broken lab equipment. Everything that is big-C Creative is also little-c creative, but not vice versa.

This book primarily adopts the little-c perspective. We are giving you the tools to solve familiar and unfamiliar problems in new ways and generate new ideas in your research process and outcomes. Some of these new ideas might reach the standard necessary for big-C Creative acclaim (which would be great for your research, career, and field!), but even if they don't there is much benefit to be gained from applying creative practices to your everyday research life.

Practicing the creative abilities will help you develop or strengthen a capacity called *creative confidence* (also known as creative self-efficacy): "a person's belief in their own ability or personal power to successfully create or produce desired change and envisioned outcomes," where the desired outcome is creating a novel or useful outcome.[19] We focus on creative confidence because it helps you act in a more creative way. Studies of creativity in the workplace have repeatedly shown that creative confidence correlates with innovative behavior and idea generation at both the individual and team level.[20] Essentially, if you know that you have the tools to solve problems creatively, logic suggests that you are more likely to both succeed in solving problems and in producing more innovative ideas.

Creative confidence relates to Albert Bandura's concept of self-efficacy and Carol Dweck's conception of a growth mindset. Self-efficacy refers to "people's beliefs about their capabilities to produce designated levels of performance that exercise influence over events that affect their lives. Self-efficacy beliefs determine how people feel, think, motivate themselves and behave."[21] A growth mindset refers to the belief that human abilities are things that one can cultivate; someone who possesses a growth mindset recognizes that their interests, strengths, and weaknesses can change as they have new experiences and gain new skills.[22] People who adopt a growth mindset are usually able to persevere in the face of the inevitable challenges that arise when they learn something new, helping them stay motivated and work toward mastery.[23] In contrast, holding a fixed mindset, wherein a person believes that individuals are born with certain traits (e.g., "I'm good at writing, but not good at math"), limits one's potential. These mindsets carry over to creativity: If you believe that some people are inherently creative and others aren't, it reduces your chances of ever becoming more creative.[24] A creative growth mindset, paired with a self-efficacious attitude, means that you believe you are capable of learning creativity. If you believe you can become more creative, you set yourself up to become so.

ON THE RELATIONSHIP BETWEEN CREATIVE AND ANALYTIC THOUGHT IN RESEARCH

"But wait!" you might say. "Doesn't doing good research require a rigorous, objective analytical process?" Yes . . . and it takes creativity too.

In the mid-twentieth century, Nobel Prize–winning biologist Peter Medawar wrote *Pluto's Republic*, a treatise on the scientific endeavor. In it, he argued that science is both ideas ("imaginative and exploratory . . . a great intellectual adventure") and critique ("a critical and analytical activity").[25] In other words, you have to have a great idea and then actually implement that idea. Research is both intuitive and analytical. This same pattern was shown in interviews of innovative scholars from diverse fields at Stanford University. When asked how they develop research projects, they emphasized the interplay between the imaginative, lateral thinking that goes into developing a good research question and the rigorous analysis necessary to test that question.[26]

Indeed, the interaction between idea generation and critique extends beyond research into other creative domains. Brain imaging shows that when you come up with creative ideas, you activate areas of your brain linked to associative, lateral thinking and areas associated with control and inhibition.[27] This highlights the continual interplay between creative and analytical thinking: Creative ideas are more likely to arise when the mind has been prepared by deep analytical thinking about a subject. The more you know, the more you have read, the more data you have worked with, and the more you have prepared the groundwork, the more fertile space there is for the generation of spontaneous connections. This link was recognized by the ancient Greeks, who used the same root word for "inventory" (i.e., the things you know) and "invention" (i.e., the things you create with what you know).[28]

In this book, we don't focus on analytical skills in the traditional sense, since there is already plenty written about how to do rigorous spectroscopy, or historiography, or radio telemetry, or grounded theory, or whatever particular methods your field uses. We offer guidance for cultivating creative research practice, which ultimately requires judgment about when to cast a wide net and when to pull it in.

WHO WE ARE, AND WHY WE'RE WRITING THIS BOOK

This book is the collective effort of a team of researchers and educators – Nicola, Amanda, Anja, Sebastian, and Adam – who came together at Stanford University with a common interest in creativity training for researchers.

We met at Stanford University's Hasso Plattner Institute for Design ("the d.school"), an institute focused on teaching innovative and creative problem solving through design. This approach includes *design thinking*, a creative problem-solving methodology that is inherently focused on addressing human needs.[29] As taught at Stanford, design thinking combines a defined innovation process with a set of mindsets and techniques for solving ill-defined problems. It emphasizes that innovation is a learnable process, not an event or an innate personality characteristic.[30] When the d.school exposes students to design thinking, its instructors aim to nurture creative confidence by teaching a set of abilities that are useful for creative work in any field. While design thinking initially grew out of product design and mechanical engineering, it has more recently been applied to solving challenges in a range of fields such as K–12 education,[31] medicine,[32] and international development.[33]

When we each converged on the d.school, it was focused on building the creative confidence and creative abilities of Stanford students through solving external problems like alleviating poverty and improving healthcare. While research students participating in these courses might gain important innovation and collaboration skills that complemented their domain expertise, for many of them, it was hard to translate those skills to their scholarly research. This is where we saw an opportunity. Because design thinking offers a learnable, repeatable method to address fundamental creative problem-solving challenges, why couldn't it be adapted for the numerous researchers at Stanford who faced creative challenges in their academic work on a daily basis? Thus, the Research as Design project – RAD for short – was born in 2010.

This book draws on our experience teaching the RAD curriculum and getting extensive iterative feedback from our students (primarily graduate students and postdocs, with occasional faculty and research staff participants) as well as from faculty colleagues in diverse disciplines and other teachers of design thinking. Beginning with our initial pilot with six students (read: "arm-twisted friends") in March 2011, we've taught RAD classes and workshops at universities and conferences on five continents. The format has varied from two-hour taster workshops to more traditional multi-week classes.

As we've taught, we've been engaged in continual evaluation of the curriculum using a technique called *design-based research* (DBR).[34] We actively observe our students and their interactions with the material, capturing real-time observations of their questions and behavior. After classes and workshops, we also obtain student feedback and capture records of the impacts of the course, through interviews, surveys, and student debriefs. This book draws on the knowledge gained through this experiential research. Throughout the text, we provide stories of scholars we have known and taught. We describe the challenges these researchers faced and how they applied the skills we've taught to develop their creative practice and bring greater ease to their work. The names and details of these stories (e.g., research field or dissertation topic) have been changed to protect anonymity, but they are based on real people. While the stories represent a handful of the hundreds of students we've worked with all over the world, we have selected them as representative of our students' common challenges and solutions. (If you're interested in a more formal evaluation of our curriculum, see the article we wrote in 2014.)[35]

Our curriculum began as a direct adaptation of the d.school's pedagogy and design thinking process to the challenges of research. Over the years that we have been teaching and investigating the creative practices of researchers, our approach has evolved in response to student feedback and our learning from our design-based research observations. Initially, we were focused almost exclusively on creative confidence as a means to greater productivity and innovative outputs. We still see this as a key benefit of creativity training for scholars. But we also found that focusing on the process of research and one's own creativity had an emotional impact on how our students approached research. We observed the same shift in ourselves as our team practiced these techniques over the years since we began working on this project. Greater facility with designing one's research process seemed to translate into less stress, greater self-efficacy, a greater sense of control, and ultimately being a happier as well as more creatively productive researcher. This link between attention to one's creative process and emotional empowerment was the most surprising outcome for us. Perhaps research doesn't have to be as painful or stressful as many PhD students and Principal Investigators seem to consider the norm.

WHO THE BOOK IS FOR

This book is written for anyone interested in creativity in research, regardless of career stage or discipline. We lay out strategies for building creativity but encourage each of you to incorporate them into your own unique practice.

Both early and established researchers should find inspiration in the book. For graduate students and postdocs, the abilities provide a concrete roadmap of what to do when feeling "stuck," thereby empowering you as a scholar and minimizing the need for protracted learning by trial and error. For more experienced researchers, the book will help develop conscious recognition of the successful strategies you already use, which can increase your ability to mentor creativity for your students. Experienced faculty may also find new techniques to try in your own research practice. Throughout the text, we provide stories of people across career stages. And in the final section, we provide chapters targeted at the types of challenges typically faced by emerging (Chapter 9) and senior scholars (Chapter 10).

The techniques presented in the book should also be useful to scientists, scholars, and academic researchers across disciplines and settings: from the physical and social sciences, to engineering, to the humanities, and including those working in universities, government, and private industry. The research process looks very different across disciplines, whether you do experiments, work in archives, or observe people or places in the field. However, because we focus on the process (of research and of solving problems), the abilities we teach work across fields: for instance, everyone has to manage relationships, develop research questions, and translate research findings into written text. Our classes have been attended by a diverse array of scholars, and we've seen the exercises work for theoretical physicists, legal scholars, chemists, and critical literary theorists, among many others.

Finally, while the book is written mostly for people actively engaged in research, Chapters 11 and 12 provide ideas for how you might use the book as a mentor, administrator, or someone otherwise engaged in helping other people (whether students, postdocs, or faculty) develop creative confidence. If you are responsible for mentoring emerging scholars, you might find the book useful as the basis for research methods courses, lab group meetings, and individualized advising or coaching.

HOW TO USE THE BOOK: TEXT, EXERCISES, AND REFLECTION

When we teach in person, we ask our students to dive into hands-on activities before we provide time for analytic thinking about what they are doing. From a pedagogical perspective, our curriculum is designed with nested cycles of experiential learning,[36] guided self-reflection on what was just experienced,[37] and brief presentations of scholarly information and stories about others' experiences that help participants develop a mental framework for understanding what they are doing and feeling. This book is organized to replicate this experience as much as possible for you, given that you do not have the interactive experience of an in-person instructor guiding you. Most chapters include text (establishing what the ability is and how it works), exercises for you to experiment with the approach, and guided questions to help you reflect on your current approaches and what you're learning. Engaging in each of these activities – reading, doing, and reflecting – can help you cultivate the cognitive, behavioral, and emotional abilities that optimize your creativity.

We recommend two possible approaches to read the book. One is to read the book chapters in order and experiment with the exercises in each chapter as you go. The second approach is to skip directly to Chapter 11 and begin the thirty-day learning progression that incorporates all the material in the book. Following this approach, you'll have the opportunity to apply the skills to your ongoing research and read each of the chapters in the context of this experimentation.

Whichever approach you choose, we encourage you to take the exercises seriously. This means not just reading the chapters, but actually trying some of the activities we suggest and then reflecting on what you learned. When you learn something new (start a new language, try a new hobby, etc.), your brain is initially challenged and you pick up the new skill rapidly. Eventually, though, you reach a cognitive plateau, where your brain shifts to autopilot because it considers the activity you're doing to be familiar and easy. However, reaching this plateau does not mean you've mastered everything you could learn about a subject. To make sure that you keep learning, you need to challenge your brain continually to overcome plateaus by being deliberate with your practice.[38] Like the sport analogy mentioned earlier, practice and game time do not necessarily contribute equally to learning; improvement will likely be much quicker with dedicated time spent practicing particular skills.

In research, PhD students are challenged by the unfamiliarity of doing things for the first time and therefore learn rapidly about the process of doing research. But for junior and senior scholars alike, as you become more familiar with research, you tend to enter autopilot regarding your research practice. If you want to learn new habits, you need intentionally to make the process of doing research new and challenging again. So, we encourage you to step out of your normal routine and try some of the activities we propose in each chapter.

A second key component of our pedagogy is reflection. Educational psychologist John Dewey defined reflection in 1938 as mental "reconstruction and reorganization which adds meaning to [one's] experience."[39] According to Donald Schön, another foundational scholar of reflective practice, professional competence is developed through a continual, dynamic process of addressing a situation based on prior experience, consciously considering how the present situation is different from previous situations, and then making sense of an event after it happened.[40] By noticing your research process, trying exercises that ask you to do research in a new way, and then reflecting on them, you build metacognition (the ability to think about your thinking) about your research process.[41] This lays a mental framework where you can store new information as you learn it. Then, as you continually do and reflect, you'll incorporate new experiences into this framework, helping you to remember new skills and apply them in the future.[42]

There are many ways to build your mental competency through reflection, but we suggest journaling, drawing, and/or discussion. The introduction to Section II provides guidance on how to use each approach and more detail about their benefits. Additionally, each chapter's exercises include a *Reflect* subsection with suggested questions to help you become aware of your assumptions, your feelings, and your reactions to the concepts and exercises.

OVERVIEW OF THE CHAPTERS

The process of creative problem solving in diverse fields including research shares fundamental similarities in the underlying mental challenges one must meet. Chapters 2 through 8, which form the heart of the book, are devoted to the seven abilities essential to innovative research. Each of these chapters includes an overview of scholarly research on how the ability works, stories that illustrate how approaching research with the ability can transform your relationship to research, and concrete techniques to practice developing it in your life.

Chapter 2 focuses on mindfulness. Researchers tend to be busy, rarely stopping to take the time to notice how they go about their research and why. This chapter argues that you can be more productive if you pay explicit attention to the behaviors, thoughts, and attitudes that comprise your research practice. By developing the ability to notice and accept what is happening, you can develop the ability to act more intentionally.

Chapter 3 discusses the role of emotions and emotional intelligence in research. While there has been increasing recognition that emotions can affect researchers' productivity, emotions are often framed as a problem to be solved. But your desires, fears, and subtle motivations can also become a source of intelligence and insight for your research. This chapter explores ways to use emotional self-awareness, self-compassion, and empathy for your colleagues and research subjects as a means to diagnose and prevent problems.

Chapter 4 focuses on making sure that you're solving the right problem. While researchers have sophisticated analytic strategies for solving problems, research can stall because you are unclear what problem needs to be solved or are trying to solve the wrong problem. This chapter explores tools for identifying and framing tractable problems. It also discusses how you can become more comfortable with ambiguity, i.e., not knowing how you'll move forward in a given situation.

Chapter 5 frames research as a continual process of experimentation and iteration. While it can be tempting to focus on finding the "right" answer in the face of challenges, moving forward in the face of a sticky research challenge often requires an iterative process of trial and error. We explore the role of divergent and convergent thinking – times when you deliberately generate numerous options or ideas, and times when you refine toward a single option – and present a variety of ways to use experimental learning to move your research forward incrementally.

Chapter 6 emphasizes how language reflects and shapes your understanding of the world. It provides guidance on ways to become aware of the language you use and the stories you tell about your research, in order to gain insight about assumptions you hold about research. Noticing these patterns provides the opportunity to craft new stories that reinforce your use of the creative abilities and your identity as a creative scholar.

Chapter 7 explores the role of human energy in creative research practice. Researchers don't necessarily work in ways that reflect or enhance available energy. In this chapter, we discuss ways to become more aware of your energy, including becoming cognizant of different types of energy and of trends in your energy over time, and provide guidance on ways to use that knowledge to work smarter. Working with your energy can also help you boost your creative abilities, by helping you cultivate the mental and emotional states that best support the types of thinking needed to be emotionally intelligent, to find and frame problems, and to ideate and experiment.

Chapter 8 focuses on finding diverse sources of feedback on your work. Researchers tend to work either independently or in project-focused teams. As a result, they may rarely get input on early ideas or interact with people in fields outside their own. This chapter highlights the benefits that diverse input can provide, including providing you with surprising insights you would not otherwise encounter, helping you develop a deeper understanding of your research process, and enabling you to see your challenges in light of others' common struggles. We present strategies for understanding your various types of feedback needs and for building a diverse support network that meets those needs.

The final section of the book is designed to help you bring the individual abilities together into a cohesive process for doing research. First, to see these skills in action, Chapters 9 and 10 apply the abilities to common research challenges, describing potential approaches to integrating the abilities to solve each challenge. Chapter 9 uses the examples of choosing a dissertation topic, cultivating your relationship with your advisor, and managing time efficiently; Chapter 10 focuses on the challenges of writing a paper, developing a team project, and designing a class.

Chapters 11 and 12 then provide suggestions for using the book (as an individual, small group, mentor/supervisor, or course designer). Chapter 11 presents a thirty-day learning progression for an individual or small group to practice with the techniques in the book; it also provides suggestions for how a faculty member or administrator might modify the curriculum to emphasize different learning objectives like productivity or emotional resilience. Chapter 12 discusses ways to use the book and the techniques it provides to mentor creative confidence in others.

The book concludes with a short reflection on our own process and suggests ideas for you to continue learning and experimenting with creativity.

ONWARD TO CREATIVITY

Hopefully, we've convinced you that cultivating creativity is worthwhile for researchers and that you can build or enhance your creative research proficiency. Now, we invite you to use this book to explore. Dig into the text, try some of the exercises, and reflect on what you already understand about your practice and what you're learning. Find the approaches that resonate with you and find the approaches that you really don't like – both contain important information about the process that works best for you.

SECTION I Develop Your Creative Abilities

Section I addresses four key abilities of creative researchers: being aware of your thoughts and behaviors, noticing and using emotions, making sure that you solve the right problem, and learning through iteration and experimentation. "Ability," per the Oxford English Dictionary, is "the quality in a person or thing which makes an action possible ... the capability or capacity to do."[1] We use the term "ability" to emphasize that these are skills that you can cultivate and which support your capacity to be creative.

These four chapters introduce each ability, describing its scientific underpinnings and providing examples of ways it can boost your research process and content. Each chapter concludes with a series of exercises for you to practice the ability. We provide three different types of exercises. *Try It* exercises are short, relatively low-investment activities for you to get an experiential taste of what the ability feels like. *Reflect* exercises are guided prompts for you to consciously consider the usual way that you go about doing research and how you've reacted to the alternative, creativity-maximizing approach we discuss (assuming it is different). Finally, the *Practice* exercises are suggestions of ways you can incorporate the ability into your day-to-day research in an ongoing way. You might think of the *Practice* category as elements you are adding to expand your toolkit throughout the chapters.

Before you dive in, the first step is to figure out where and how you will capture your work. You want a single place to capture your reflections, both on the guided *Reflect* prompts and on what you're learning through reading, the *Try It*s, and the *Practice*s. While this could be a computer file or a pile of Post-it notes by your desk, we recommend using a good old-fashioned notebook. When you write by hand, you activate different neural networks than when you type on a computer, triggering your working memory and helping you retain information longer.[2] If you use a blank notebook, it will give you the most flexibility for capturing both text and drawings.

For the *Try It*s and the *Practice*s, the key is to actually do them. As a scholar, you're probably really good at reading and thinking about things. For the time you're engaging with this book, we encourage you to focus on action – implementing new ideas and exercises – and save in-depth consideration of them for afterwards. The *Try It*s are designed to be quick and easy so you can fit them into a busy schedule. Some of them you can put the book down and try before continuing to read the next chapter, while others ask you to make small modifications to your daily research practice. However, the fact that you can complete the *Try It*s in only a few minutes doesn't make them fluffy; we've seen our students' thinking evolve substantially by taking ten minutes to sketch their ideas or incorporate a mindfulness technique. Because the *Practice*s are longer-term shifts in how you go about your research, it's up to you to decide how deep you want to go with them. Some you may experiment with and then drop; others may become a long-term tool in your research toolbox. But you won't know which tools you want to retain if you don't try them out.

Any time we say *Reflect*, you can choose to freewrite your insights, draw them, or both. We provide some suggestions about best practices for journaling and visual thinking in the rest of this section introduction. Once you've done some individual reflection, you could also consider discussing your ideas and learning with colleagues, friends, or other people who are reading this book. The thirty-day program in Chapter 11 provides ideas for using the *Reflect* exercises as discussion prompts but urges you to first consider them individually.

Finally, to really get the most bang for your buck, we suggest that you build dedicated time for doing the exercises and reflection into your research calendar or planner. In our experience, it's easy to keep putting off this kind of self-directed experiential learning unless you make a clear plan for when you will devote time to it.

WRITING TO THINK: JOURNALING AND FREEWRITING IOI

While most researchers write frequently, if not daily, much of that writing is produced with the intent to communicate – to convince people to give you money, to share your findings with a broader audience, to show that you know a field, or simply to respond to the many emails you receive every day. In contrast, journaling and freewriting are related practices that use the act of writing as a way to think.

Journal keeping is an ancient practice that allows writers to have ongoing conversations with themselves.[3] Ongoing use of a journal can help with "develop[ing] the kind of skills, thinking, and spontaneous creativity expected in academic work."[4] By serving as an evolving record of its author's thinking, a journal becomes "concrete evidence" to capture "fleeting glimpses of understanding."[5] Journals serve as a valuable aid for reflection-based learning;[6] as a result they are frequently used in professional training settings such as teacher or nursing education.[7]

In their book *Journal Keeping: How to Use Reflective Writing for Learning, Teaching, Professional Insight, and Positive Change*, Dannelle Stevens and Joanne Cooper define a journal by six attributes: "It is written, dated, informal, flexible, private, and archival."[8] While the form of two individual's journals might look very different, what makes something a journal is the sustained record of reflection created over time. Stevens and Cooper also provide concrete techniques for elements that might appear within a journal:[9]

- Freewriting and focused freewriting [discussed in this section introduction]
- Lists or brainstorms of responses to a question or prompt [discussed in Chapter 5]
- Logs of dated events to record behavior or what happened
- Dialogues, written in the form of lines as in a play script
- Concept maps or other visual depictions [discussed in this section introduction]
- Metaphorical explorations
- Meta-reflection based on rereading entries from the preceding week or month

We'd like to call particular attention to the first element on this list: freewriting. *Freewriting* is a writing practice where you write to reach a predefined goal, either a given amount of time (say, fifteen minutes) or a given number of words (say, 500 words). You might or might not use a prompt (e.g., "What is the benefit of freewriting for creativity?"), which is how Stevens and Cooper distinguish freewriting (no prompt) from focused freewriting (with a starting prompt). Beyond a possible starting prompt, there are no rules, no boundaries, no judgment, and definitely no spell checking or editing. Your goal is to write without stopping (to the extent you can) until you reach the time or word count that you set. You are not aiming to produce content that you will keep. If it helps you feel more free, you can freewrite outside of your journal and destroy the pages or the computer file afterward. The point is to keep the pen moving or your fingers typing in order to let those "fleeting glimpse[s] of understanding" rise to the surface and to let your mind make associative connections you might not usually make.[10]

Freewriting helps create just enough distance to allow you to see your ideas in a new light. It starts from the inverse premise of most writing tasks: Rather than writing once you have ideas or results or know what you want to say, freewriting uses the act of putting words on paper to let the story emerge. In her book that details how to use freewriting in academic writing, Joan Bolker, former Director of the Harvard Writing Center, describes the power of this continuous commitment to emergent writing: "Writing is at the center of producing a dissertation [or any other piece of scholarship]. [You must learn] how not to talk away your ideas or lose them in mental gymnastics. You will learn to write in order to think, to encourage thought, to tease thought out of chaos or out of fright. You will write constantly, and continuously, at every stage, to name your topic and to find your way into it. You will learn to write past certainty, past prejudice, through contradiction, and into complexity ... If you're to do all of this, you need to write every day, even if it's only for fifteen minutes a day."[11]

Freewriting provides designated space and time for creative thinking to occur. Like journaling, the way an individual uses that time will vary on any given day and with different projects. Sometimes freewriting might give you space to develop ideas, explore tangents, ask yourself new questions, or brainstorm how to address difficulties. Other times it could lead to new associations in your data or new evidence to support your argument. By committing yourself to reflection through freewriting, you might identify flaws in your logic or possible criticisms of ideas before anyone else sees a draft. At its best, freewriting allows you to use your own mind as a teammate, literally carrying on a conversation with yourself that helps you see your own ideas in a new light.

We encourage you to think of the notebook you keep for your creativity in research exploration as a journal. The exercises suggest specific ways to use this tool. Another idea is to set aside designated freewriting time each day or week and reflect on what you've learned. Thinking of the notebook as a record of your evolving reflection and understanding of yourself as a creative scholar will hopefully inspire you to find other ways to reflect through the act of writing.

DRAWING TO THINK: VISUAL THINKING 101

Journals can also capture visual elements. Like written reflection, images can be used to think: "the purpose of visualization is insight, not pictures."[12]

As with writing, many researchers use visualizations, but generally with the purpose to communicate: the visual elements in papers, presentations, and proposals. However, visual thinking can support every part of the research process, from drafting early ideas or honing the plan of a research proposal to visually summarizing the key aspects of a paper or dissertation. Visual thinking can also help you explore your research process; many of our exercises ask you to make sketches, like drawing your feedback network or your energy curve.

More formally, using visual thinking and creating visual artifacts helps you transform implicit or tacit knowledge into explicit knowledge.[13] Visual artifacts help extend your brain's capacity "to store and process information," helping to overcome cognitive load and freeing up space for you to derive new insights.[14] Visual thinking provides an important complement to language and text, as drawing (and related visual expressions like painting or creating a PowerPoint slide) engages different parts of your brain from when you talk or write.[15] Thus visual thinking can often help you see things from new perspectives.

How can you bring visual thinking into practice? The key is to find a way to transfer what is in your mind into a visual representation. You do not need to be "good at drawing" to do this effectively. As one participant in our class expressed, "I'm a computer scientist, my life consists of one's and zero's." Sebastian, whose research focuses on visual thinking, replied, "Well, if you can draw a box and an arrow, you are perfectly equipped to use visual thinking as a tool for your research."

As you use visual thinking to enhance your thinking and reflection, there are several basic techniques that can help you augment your thinking and communicating efforts. Two key distinctions can help you be more conscious in choosing what to depict and how to depict it. First, consider whether you're trying to visualize some kind of process (e.g., the steps you used in conducting an experiment, or a timeline of how your field has evolved over time) or a type of structure (e.g., how different authors contribute to your argument, or the relationship between elements of data). How might you depict the structure of something differently than the process used to get there? Second, you might choose to represent either processes or structures in an abstract way (e.g., a Venn Diagram or 2x2 matrix) or by linking them to a real-world metaphor (e.g., drawing your research journey as a trek up a mountain). As you use visual thinking, play with drawing the same concept multiple ways or depicting different dimensions of it, and see what new insights you might uncover. For inspiration, see Figure 2.1.

Regardless of the overarching choices you have made about how to portray your ideas, there are also a number of visualization conventions (Figure 2.2) that help translate thoughts into visuals. You can use

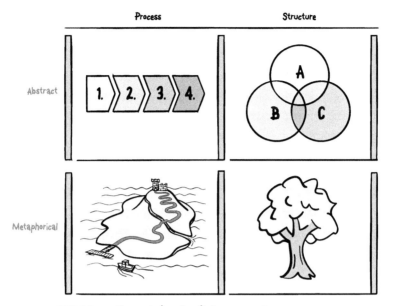

FIGURE 2.1 Formats for visualizing concepts

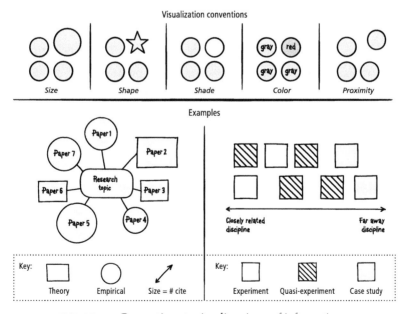

FIGURE 2.2 Conventions to visualize pieces of information

size, shape, shading, color, and location/proximity to differentiate between different ideas or types of information.[16] For example, you might use size to indicate the number of citations of an author or a field, or you might use color or shape to capture different categories of ideas (e.g., activities related to different research projects).

A final strategy that is particularly helpful when dealing with complex information is to create visuals that provide an "overview first, [then] details on demand."[17] Start by focusing on the big picture and distill your idea into the key concepts or connections. In concrete terms, try to represent the whole project or problem visually on one page or one PowerPoint slide. This helps you identify core ideas and not be overwhelmed by too much information. Then, if you feel that you want more detail, you can always draw additional visuals that support the big idea by providing additional details.

We encourage you to experiment with visual thinking as well as written reflection in your notebook. If you get stuck how to depict something visually, you might try these three approaches as ideas to help you explore, learn, and reflect through visual means.

2 Mind Your Process and Be Intentional

Stephanie was always complaining about how she never had time to get research done – about all of her backlogged papers, or not having a spare afternoon to schedule interviews for an ongoing project. This was a source of great stress, as she always felt behind. But somehow she always had time to meet with friends or colleagues. She was in the campus coffee shop almost every day. Colleagues in her department started teasingly taking note of how frequently she could be found there and tallying the times that Stephanie *wasn't* there.

While it would be easy to fault Stephanie for her obvious disconnect, we tell her story as an example of the blindness many researchers (and humans, to be fair) carry about what they do and why and how they do it. If you're like a lot of the scholars we know, you probably tend to focus on getting things done. Being admitted to graduate school by definition required that you were someone who accomplished things, excelled at completing predefined assignments, and finished projects. As a PhD student and later as a faculty member or practicing researcher, the number of things to accomplish tends to be greater than the available hours in a day. External evaluation metrics often focus on products: papers published, grants funded, and classes taught. Many researchers have thus developed a tendency to focus on concrete outcomes – tasks accomplished, papers submitted, data collected, etc. – as a metric of productivity. Often these outcomes are defined by other people, such as hiring committees, dissertation advisors, or grant review boards, rather than by you.

Outcome metrics provide structure to research. However, focusing on these metrics does not always encourage researchers to work in a manner that leads to production of their best work. When was the last time you thought about *how* you were working: about details like where you like to write, or at what time of day you are most alert, or why you tend to procrastinate on certain tasks, or how a particular project was making you feel? If you're like most busy researchers, it's probably been a while since you've considered your research process. Instead, like Stephanie, you likely plow ahead with your routine practice – write when you're under a deadline, hurry from meeting to meeting and project to project, always feeling behind and never stopping to consider if there's a better way to meet your goals. In contrast, paying careful attention to your process can help you optimize your workflow and enjoy yourself more while doing so.

Mindfulness is the skill of observing what you are doing, thinking, and feeling to inform your best process as a researcher. Being mindful of your process for doing research is a fundamental tool to help you think about aspects of your work you may rarely or never consider; it is the first step in building deliberate creativity into your research process. Learning to be more mindful of your research process can help you diagnose your current thoughts and behaviors and use that understanding to intentionally chart a path forward.

MINDFULNESS: LEARNING TO WATCH YOUR PROCESS

While mindfulness is sometimes associated with Buddhism or New Age thought, at its simplest, mindfulness means the habit of (1) pausing to notice what is happening as it occurs and (2) accepting that it is happening without trying to change it. By noticing and accepting without judgment, you build awareness about how you tend to act or react in different settings, which creates the foundation to decide consciously what you want to do next.

Mindfulness can first be applied to your actions or behaviors. By noticing what you are doing, you start to notice how you spend your time and any unconscious habits you may have. By being aware of her behaviors, Stephanie might have noticed that she spent a lot of time socializing in the coffee shop. An important component of a mindful approach, though, is to avoid evaluating whether spending time at the coffee shop is good or bad; the goal is just to notice that it's a tendency. Similarly, you might notice ways you may be acting that are influencing your research process.

A deeper form of mindfulness training focuses on learning to notice, accept, and be more intentional about cognitive patterns – what your thoughts are doing. Humans spend as much time ruminating on things that aren't happening as thinking about things that they're actively doing.[1] In other words, you're not fully in control of your thoughts. However, training your ability to pay attention to your thoughts can be achieved through various forms of mindfulness meditation, where you train yourself to focus on a single object (e.g., your breath, a visualization, the sensations in your body) and practice coming back from whatever unconscious train of thought your mind decides to take. On a shorter timescale, it can mean building a habit of pausing, shifting to look internally, and noticing what you're thinking and how it makes you feel.

A lot of popular and scientific literature on mindfulness tends to focus on this second incarnation: awareness of your thoughts. This is because mindfulness of thoughts and mindfulness of behaviors are deeply intertwined. Learning to notice your behaviors requires enough mental awareness to stop following whatever automatic train of thought you're on and turn your attention to whatever activities you're engaged in.

Mindfulness and Creativity

The growing scientific literature on mindfulness practice points to a diverse array of potential benefits for creativity. First, it helps sharpen your attention, helping you focus by consciously tuning out superfluous distractions and not following your thoughts automatically down whatever path those distractions create.[2] Second, mindfulness reduces psychological biases like sunk-cost biases, allowing you to make more rational decisions and helping your mind avoid incorrect beliefs that may limit the ideas you generate.[3] Paying attention to your thought patterns also helps you notice what unconscious assumptions you might be making, helping you avoid getting stuck in rigid thought patterns and allowing you to think outside the box.[4] This means that mindfulness meditation can help you develop more creative and divergent styles of thinking.[5]

Mindfulness can also help boost creativity in less direct ways. First, individuals who engage in long-term meditation practices have been shown to be more resilient to stress and have lower rates of psychological burnout.[6] While this is immediately beneficial for people in the high-stress, high-burnout field of research,[7] reducing stress also enables your brain to be in a less reactive, more excited state, freeing it for creative problem solving.[8] Mindfulness practice also helps you be less judgmental of yourself and other people, helping you approach ideas with an open mind and work more effectively with other people.[9]

Components of Mindfulness: Intention, Attention, Attitude

Mindfulness generally entails three things (Figure 2.3): "the Intention to pay Attention with a certain Attitude" (of curiosity and compassion).[10]

Intention simply means that you are making a conscious choice to try. You'll forget, a lot (trust us, we've been working on this for years), but every day is a new day to try once again to be present and simply notice what you're doing.

Attention means slowing down to pay attention to whatever is happening in your life – the external noises, colors, people, and the internal thoughts and feelings – as it happens. It can be as simple as pausing, taking a slow breath, and asking, "What's going on right now?" And when you catch yourself on an automatic train of thought, do that: Pause, take a slow breath, and ask, "What's going on right now?" The more times you do this, the easier it will get.

Attitude means approaching the present moment with non-judging curiosity and compassion for yourself and others. Whatever you notice yourself doing or thinking, try to accept it as it is.

And how does this relate to your research? The next time you're feeling stuck, or unsure what to do next, or have a big conversation coming up with your advisor, or realize you just sat at your computer for five hours and have no idea where the time went, pause, take a slow breath, and ask, "What's going on right now?" Notice what you're doing, what you're thinking, and what you're feeling. Notice any assumptions or judgments you're making about yourself, your research, or the people around you. After you've noticed, you can reflect on what these assumptions or thoughts are leading you to do, or whether they're accurate, but always try to maintain an air of curiosity and self-compassion as you do so.

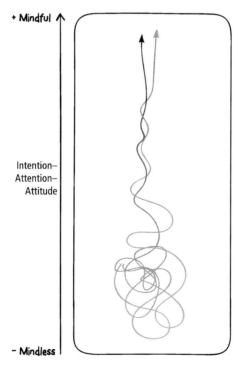

FIGURE 2.3 Intention, attention, attitude

HOW MINDFULNESS HELPS YOU DO BETTER RESEARCH

For researchers, mindfulness builds awareness of how you react to challenges and approach your research practice. At the most basic, mindfulness for researchers means developing conscious awareness of what you are doing, thinking, and feeling moment by moment. This practice of continually asking, "What is happening right now?" puts you more in control of your actions. By becoming aware of what is happening, you develop the ability to choose how you will act in response, whether you need to react cognitively in the course of solving a problem or emotionally in response to your feelings or others' actions.

Mindfulness Helps You Recognize Behavioral Patterns

Research requires constant decisions about what you are doing to move projects forward and how you are spending your time. You must be able to move fluidly between short-term task orientations (e.g., reviewing literature, writing a conference paper, leading a lab meeting) and long-term orientations (finishing the thesis, getting a tenure-track job, funding a research agenda). And once you become a Principal Investigator (and often much earlier), there is rarely anyone besides you directing your day-to-day tasks. Thus, knowing what you are doing, being aware of where you are in your research process, and relating the task at hand to your big picture goals is vital ability of researchers.

Mindfulness helps you notice what you are doing, which is the first step in actively choosing behaviors that progress your goals. When Alyssa accepted her dream job as a postdoc in a new city, she realized almost immediately that she loved the job and hated the city. She felt unbearably trapped and lonely, leaving work each night and bursting into tears as soon as she was alone in her car driving home. Working hard to impress her colleagues, she didn't feel like she could tell anyone how much she hated the city. One day at lunch with a visiting speaker, the guest asked everyone what the city was like.

Her coworkers gave glowing reviews as they went around the table. When someone looked at Alyssa for her opinion, her face must have told some part of the truth. "You don't like it here?" they asked. Fumbling to recover, she punted, feebly explaining that it was a challenging transition coming from a small town on the West Coast.

While Alyssa was initially furious that she'd let her secret show, the incident actually made her realize that her negativity about the new city was impacting her relationships with her new colleagues. Because she was afraid of being "found out," she wasn't actively getting to know the people she worked with, so she wasn't really becoming a colleague. Even though her opinion of the city didn't change, after she became aware that she'd been avoiding personal conversations with her colleagues, Alyssa made an active attempt to become a better colleague.

Another way to use mindfulness to direct action is to become aware when a change in course is necessary. When Paul was in the middle of writing his dissertation, he was stuck trying to write a research memo he had promised his advisor at a committee meeting. The advisor was excited that Paul had finished analyzing data, and they had agreed that Paul would summarize major findings into a two-page memo so they could discuss them and plan the outline for a paper. Paul could not understand why he was so overwhelmed by such a simple writing task. He sat down and asked himself why the memo felt overwhelming. He realized that the problem was actually an abundance of riches: He had so much data and so many ideas that they wouldn't fit into a short memo. Instead of writing a memo, the next action he needed to take was to write an outline and then start writing the actual paper. What had seemed like the easy option when his advisor suggested it turned out to be more difficult when he tried it. So, Paul wrote his advisor an email explaining the situation and they set a deadline for a month out to discuss a draft paper instead. For many students, the research memo would have been the perfect suggestion to support writing up data for the first time, but in this case, it turned out to be counterproductive to what Paul needed. Mindfulness allowed him to recognize what steps he needed to take next and gave him the confidence to change plans with his advisor.

By intentionally observing what you are doing, you can identify what behaviors are helping you (or not) and figure out what your next best action might be. You also empower yourself to understand what your research process looks like. You can practice this mindfulness at multiple different timescales: from moment to moment or month to month. As you become more familiar with mindfulness, this understanding develops into active steering of your research.

Mindfulness Helps You Recognize Thought Patterns

Your mind is constantly producing thoughts to interpret your world. These thoughts shape how you understand events and experiences.[11] By becoming aware of your thought patterns, you develop the opportunity to notice any automatic assumptions or associations you are making. Becoming aware of these assumptions enables you to interrogate whether those assumptions are in fact true.

One set of assumptions that can be helpful to examine is thoughts you have about how you work or why you work the way you do. When Chris was in the dissertation-writing years of his PhD, he had a severe case of writer's block. He never sat down to write because he didn't feel like he could start writing until he gathered more data, and when he did try to write, a nagging feeling that his advisors were not pleased with his results to date kept him from producing much text. However, when he started paying careful attention to these unconscious assumptions that arose when he thought about writing, he realized his assumptions about his advisors' judgments were not based on facts. The idea that the solution to his writer's block was external (getting more data so his advisors would like his project) was simply an assumption, and it was not helping his progress. Once he addressed this assumption, he realized that what he actually needed to do was find ways to motivate himself to write. He started tracking his writing time, so he could quantitatively see more writing happening over time. He also developed a series of carrot-and-stick strategies, like a rule that he was not allowed to do anything but make tea and write until he had produced a thousand words that day. The rest of the day would then be free to do whatever else he wanted. By noticing the automatic assumptions he made whenever he sat down to (try to) write, Chris realized that these habitual thoughts were pointing him in a wrong direction. It wasn't his advisors or the data that was keeping him from writing: He simply was struggling with motivation.

Mindfulness can also help you become aware of how your thinking about your research content is evolving. Often, when you start analyzing data, it can feel like you're living in a state of chaos. Sam, a sociologist, has found this is to be especially true for qualitative data like interviews. When he first starts the analysis phase of a project, there are infinite possible directions and no clear path, and it often feels overwhelming. While he of course follows best practices for applying analytical categories to this messy information (qualitative researchers call this process "coding"), Sam has found that his best insights come when he consciously leans into the ambiguity of the data and stays aware of how his thinking is evolving as his evidence base grows. By trying to understand precisely what each bit of text is saying and how it links to his growing understanding, he is able to move from not knowing what story the data are telling to making clear arguments about the patterns that exist in his data.

By being aware of what you are thinking about your research and your research practice, you gain knowledge about your research process and provide yourself with the opportunity to consciously choose how to go about your work.

Mindfulness Helps You Recognize Emotional Patterns

Finally, mindfulness can help you recognize when emotions may be playing a role in what you are doing, providing the opportunity to learn from and shape how you react to emotions. One of the insights of mindfulness is that emotions themselves simply exist; it is the way one reacts to them that causes much of the stress or dissatisfaction generally associated with negative emotions.[12] Thus becoming aware of your emotional reactions also gives you the opportunity to be more intentional in your responses. In research, mindfulness can be particularly helpful to notice when other types of challenges have an emotional component you did not previously recognize. Often this is what is keeping you from moving forward.

Ziyi was a new assistant professor and was asked to join a team writing a large National Science Foundation grant proposal. The team divvied up the writing tasks, and – unbeknownst to the lead Principal Investigator – Ziyi was assigned to write a section that was closely tied to her dissertation project and core research interests. However, she had severe writer's block when she sat down at the computer – no clue even where to start the narrative. She pulled her husband in to help brainstorm a conceptual framework, which helped but didn't get words on the page. And she spent several sleepless nights worrying about the proposal and her inability to write. The next day, instead of staring at a blank Word document, she decided to pause and ask why she felt so stuck. As she turned her attention inward, she realized her inability to write had an emotional foundation: She felt underappreciated. Despite the work being in her core area of expertise, Ziyi had been added to the team very late in the process, was added as a collaborator rather than a co-investigator and was working with a full professor who would likely do little work but take most of the credit. So, she picked up the phone and called the grant lead to discuss her concerns: that she wanted to be a part of the project but only if she were treated as an equal player (especially since she was pre-tenure and it mattered more for her than for the more senior colleagues). After that conversation, Ziyi was added as a Principal Investigator on the grant, and the writing flowed freely now that she had addressed her deeper concern of being undervalued.

In this example, Ziyi first focused on the behavior and why she was stuck – assuming if she just had a good conceptual framework, then she could write. But instead, taking the time to pause and ask,

"What else is going on here?" helped Ziyi identify a deeper emotional reason for the trouble she was having, along with a way to start resolving it. Mindfulness provides the space and attention that helps you tell when your emotions are signaling something important. (Chapter 3 covers the skill of emotional intelligence in detail, providing tools to use and manage the emotions you uncover through mindfulness.)

HOW TO BUILD MINDFUL AWARENESS

As easy way to start being more aware of your research process is to track your behaviors in order to gather empirical evidence about how you are actually acting. A low-tech way to do this is just to set a timer throughout the day, and when it goes off note what you're doing and how you feel on a piece of paper or a spreadsheet. There are also a variety of time-tracking and similar apps you can use. As you start collecting data on what you're doing, you'll learn more about your patterns of behavior and how you spend your time.

However, the fastest way to build your brain's ability to pay attention – which is particularly important for noticing thoughts and emotions – is through mindfulness meditation. There are a number of different guides you can find on how to meditate and no single right way to do it. Nicola likes to simply sit and follow her breath; thinking "In" on the inhale and "Out" on the exhale. Sebastian prefers guided meditations, where someone else tells you what to focus on for the duration of the exercise; a range of apps, like Headspace or Calm provide guided meditations.[13] He likes to think about meditation as a metaphor of sitting by the highway: Each thought is a car, and you're simply watching them come and go. Amanda often meditates as part of her yoga practice, consciously noticing what is happening in her body, but she also appreciates a tip she was given in a course she took while a busy PhD student: Every shower you take is a chance to be exquisitely aware of the present moment.[14] The details of *how* you practice focusing your brain matter less than the fact that you're trying – and that you're trying regularly.

Anja is an overthinker whose brain rarely pauses to relax. She is constantly processing, analyzing things that happened in the past, or thinking about possible scenarios that might happen in the future. This rarely leaves her in the state of being aware of the present moment. For many years she attended yoga classes with the goal to master mindfulness, but even the five-minute meditation at the beginning of class was painful: Her to-do list would start to visually run through her mind no matter how hard she tried to stay focused on her breath. This left her feeling frustrated and incompetent. Last year, Anja visited a friend who is a Zen master in Japan. After leading a meditation session for a group of high-achieving executives, he joked about how many people often do meditation and spend the entire session they berating themselves for not being able to stop thinking, treating meditation as another project to perfect as soon as possible. This made Anja realize that meditation practice itself is a journey and being imperfect is part of it. Some days it goes easier and some days it is harder. Thinking about meditation this way helps Anja cherish her quiet minutes spent trying each day. The only goal is to show up on the mat or cushion for ten minutes a day to practice. Not to be the best, not to prove anything to others, but just to show up for herself. (For those of you who are empirically driven, there is no science-based consensus on exactly how much meditation is "enough," so we suggest you tackle an amount that you can follow through with over time, be it five minutes, twenty minutes, or more.)[15]

This story also ties to the importance of having a nonjudgmental attitude toward yourself. Effort and intention count, and even if you feel totally incompetent, simply trying again and again means you are learning to have more control and intentionality over your thought patterns.

Finally, as a caveat, while meditation is often challenging and can definitely be frustrating for everyone at times, in rare cases it can uncover buried traumas.[16] If meditating feels extremely challenging or traumatizing, please work with a trained teacher, clinician, or mediator to ensure that you're approaching it safely.

SUMMARY

As the stories in this chapter have illustrated, mindfulness is the habit of paying attention to what you are doing. In order to change your research process, you have to first be aware of what it looks like now and be curious about why it is that way. By being mindful of your process, you also slow down and create space so that you can begin having the power to choose where to go next, rather than blindly following your behavioral and mental habits.

EXERCISES

Try It

2.1 **Mindful email:** Take an everyday activity (like checking your email) and try doing it with as much attention as you can. Notice how your fingers feel on the keyboard or phone screen. Notice where your eyes go first on the screen, and then where your attention moves. Pause before you click any buttons or links, and notice what happens as you click. Notice if you have any emotional reactions as you read: Do you feel happy or excited? Relieved? Overwhelmed by the number of unread messages? Notice where and how you feel these emotions in your body: a knot in your stomach? A faster heart rate? A smile on your face? What was it like being mindful while doing something you do every day?[17]

2.2 **Notice your research:** Practice checking in on your research process for the next three days. Get a notebook, pad of Post-its, Evernote file, Word document, etc., and keep it sitting next to you on your desk (or open on your computer). Set an alarm to go off a couple times a day. When it goes off, record what you are doing (for instance, "Reading Smith et al. paper," "Making my sixth cup of tea," "Talking through the model with my advisor"). How is this activity related to your research content or process? How does it fit with your goal for the week? For the month? How do you feel about it?

2.3 **Break a habit:** Pick a small, frequent habit to break. Try remembering to open the door with the opposite hand you usually use. Or if you take the stairs regularly, try stepping first with the opposite foot.[18] Approach this with curiosity: What feels familiar or strange about this? What happens when you bring attention to what is usually automatic?

2.4 **Notice creativity:** Consciously notice your most and least creative moments over the course of a day (or even a week). One way to make this concrete is to take a photo of each moment with your phone or a camera. Gather these moments into a file and give them captions that describe what did or did not feel creative about the situation and/or setting. How are these moments similar or different?

Practice

2.5 **Pause and breathe:** Start to develop the habit of pausing as the first thing you do when you need to make a decision in your research practice or realize you are facing a challenge. Notice what you're doing and thinking, and consider how you got there. Take a deep breath or two and then proceed.

2.6 **Mindfulness cue:** Develop a cue that reminds you to turn your attention to the present. This should be something that happens fairly often but not constantly (like the phone ringing, a popup on your computer, or a sticker you put on the refrigerator). When you notice the cue, pause, take a deep breath, and notice what you are doing. You may also want to experiment with a more formal regular mindfulness practice, whether using an app, visiting a local meditation center, or simply on your own at home.

2.7 **Three good things:** At the end of the day, write down three research-related things that went well during that day. Write down what happened in as much detail as possible, including what you did or said and, if others were involved, what they did or said. Note how this event made you feel at the time and how this event made you feel later (including now, as you remember it).

Reflect

2.8 Are there times in your life when you feel deeply engaged in the present moment? When do they happen? What are you doing at those times?

2.9 Think about a research-related decision you made in the last week. How did you make the decision? How did you realize that you needed to make a decision? How did you choose what steps to take next? Did you consciously consider any alternative steps?

2.10 Draw the process that you used to take your most recent research project from an initial idea to a completed product. First, draw the beginning, middle, and end – where did you start, and how did you progress? Now, go deeper: What specific tasks happened in each stage? What triggered transitions between the stages? Were there times when you cycled back to an earlier stage? Now compare this project to your general process: How do the tasks, stages, or triggers vary between projects?

3 Use Emotions to Diagnose Problems and Move Forward

When Emotions Are a "Problem" to Be Solved

Amber was a first year PhD student who planned to study the health impacts of mining in Peru. By all objective measures, she was in a great spot to start her research: She had a National Science Foundation Graduate Research Fellowship, great advisors with local connections, and a clear idea of her research direction. Over spring break, Amber went back to New York City (where she had lived before starting the PhD) to visit friends. When she arrived back on campus in late March, it was time to start planning summer fieldwork in Peru. The only problem was, she was not at all excited. She couldn't stop thinking about New York. After a number of sleepless nights and asking herself what was wrong, she realized that her heart was still in New York. She couldn't imagine spending the next five years only going back for short visits, and she'd lost all interest in a new scientific field that would have no relevance in the place she cared most about. But she struggled with the implications of what she was feeling. She worried she was making an irrational decision, since she knew changing directions would set her back drastically, from finding new advisors to figuring out a whole new area of research. She tried to ignore her desire to be in New York and move forward with her summer plans. Ultimately, though, Amber listened to her emotions, changing advisors and changing her research focus to asthma. Her PhD took a year longer than it likely would have had she continued with her original plan. But she was excited and happy, working on problems she cared about in a place she wanted to be.

During much of the time that she struggled to decide about changing her topic, Amber was doing what researchers often do: treating her emotions as a problem to be solved so she could get on with doing the real research. There is an old but persistent myth that research is rigorous, rational, analytical, and thus – implicitly – not emotional.[1] Within natural science fields in particular, emotion and the scientific method are often painted as mutually exclusive, so many researchers seem to assume that doing quality research means not being emotional. Of course, emotions are acknowledged when they rise to the level of a problem preventing you from accomplishing what needs to be accomplished: a death in the family, a devastating break-up, an injury or illness. Or more positively, getting married, having a baby, or getting tenure might be recognized as emotional milestones. But limiting the public discussion of emotions to life's big celebrations and tragedies reinforces the common belief that emotions play a minimal role in day-to-day research life.

Certainly, unless you are in a field where emotion and reflexivity play a role in shaping or interpreting your research, evidence is not and absolutely should not be based on emotional "truth" or instinct in the same way certain personal decisions might sometimes be; the source of scientific rigor comes from scientific conclusions being as unbiased as possible. But human feelings, needs, and emotions are inevitably a part of the process of producing research, simply because research is a challenging human enterprise. Research is carried out by people with the same evolutionary urges, drives, and reactions as any other human being, so by ignoring emotions you lose access to an important source of knowledge about yourself and your environment.

Learning to pay attention to emotions allows you to reclaim this source of knowledge, helping you to diagnose challenges that arise in your research and sometimes to proactively prevent them. By developing the skills of emotional intelligence, including self-awareness, self-compassion, and empathy, you can increase your ability to understand your own actions and the actions of others.

Being Human Means Having Emotions

Humans' emotional capacity originally evolved as a mechanism to allow quick reactions in settings where taking time to think could be deadly, making it more likely that your ancestors survived to produce more offspring. When someone is afraid, for instance, a fight-or-flight response triggers, helping them face down a predator or find a safe hiding spot. When someone sees (or smells) rotten food, they feel disgust. In these cases, emotions – driven by floods of hormones to the brain – are bypassing the thinking brain to force the person to act more quickly than they would if they used their rational problem-solving skills. Today, you rarely face the kinds of situations your ancestors faced on the savannah, but you retain a brain and body that was built for split-second action. And beyond fight or flight, automatic responses to external stimuli, which are cued through the emotions, provide important basic information about the world, like when a potential mate is interested or whether a stranger is hostile. This means that emotions play a substantial role, often shaping your behavior and actions even when you are not aware of them.[2]

One substantial place where emotions play a role in research is in how you make decisions. While philosophers and economists have long held that people are rational, research into how "rational" humans actually behave in the world and how they make decisions has demonstrated that human beings are not very rational at all. Instead, people are driven greatly by emotions. When you make a decision or are faced with a new challenge, your body first reacts instinctually, with floods of hormones that signal to you whether a situation is desirable or to be avoided. Then, your thinking brain – the prefrontal cortex – takes over, allowing you to work through a problem or situation logically.[3]

What this all means is that before you can start making decisions rationally, your body has already introduced a host of internal intuitions, assumptions, and biases about the nature of the problem you're facing, so you're not starting from an objective viewpoint. Emotions influence your perception of the physical reality surrounding you. For instance, experimental participants overestimated the incline of a hill when listening to music that primed sad emotions.[4] Emotions shape how large you perceive risks to be.[5] And they shape your assumptions about your motivations and the motivations of other people.[6] Because you cannot make decisions without emotions to some extent playing a role, emotions necessarily play a role in the practice and production of scholarly research.

The ubiquity of emotions in the human experience also means that trying to ignore emotions and banish them from research practice is often counterproductive or even destructive to your work and health. Because emotions provide important cues about what is happening, ignoring them means you lose a valuable source of information about your world – when you are facing a threat, whether another person is friendly or hostile, when you are safe or not. For instance, when you meet a new person, you have little information about who they are or whether to trust them, so you draw on instincts to guide your decision.[7] Of course, this may result in a biased assessment, but your body is giving you clues about this new, unfamiliar stimulus.

Burying emotions can also be dangerous to your mental and physical health. When a surprise or fearful event triggers the fight-or-flight responses that evolved to help keep your ancestors safe, your body can be hijacked by a flood of anger or fear that overwhelms any logical or rational responses you might desire. When this happens, you literally lose control of your body and may do or say things that you later regret.[8] When someone is not able to express strong emotions following a traumatic event, the unexpressed and/or unrecognized emotions can have lasting and drastic effects on brain and body.[9] Even in less traumatic situations, buried emotions can influence your health. While much research has focused on more extreme mental conditions like depression, a national survey in Australia found that people who often felt fear and distress had significantly higher incidence of a number of physical conditions, including asthma, stroke, cancer, heart conditions, arthritis, and diabetes.[10] Ignoring negative emotions can have very real health consequences.

Whether acknowledged or not, emotions exist, and they continue to influence your health, well-being, research productivity, relationships, and how others perceive you. In recent years, there has been an encouraging and growing recognition of the link between emotions and the demands of research. For example, a careers column in *Nature* reported on what it calls "a harsh reality," a study documenting that "PhD students are more likely to experience mental health distress than other highly educated individuals," due to high workloads, a perceived lack of control over their work, and an imbalance between work and the rest of their lives. The study's authors conclude that the results "highlight the need for universities to offer counselling services and other resources to PhD students."[11] But this *Nature* report is typical in its characterization of emotions as a mental health issue. Too often, when emotions are recognized as playing a role in research, they are framed as a problem that needs to be solved, usually through mental health interventions offered by outside professionals.

To be sure, depression and other mental illnesses are very real, and efforts to provide counselling are critical for the well-being of students and practicing scholars. But we argue that's only a fraction of the role emotions can play.

This chapter argues for using emotions as a guide to point the way to greater research productivity and well-being – or at least as a guide to identify how and why you are stuck. Rather than viewing emotions in research as a problem to solve, we suggest that emotions can actually be a tool to become a more effective scholar. The former approach assumes emotions are negative and sometimes associates them with mental health impairments. We present an alternative:

a way of intentionally using emotions in research as a form of empowerment based upon developing and practicing the skills of emotional intelligence.

EMOTIONAL INTELLIGENCE: THE POWER OF NOTICING, UNDERSTANDING, AND REGULATING EMOTIONS

The ability to notice, understand, and respond to your own emotions and other people's emotions is commonly called *emotional intelligence*. Emotional intelligence (EI) is the ability to notice what emotions are happening, make sense of what they're telling you about the world, and then regulate those emotions to make sure that you are responding in an intentional (not just automatic) way.[12] In other words, EI is a way to tap into the information emotions are providing while still allowing your conscious brain to plan or act with more control. This means that rather than letting emotions unconsciously drive decisions, you acknowledge and incorporate the information your emotions provide.

The skill of EI can be applied to yourself and to other people. The abilities to understand your own emotions and react intentionally are called *self-awareness* and *self-regulation*. The closely linked ability to approach your own emotions with care and without judgment is called *self-compassion*. The ability to understand and appropriately respond to the feelings and needs of others is known as *social awareness* or *empathy*.

Self-awareness gives you the tools to observe and use your own emotions, rather than burying them or being carried unconsciously by the chemicals they trigger. When you are emotionally self-aware, you are conscious of your feelings and understand how they affect you and your behaviors.[13] Self-awareness also helps you in group settings, as emotions help you act more morally (e.g., feeling shame or disgust when you or someone else transgresses norms).[14]

Self-compassion – holding kindness for yourself without judgment – supports your ability to be self-aware.[15] As you notice your emotions, being compassionate toward yourself allows you to accept whatever emotions you are actually having, even if you would rather not be having them. In particular, self-compassion enhances your ability to accurately perceive negative emotions without being overwhelmed with self-criticism.[16]

Finally, empathy, the ability to recognize and engage with another person's emotions, helps you build and manage relationships with other people. For most of the species' history, humans have lived and worked in small groups, and thus by necessity they have learned how to interact effectively with other people. With this came many automatic and learned reactions to social interaction – the ability to read social cues, recognize faces and the information contained in those faces, and respond to these cues in an appropriate manner. People who were more skilled in these responses were more likely to be included, respected, and cared for by the group, and therefore more likely to survive and pass on their genes.[17]

Emotional intelligence has been shown to enhance well-being and productivity. In a meta-analysis of the impacts of emotional intelligence, Nicola Schutte and coauthors found positive associations between emotional intelligence and mental, physical, and psychosomatic health.[18] EI also helps increase productivity through reduced procrastination (like checking emails) and boredom because you're more willing to sit with negative or uncomfortable emotions.[19] People who are self-aware tend to be higher performing at their jobs, partly because they are more conscientious.[20] Similarly, in the largest study of business leaders ever undertaken, self-awareness was identified as a key ability contributing to participants' success in their respective roles.[21]

EI also has a positive influence on creativity. Self-compassion increases your curiosity and optimism, both of which are correlated with creativity.[22] Empathy, specifically the ability to read someone's emotions through their eyes, likewise correlates with creativity metrics.[23] Finally, teams that have emotionally intelligent members generally share greater trust and a more collaborative work environment, which improves their ability to come up with more creative ideas.[24]

HOW EMOTIONAL INTELLIGENCE HELPS YOU DO BETTER RESEARCH

What all this means is that your professional research self is inseparable from your emotional needs. As a result, scholarly research requires and benefits from emotional intelligence, just like other professional and creative endeavors. Here, we describe four distinct applications of understanding human needs and using emotional intelligence to help you in research settings (see Figure 3.1). We divide these applications into those that use self-awareness and self-compassion – helping you recognize and accept your own wants, needs, and interests – and those founded on empathy – helping you work more effectively with research colleagues and research subjects.

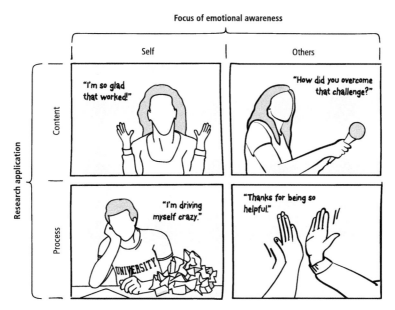

FIGURE 3.1 Applying emotional intelligence to research process and content, for yourself and others

Understand Your Research Process through Self-Awareness and Self-Compassion

The first benefit of using emotions is as a window into your own needs, interests, and traits that might otherwise remain hidden. Noticing the emotions that emerge as you do your research can provide valuable feedback in helping you discover your own idiosyncratic research process, including time management issues, goal setting, and which analytic methods will mesh best with your personality. At their core, these process issues are ultimately about your individual preferences, skills, talents, quirks, and how they can best be channeled to produce interesting scholarship. The way you feel about your current research process – whether exuberant or despairing – can yield important clues about your strengths and/or reveal mismatches in your current work style. This helps you decide how you might redesign your process in response.

Sometimes this occurs on a small scale. As I (Nicola) write this, I am procrastinating turning my attention to revising a journal manuscript that was rejected three days ago. Being rejected is not pleasant under any circumstances, but underlying the raw procrastination is a deeper fear: If this paper (a sole-authored piece I've been working on for two years) doesn't get accepted, maybe I won't get tenure. As I admit that fear is underlying the procrastination, it is important that I exercise self-compassion: There's no point in punishing myself for procrastinating on the revisions. It also helps me find a way forward. Brute force alone probably won't help me do the revisions (since that could just reinforce the fear). Instead, I'm trying to remind myself of the strengths of this manuscript and the research it is based on: It is reporting novel results and with some editing it is likely I will be able to publish it, whether in this journal or another. By explicitly addressing this fear, I can help myself reframe my relationship to the paper and make progress on it.

Similarly, many PhDs know the experience of worry before meeting with their advisor. Li Jie, a PhD student who had transferred from another university and then took one of our classes, regularly fretted about meeting with his advisor. In the course of exploring the underlying emotional causes for his hesitation, he realized that he was unconsciously putting pressure on himself to be the perfect student in order to pay his advisor back, since the advisor had helped him transfer to his prestigious new university. Recognizing his unconscious desire to pay his advisor back was freeing for Li Jie, as it helped him separate his gratitude for the help in transferring from his desire to impress his advisor.

In both of these examples, the researcher could have moved forward without recognizing the underlying emotions, but doing so would likely have been slower and more painful. By understanding when you feel afraid, angry, or sad about a task, an interaction, or your work more generally, you can gain greater insight into your research process and learn how to move forward more efficiently, effectively, and happily.

Particularly when negative emotions are involved, noticing emotions may only be the first step. It is absolutely possible to understand that you are insecure or unhappy and then respond unkindly to yourself or others: with criticism, frustration, or anger. That's where self-compassion comes in.

Adam learned this lesson poignantly when his first child was born. Before he became a parent, he could outwork almost any challenge he faced. If he was overwhelmed with teaching and research, he would just work as late into the night and as much of the weekend as it took to get the work done. After his daughter was born, the importance of spending time with his family added a new constraint. But Adam was often frustrated at himself that he was less capable of solving problems that he would have solved in the past through sheer application of hours. Through self-reflection and some long hard conversations with his wife, he realized that it was OK that he could not always be the perfect researcher at work. By treating himself with self-compassion, he gained a more realistic sense of the very real trade-offs he faced. And as he then looked at those trade-offs and considered his emotions, he knew that quality time with his family far outweighed solving every single problem faced at work. The combination of self-awareness and self-compassion helps him make smart choices about which select occasions he will let work eat into family time and about the majority of times when he says no much more often than he used to.

Positive emotions can also help guide your research process. Noticing what inspires you can provide insight for selecting between projects or charting the best path forward. Or you might want to track your process so you learn when you are really in a groove. *Flow* is a state of focused concentration, often where you are so immersed in an activity that you stop noticing that time has passed. When you are in a state of flow, your level of skill is well-matched with the task at hand. Work feels effortless, you show high levels of performance, and you can learn new information quickly.[25] Flow is often accompanied by high levels of happiness or satisfaction. By becoming aware of when you feel flow doing research, you can begin to mimic the work settings and activities that help you enter that state more quickly.

Develop Your Project through Self-Awareness and Self-Compassion

Emotional intelligence can also help you develop the content of your research, as emotions can be a useful tool for identifying important research questions. At an individual level, learning to recognize excitement can indicate a promising direction for a new research project. In the story that introduced this chapter, part of Amber's insight in embracing her emotions was listening to the excitement she felt when she returned to New York City after ten months away. Even though the direction of research was uncertain when she made her decision to change topics, she was excited to move forward knowing she would get to work in a place about which she cared deeply.

Likewise, anger, frustration, indignation, and sadness can all inspire and motivate high-quality research. For instance, when Jorge was starting his PhD program, his home country of Mexico was struck by an earthquake. Seeing his hometown flattened and his family struggling to get assistance frustrated and saddened him. It also pushed him to change the planned direction of his research, leading him to investigate what motivates governments to respond to disasters in the way they do and what that means for the people affected. In this example, by listening to his emotions, Jorge found a project he found meaningful and that would have a real impact in the world.

Finally, some academic disciplines have rich traditions of using the researcher's emotions as part of the research inquiry itself. For instance, anthropologists have traditionally gone into the field to observe people living and working in action. As postmodern critique destroyed the myth of an "objective" observer, the researcher's own reactions as observer became part of how an anthropologist came to understand encounters with their subjects.[26] Many disciplines with familial ties to anthropology – including public health, sociology, and human geography – similarly use the researcher's own perceptions and emotions as part of their data.

Understand a Team's Process through Empathy

It is not only your own emotions that can provide insight when doing research. Exploring the feelings, wants, and needs of others involved in a situation and how those emotions might be shaping their behavior can also lead to greater understanding. When seeking to understand the emotions of others, researchers must draw on empathy, figuratively placing themselves into someone else's shoes and imagining what the world looks like from that position. Active listening – focusing on hearing another person's story, including their wants and needs, without interjecting your own opinion or story – is another skill to build empathy. Exercises 3.3 and 3.7 give you ideas to practice both of these approaches.

One use of empathy is to assist in managing relationships with mentors or mentees. (This is covered in greater detail from the mentee perspective in Chapter 9 and from the mentor perspective in Chapter 12.) Both advisor and student may feel work-related pressure as well as stress in their personal lives. From the graduate student point of view, interactions with advisors can be fraught with a variety of emotions, including anxiety, frustration, disappointment, guilt, and sometimes anger. But what the student may not understand is that in almost all cases (apart from the worst examples of negligence or abuse of position), the advisor's world is shaped by constraints and pressures that generally explain whatever caused the student's frustration. An advisor might be acting out of their own anxiety about tenure decisions, for example, or setting demanding standards because of their faith in their students' talents. Similarly, from the advisor's point of view, a student might appear to be underperforming but might actually be having difficulty adjusting to graduate school or dealing with difficulties with a spouse. By considering the other person's emotional experience, you might find that your own feelings about the situation become more complex and you develop greater understanding. Or, even if your own anger, frustration, or worry persist, which is perfectly natural – remember, mindfulness asks us to start from the feelings that exist without judging them – the exercise of considering the other person's point of view might still be helpful for suggesting strategies to frame the problem from a mutual point of view that helps move toward a solution.

Empathy and talking about your emotions are also tools to keep a team functioning at its best. Collaborators on a research project or coauthors on a paper, for example, are engaged in a joint research process influenced not only by the team's progress, but also by the emotional well-being of the individual members. Given the potential for periods of stress, strain, busyness, and plain old bad days to derail progress, one technique we have found helpful is to pay explicit attention to the emotional state of our team members and shape our expectations for the day or week or month accordingly. Some might say this is allowing emotions to get in the way of making research programs; we see it as meeting the team members where they are. If a team persists in moving forward without recognizing when individual members are stressed about another project, or dealing with a difficult family situation, or simply too busy with the end of a semester to contribute as they promised, issues that began outside the team will inevitably begin to affect the team's productivity and, eventually and even worse, the relationship among team members.

The author team has learned through experience about the importance of making a space for emotions as a way to build good working relationships. In each of our research lives, we have had occasions when we were not as explicit about emotions as we wished we would have been in hindsight. But as a result of those experiences on other projects, the five of us writing this book have made it a priority to know what is going on in one another's personal and professional lives and understand how much space has thus been left for this project. The space available has fluctuated at different times for each of us. Adam and his wife moved across the country and had two babies. Nicola got married and started a tenure-track position. Amanda also transitioned to a permanent research position in a government agency and dealt with significant health issues. Anja has two kids and teaching positions on two continents. Sebastian joined the team after the rest of us had well-established working relationships, and we had to consciously integrate him into our existing team norms and traditions. Yet over the ten years between when we started working with each other and when we delivered the final manuscript of this book, we maintained clear lines of communication about our needs and feelings. This ultimately strengthened our working relationships, which allowed us to write this book with authors scattered across two continents.

Paying attention to emotions can be used explicitly and proactively at the beginning of a collaboration as well. Research collaboration is about intellectual exchange, but that intellectual exchange rests on a foundation of effective team dynamics.[27] The formation of a research collaboration requires forming a set of interpersonal relationships and building a set of team norms and expectations, just like any other team formation process (see Chapter 10 for more). It can be an exciting time, but also a time of uncertainty and lack of clarity. By paying attention to the emotions and even explicitly marking for the team when you sense confusion or a breakthrough, the relationship and the content of the collaboration can unfold together.

One of Justin's most fulfilling collaborations was as a member of an interdisciplinary working group. One of the Principal Investigators set the tone for the working group from the first meeting when he opened with this statement: "I have three rules for this group. We're going to do good science, have fun, and no assholes." The "no assholes rule" and the tone set by the lead scientists to value interpersonal relationships carried through the project.[28] The group dynamic was frank and honest, with members able to offer one another critical feedback, but also able to ask questions about one another's workloads and much more likely to give others credit for ideas than to seek the limelight.

Develop Your Project through Empathy

Finally, understanding others' emotions can be a tool for the actual conduct of research, in order to better pose and then answer questions that matter to people in the world. This draws on the same empathy skills as working in a team but is applied to people who may be more diverse or hold different worldviews than you and your research colleagues.

First, many researchers are increasingly working with "lay" citizens in the practice of research. Given various names depending on how the engagement is structured (including coproduction, community-based research, or citizen science),[29] these processes entail researchers and nonscientists working together to (1) define what an interesting or relevant research question is; (2) decide how to answer that question; (3) collect or analyze the needed data; and/or (4) interpret data to solve real-world problems. When using this approach, a researcher has to be able to interact and empathize with everyone involved as if it is an extended research team. Exactly what this will look like will differ depending on the approach used. Scientists overseeing the Audubon Society's annual bird count have minimal contact with birders sending in their counts yet do need to make sure that these birders feel engaged and useful enough that they continue participating year after year.[30] In contrast, research produced in collaboration with indigenous or local communities can require explicit emotional investment and relationship building over a period of years.[31]

In interpretivist research in the humanities and social sciences, people's experience of the world – their worldviews, beliefs, and emotions – are the primary evidence used by researchers. In these settings, the researcher often lives, works, and builds rapport with the people who are being researched, in order to build trust and gain an insider's view of how their subjects' world works.[32] In other words, researchers in these disciplines may make use of empathy as a method and emotions as a data source (though they may not term their evidence "data").

Similarly, a number of fields that design interventions, technology, or products have also come to recognize the importance of considering human emotions, preferences, and relationships. For instance, a group of bioengineering students sought to improve the treatment of cystic fibrosis. After discovering that one of the biggest challenges is patient compliance, the students spent hours meeting directly with patients, doctors, and nurses to understand why patients weren't following through on their treatment. By using empathy to understand patient experiences, they learned that the biggest barriers were that treatment took a lot of time, was difficult to do alone, and was incredibly painful. Based on this knowledge, the students are developing a portable and passive device to treat cystic fibrosis.[33]

Empathy as a research tool can even extend beyond the human subjects or beneficiaries of the work to nonhuman entities. In one of our classes, Leah, a marine ecologist, wrote a short story from the perspective of an alga as a way to understand its needs and constraints. This led her to a series of researchable questions about how warming ocean water would affect these needs.

HOW TO USE EMOTIONS IN YOUR RESEARCH

Whether you are engaging in self-awareness and self-compassion or empathy, and whether you're applying these tools to your research process or content, you'll move through the same general series of steps to work with the emotions held by you and others. The stories we have told in the text above illustrate these steps in practice, but we call them out explicitly here to make them easier to apply to your own work.

Before you can work effectively with emotions, you have to accept that emotions play a role in research. For some people, this will come naturally, so you won't have to spend too much energy here. For other people, this may be challenging. If you have balked at or internally pushed back against this chapter, it may suggest that you need to work on consciously accepting that researchers – including you – are human, that being human means having emotions, and that therefore emotions inevitably play a role in your research process. We suggest four steps for harnessing the power of emotional intelligence in your process (Table 3.1 and Figure 3.2).

Steps for Emotional Intelligence

FIGURE 3.2 Four steps for using emotional intelligence

Table 3.1 *Four steps for using emotional intelligence*

Step	Self-awareness and self-compassion	Empathy
1. Notice	Start noticing consciously when and where emotions crop up in your research. For this step, you'll draw heavily on the tools of mindfulness introduced in Chapter 2 to notice how you feel as you move through your research. Try stopping and considering how you are feeling in situations when you might be used to being "rational" or "scientific" and not paying attention to your emotions. Notice the feedback your body is providing: when you feel tense, when you feel like you have butterflies in your stomach, when you feel relaxed.	Notice when your colleagues seem tense or agitated or happy. Sometimes this will show up in their words, sometimes in their body language, and sometimes you might need to explicitly ask someone for more information about what they are feeling. In the case of your research subjects, the ability to notice (though not necessarily discuss) emotions might even be a skill that you cultivate as part of your data-collection process, for example, when conducting interviews.
2. Name	As you notice different feelings and reactions in your body, it helps to name the specific emotion you are feeling. By naming the emotion, you pause the automatic response your body has learned. You assert some control over your emotions when you say, "I am angry" or "I am sad." Similarly, when you consciously note, "I am content," you become more aware of it. Naming your emotions helps your brain approach them cognitively.[34]	Depending on the situation, you might try explicitly naming the emotions you notice in others, though you'll want to remember that only the person experiencing it can actually name an emotion with authority. This means it is generally best to phrase it as a suggestion or question, for example, "You seem a bit stressed today, is everything OK?"

Table 3.1 (cont.)

Step	Self-awareness and self-compassion	Empathy
3. Understand	Next, you can start to notice whether your emotions are furthering your goals at that instant or whether they're hindering you, and in what ways. Try to bring a curiosity to your research challenges and consider how your emotions might be influencing them. The emotion is often like a tip of an iceberg to a set of assumptions you may be making about what is wrong.	If you notice those you are interacting with, such as a colleague or a mentee, experiencing strong emotions, you can experiment with techniques like an empathy map (see Exercise 3.7) to help them explore why they might be feeling that way. Or, depending on your relationship, you could ask gently for more information about the situation and what might be making them upset, excited, or sad.
4. Choose how you want to act or react	At this point, play with choosing how you want to react to this emotion. It's important to note that you *always* react, as this is a biological inevitability. However, by adding steps 1–3, you can generally make a more conscious choice of how you want to respond. Especially in the face of negative emotions, this is the stage where you have the choice to actively choose an attitude of self-compassion. While that won't make the cause go away, research suggests the non-judgmental attitude can actually shift how you experience the negative emotion.[35]	As you engage in empathy, notice how it makes you feel. Are you becoming sympathetic to your colleagues or subjects? Do you feel annoyed? Do you want to choose a different way to react? This might also be a moment for self-compassion. Perhaps you can't choose a different reaction right now. That means you have a chance to practice meeting yourself where you are without judgment.

In naming your emotions, it helps to know what you're looking for. Humans are generally considered to have four basic categories of emotions: happy, sad, afraid, and angry (though there is some debate over exactly how to divide emotions and into how many categories).[36] Within each type, however, there are many nuances. For instance, consider the ways different varieties of happiness feel: joy comes with a quick rush of dopamine, while serenity is much calmer. There are also second-order emotions, including shame, guilt, pride, and embarrassment; these more complex emotions arise based on the way you cognitively process an experience through self-reflection and self-evaluation, rather than happening automatically.[37]

As you practice observing your emotions, try to be as precise as you can in describing what you're feeling. Table 3.2 provides an overview of the common categories of emotions, with a few examples of ways we've seen them show up in research. Remember, though, that the same event can lead to different emotions, depending on the person and the circumstances. For instance, having a paper rejected might variably lead to anger, fear, or embarrassment – or perhaps even occasionally relief.

TWO ROLES FOR EMOTIONS: DIAGNOSIS AND PREVENTION

Emotional intelligence plays two distinct roles. One is diagnostic, based on noticing (usually unpleasant) emotions and tracing back their root causes. The other is preventative, using self-awareness, self-compassion, and empathy to preempt emotionally difficult situations. While this second role for emotional intelligence is often more challenging, with practice you can achieve it more often.

Diagnose Problems, Including Problems You Don't Want to Be Having

Emotions can help you identify problems. When feelings are serving this function, they tend to be unpleasant feelings: fear, anger, frustration, and so on. This signaling function of feelings, with the often negative emotions involved, is why the feelings themselves often get

Table 3.2 *How emotions might manifest in research*

Emotion	Examples of ways the emotions could manifest in research		
	Self	Colleagues	Research subjects
Basic emotions			
Anger (rage, frustration, disgust)	Messing up a presentation; Getting scooped; Running out of time for PhD work because you have too many other things you are responsible for	Finding out that teammates are not taking a collaborative project deadline seriously; Receiving conflicting feedback from your mentor; Learning someone used your ideas without attribution	Disagreeing fundamentally with research subjects (e.g., on politics); Having subjects not follow through during an intervention
Happiness (joy, serenity, gratitude)	Getting on the plane to go begin fieldwork; Having a novel insight that builds off your prior work; Identifying the argument that describes your data	Having a productive team meeting; Receiving support from a mentor or colleague	Connecting on a deeper level with a research interviewee; Meeting the leaders of a community initiative you are studying and hearing their stories
Sadness (grief, dissatisfaction, neglect)	Losing notes or data (e.g., in a lab flood or due to a computer glitch); Spending days lonely or isolated on your new campus; Discovering that your data don't support a hypothesis	Interacting with a colleague who is struggling; Seeing someone else's success or achievements and wishing you had them	Hearing tragic stories from interviewees or research subjects; Dealing with loss related to your research topic (e.g., climate change, poverty)

Table 3.2 (cont.)

Emotion	Examples of ways the emotions could manifest in research		
	Self	Colleagues	Research subjects
Fear (anxiety, panic, horror)	Being convinced your ideas aren't good enough Worrying about getting funding to do your work Wondering whether you will ever get a job	Worrying about your ability to get funding to pay for students Wanting not to let your teammates down	Being unsure if you are acting unethically or betraying confidentiality in your interactions with subjects Worrying that your results won't show anything worthwhile
Complex emotions			
Guilt	Not getting as much done over the weekend as you planned Taking time off to go on vacation or to a friend's wedding	Showing up to a meeting without any new results Deciding to quit a collaborative project midstream	Forgetting to send thank you emails after an interview Not writing up results in a way that is useful to the community members who participated in the research
Pride	Getting your first paper published Receiving a major award	Hearing someone say your work is impactful Feeling more successful than a struggling colleague	Learning that your work made a difference to someone
Boredom	Entering the 3000th data point into Excel Rereading the sixth draft of a manuscript Checking email	Sitting through a long-winded colleague's presentation Explaining statistical significance (again) to your advisee	Waiting for research subjects to finish a test

framed as a "problem" to be solved. But it is not the emotions them-selves that are the problem. The emotions simply exist, without being inherently good or bad: They are reactions that arise in the brain and body in response to stimuli from the world.

By consciously noticing them, your feelings can become an indicator: a source of feedback about what you think or need that you might not have previously been paying attention to or realized. By learning to recognize your emotional responses, you get access to a rich source of information about subtle tensions that are acting in your life.[38]

One of the most important sources of information that emo-tions provide is helping you become conscious of problems, even when they are problems you wish you were not having. Our colleagues Bill Burnett and Dave Evans, authors of the best-selling book *Designing Your Life*, call this the "accept" phase of problem solving, emphasizing that mindful acceptance of undesired emotions is a necessary prerequisite to intentional action.[39] Self-compassion also helps in the diagnosis of problems, since even when you recognize a problem, that doesn't always translate into acceptance. Cultivating self-compassion eventually results in acceptance of your emotions, whatever they are, thereby letting you move forward.

Daphne was a British postdoc studying the role of race in devel-opment policy in Kenya, a challenging topic for a white woman coming from a former colonial power to undertake. Midway through her pro-ject, she presented preliminary results at a conference in-country and received a harsh reaction. In short, multiple audience members sug-gested her study was culturally insensitive; one even hinted that she was replicating colonial power relations in her research design. Understandably, Daphne was devastated. For the first two or three days after this nightmare conference presentation, she could barely keep from crying when she thought about her research. But as she brought a combination of self-awareness and self-compassion to the situation, she began to feel less miserable. She first focused on noticing what she was feeling and also on engaging with the contents of the criticism. While she recognized that the study was certainly not perfect, she also reminded herself that she was working on challenging topics in a difficult context. She knew she had made mistakes and might have designed certain elements of the study differently if she had known in the beginning everything she knew now. But she also recognized that she was genuinely doing her best, that she had carefully sought the advice of many people of various races in Kenya in the early stages of the research, and that no study in that context would ever please everyone. By approaching herself gently in what turned out to be the toughest single moment of her study, Daphne was able to move forward in the face of what might otherwise have been paralyzing criticism. Her self-compassion also helped her stay open about the content of the critiques and incorporate the parts she felt were justified into how she presented her final results. Given the challenging environment in which Daphne was working, self-compassion became a tool not only to manage her own emotions but also to grapple with the inherent contradictions of being white and British working in postcolonial Kenya.

Prevent Problems Before They Emerge

Eventually, the regular practice of mindfulness, self-awareness, self-compassion, and empathy helps you recognize how emotions might influence a situation in advance, before a problem actually develops. You learn to watch your feelings about your research process or content and continually ask how they are changing and why. This self-awareness allows you to identify patterns in your emotions, including situations that psychologists sometimes call "triggers," or which you might think of as landmines.[40] Unaddressed, these will blow up and leave you angry or stressed or stuck with a problem. Self-compassion, too, aids in preventing problems, as you come to accept limits on your energy or capacity and be kind to yourself.

When Marco started his graduate work, he really enjoyed the literature review – digging into new topics – and doing the field research. But he was struggling deeply with writing. He was afraid to bring his own opinions to the writing, as all the authors he was citing sounded so smart and he felt that he didn't have anything original to say. But he persisted, trying hard to write. The more he pushed himself, though, the more he felt that what he was producing wasn't as good as he'd like it to be. One day, Marco went to a lecture on campus, and the speaker said that many people spend their lives comparing themselves to others and then beating themselves up for not being as smart or strong or wealthy as their neighbor. He realized this was exactly how he was treating his writing – judging himself for not being smart enough or good enough. He realized it was OK to feel inadequate – it was human! – and that instead of berating himself, he could try being less harsh. He could try just opening his notebook every day and writing: one word at a time, one page at a time. This moment was transformative for Marco, helping him incorporate self-compassion to help himself write freely. While today Marco is still harder on himself than he might like when he starts a new project and can't easily put words on the page, he proactively works to avoid it. He has a quote from a classic book on writing taped to his desk to remind himself that the goal is to write, not to be perfect: "Almost all good writing begins with terrible first efforts. You need to start somewhere."[41] By reading this quote before he sits down to write, he helps himself write proactively despite his tendency toward self-criticism.

In interactions with team members and research subjects, empathy can similarly head off difficult situations before they develop. Being aware of emotions can suggest when others are not getting their needs met, such as when they are feeling unappreciated. By recognizing early on how others' feelings are influencing teamwork or research interactions with subjects, you can take steps to prevent issues from escalating.

When she started her postdoc, Nadia wasn't really sure what she should expect from her new supervisor. While she had had a great relationship with her PhD advisor, she hadn't really gotten the career guidance she hoped for, and she was anxious that her new mentor would serve that role. This worry, plus the fact that her supervisor was famous and would be traveling a lot, made Nadia quite nervous before their first meeting. In fact, she was losing sleep, worrying about how to express all of her needs to her mentor. However, she decided to address this worry face on. She put herself in her new supervisor's shoes and explored his needs, wants, constraints, and interests in his position as her postdoc mentor. She realized that he would benefit from landing her in a good job – he kept a list of recent placements on his website – which made it not seem quite so scary for her to broach the idea of career mentoring. And, once that fear was out of the way, Nadia also felt empowered to ask how she could get regular meetings even while her mentor was traveling, rather than waiting until she needed guidance. Empathy gave her the impetus to be proactive in managing her relationship with her mentor.

SUMMARY

In this chapter, we have argued that emotions play a central role in research. By acknowledging them, you gain more intentional control over how you do your research and can tap into an important source of information about your motivations and implicit reactions to the world around you. With the skill of emotional intelligence – including self-awareness, self-compassion, and empathy – you can fundamentally reshape the role that emotions play in your work.

EXERCISES

Try It

3.1 **Notice your emotions:** Set three timers to go off sometime during your workday. When they go off, try to recall the last emotion you felt before you heard the alarm. Notice also how you are feeling about your research in general. Try this every day for a week, varying the times the alarm is set for. At the end of the week, look for emotional patterns across the week. How have you been feeling about research? About life? How are they related, or not? If you like, draw a map of your emotional journey, noting the inflection points of when your mood went up or down and what triggered this change.

3.2 **Name your emotions:** When you check in with a close friend or colleague about your work, practice naming the emotions you feel. Go beyond the basics like happy and sad. Experiment with representing the full spectrum and intensity of your emotions by precisely describing what you are experiencing. For example, instead of just saying you are mad, be specific. Are you angry, upset, irritated, furious, irate, etc.? Don't forget about positive emotions, like excitement, relief, wonder, and gratitude. How does naming your emotions affect your experience of them?

3.3 **Practice active listening:** Find a close friend or colleague and take turns discussing a topic like your goals for the year or relationships with mentees or mentors.[42] When you are listening, you are only allowed to express sympathy, ask clarifying questions about your partner's topic, or say, "Tell me more," to encourage more detail. Consciously refrain from offering advice or sharing your own story until it is your turn. What was it like to stay fully present and focused on listening to your partner?

3.4 **Practice self-compassion:** Sometimes practicing spontaneous self-compassion is difficult. Try writing a letter to yourself where you speak in a forgiving way about your strengths and weaknesses in the same generous tone you would use to speak to a friend who was being hard on themselves. You might like to use the following sentence starters to help you:

- I remember I don't need to be perfect when . . . (or because . . .)
- I forgive myself for making a mistake when I . . . (or because . . .)
- A self-compassionate behavior I noticed in myself today that I am excited to nurture is . . .
- When I've had a hard day, I take care of myself by . . .

Alternatively, you can try writing the letter from the perspective of a close friend. What would they say to you?[43]

Practices

3.5 **Five why's for emotions:** As you go through your work (for instance, if you have a decision to make, or if you find yourself bored and procrastinating), build a habit of pausing to ask, "What am I feeling about this?" and naming the emotion you feel. If a specific emotion isn't immediately obvious, try asking, "Why?" successively to uncover any hidden emotions. For instance, "I don't know whether to start collecting data. *Why don't I know?* I'm not sure if I have done enough background reading. *Why do I think I need background reading?* My advisor hasn't given me an indication that I'm ready. *Why do I want my advisor's approval?* I'm scared that I don't have a good idea." (If you have worked through Chapter 2, notice that this pause to notice emotions naturally complements the pause to build awareness introduced in Exercise 2.5.)[44]

3.6 **Reframe three things:** Deliberately practice self-compassion. At the end of the day, write down two or three things that didn't go well or that you are worried, scared, or angry about. Describe what happened and what you're feeling about it. Now, imagine that a close friend (not you) were feeling these things. Write one or two sentences in the same compassionate tone you might use to comfort your friend to support the emotions that you're feeling.

3.7 **Walk in someone else's shoes:** Imagine that you are walking in someone else's shoes and try to see the world from their point of view. Draw that person or write their name at the center of a sheet of paper. Then answer these questions: What do they need to do? What do they say? How do they spend their time? What do they hear? What do they think and feel? What keeps them up at night? How do they see you? You can either focus this exercise on their experiences in general or on their perspective on a given situation.

Reflect

3.8 How emotionally aware are you in general? How do you tend to express your emotions? How comfortable are you talking about emotions?

3.9 To what extent do you currently make use of emotions in your research practice? In general, do you think emotions help, or are they a distraction? How do emotions affect your research process on a day-to-day basis? Does this answer vary for different types of emotions?

3.10 When are you the most fulfilled as a researcher? What actions, behaviors, or events lead you to feel fulfilled? Conversely, when do you feel the most challenged or frustrated as a researcher? Are there particular actions, behaviors, or events that generally cause you to feel frustrated?

3.11   To what extent do the people around you support emotional intelligence? Are your coworkers willing to be vulnerable with each other? To what extent do your department, colleagues, and/or teams support emotional intelligence? How about your field of study? Are certain emotions more acceptable than others? How does this context influence you?

4   Solve the Right Problem

Richard was the Principal Investigator of a large biology lab. And he was worried. He was coming up for promotion to full professor, and his group had published half as many papers in the last two years as they had in any previous two-year period. Without publications, he didn't know if he'd be able to renew the National Institutes of Health (NIH) grant that funded most of the lab; without the grant, it was unlikely he'd receive his promotion. He tried to figure out what was going on but didn't really see any trends that could explain the drop: The group size hadn't declined (it had actually grown), and they were working on similar types of questions as they'd always studied. So, he concluded that his team just must not be working hard enough. He called a lab meeting, shared his concerns with the group, and asked everyone to push forward. But a few months later, the lab's morale was low, people were putting in long hours, and the productivity didn't seem to have changed much.

When you are facing "a problem," it can feel big and scary. Just like Richard, your first instinct is often to try to address it as quickly as possible or just to work harder and longer until the situation is resolved. Or think about the last time a friend came to you with a problem. If you're like most people, after they told you what was going on, you likely suggested solutions they could try – again working them toward a resolution as quickly as possible. The challenge, though, is that by jumping to a (re)solution, you may end up missing important contextual clues and thus choose a less than optimal solution.

The way that you understand the problem you are facing is intimately connected to the way you approach solving it. While there are numerous definitions of what a problem is,[1] at its most basic a problem is "a perceived gap between the existing state and a desired state" of the world.[2] How you view the gap between the existing state and your desired state fundamentally influences your view of the challenge you are facing. Most often the word *problem* is associated with a deficiency that needs to be remedied. But that gap can also be viewed as an opportunity to improve the existing state to something better than currently exists. In research there are plenty of opportunities where your challenge is to figure out how to improve an existing situation. In this chapter, we use the term *problems* to refer to both these instances and the more traditional "problems to be solved," as they can be addressed using similar cognitive approaches.

You carry assumptions about what the problem is and about whether the problem is positive or negative; these assumptions have a certain path dependence that leads you to a pre-constrained set of possible solutions.[3] Imagine you're struggling to make a figure for a paper, perhaps because your software keeps crashing. If you consider that the problem is, "I need to fix the software so I can make this figure," all of your solutions will be focused on debugging the software (generally an incredibly frustrating task). But if you were instead to say, "I need a way to make this figure by tomorrow," there are many more possible solutions at your disposal (like drawing it by hand, using a different software program, or asking a coauthor to take over).

The same challenge arises when you jump to conclusions related to your research content. Let's say you study drug use. If you define the problem as, "There are not enough low-cost drug treatment centers," your research will focus on questions like why there aren't more treatment centers or on how to make existing treatment centers cheaper. But if you take a broader framing of the problem – "Drug users lack places to seek treatment" – you open up many more possible directions for your research to explore.[4] It's like the old joke about someone looking for their keys under a street lamp. Their friend comes along and asks, "Did you lose them under the lamp?" The searcher responds, "No, but I can see under the light here." Your framing of a problem is like a street lamp; it shines your problem-solving attention in one particular direction and makes it much harder to see things outside that cone of light.

By rushing to a solution, you may even end up solving the wrong problem! When you define a problem in what seems to be the most obvious way, you make yourself susceptible to premature closure – a cognitive error where your initial assumption about the nature of the problem blinds you to alternative (and possibly more accurate or help-ful) explanations.[5] Indeed, in studies of doctors, premature closure (latching onto an initial diagnosis) can lead to misdiagnosis.[6]

You'll be more efficient and effective if you first slow down to explore your problem, consider multiple potential views of the pro-blem, and then are intentional in selecting one. Albert Einstein – some-one considered to have been a fairly creative person – is apocryphally quoted as saying: "If I had only one hour to save the world, I would spend fifty-five minutes defining the problem, and only five minutes finding the solution." Even if he didn't say it, it's worthwhile advice to heed. By finding ways to more fully understand a problem and the assumptions you have about its causes and/or solutions, you can be more flexible, find more options for solving the problem, move much faster once you switch to solving mode, and make sure you spend your time on more meaningful (rather than simply obvious) problems.

USE AMBIGUITY TO YOUR ADVANTAGE: FIND AND FRAME PROBLEMS TO DO BETTER RESEARCH

Humans are what psychologists call ambiguity intolerant.[7] People don't like being in situations where the outcome is uncertain, where they don't know the answer, or they don't feel like they are in control of what happens next. Ambiguity challenges the brain, specifically the dorsolateral prefrontal cortex, which receives and processes new infor-mation. Because ambiguity by definition is a situation in which too little information exists, your brain cannot understand it immediately or classify it into a mental model to guide your decision-making. When the brain is not able to make an informed decision quickly, you feel anxious, which only increases the cognitive effort needed to make a decision or solve a problem.[8] When faced with ambiguity, human brains try to resolve it quickly, to help you escape the feeling of not being in control. Specifically, you tend to jump into finding a solution to your malaise as quickly as possible.

Taking time to consider problems before rushing to solve them means becoming comfortable with ambiguity – learning to stay in uncertain situations, where you don't know the answer and are unsure where you are headed. *Ambiguity tolerance* "refers to the way an individual (or group) perceives and processes information about ambiguous situations or stimuli when confronted by an array of unfamiliar, complex, or incongruent clues."[9] People who are more ambiguity tolerant seek unexpected or unfamiliar people and settings and avoid settling into a routine, and they are comfortable when they don't know the answer.[10] Ambiguity tolerance is generally considered to be beneficial for creativity. In surveys, people who are more tolerant of ambiguity score higher on creativity indices.[11] Tolerance for ambiguity likewise may contribute to the generation of ideas in the process of creative problem solving, enabling you to explore new possibilities, unusual ideas, and uncommon paths.[12]

The good news is that, even if you are someone who loves routine and familiarity, you can develop your ability to lean into ambiguity.[13] Because research – both its process and content – is essentially all about solving problems, learning to work with ambiguity in research means slowing down when you are faced with a new problem. The skill that creativity scholars call problem finding "includes the anticipation of problems, identifying problems when none exist, and structuring an ill-defined problem so problem solving efforts can proceed."[14] Specifically, learning how to (1) find the right problem to solve and (2) frame it in an effective manner will help you be more efficient in moving through your research and ultimately help you develop more creative, impactful solutions.[15]

Understand Your Problem Space

The first step in figuring out what problem you are facing is to step back and consider the whole set of questions or components that are relevant to the dilemma you're facing. There are always multiple potential "problems" behind what you immediately see. Scholars of decision-making call this suite of questions your *problem space*.[16] For instance, if your problem is what to eat for dinner, your problem space might include questions about what food you have in the fridge, whether you have time to go shopping, whether you want to go out to eat, whether a friend or spouse or children are also included and what they want, what your budget is, whether you are craving your mom's chicken noodle soup, etc. Each of these questions is relevant, but not all are necessary to answer every time you eat dinner. Your solution – what you end up eating for dinner – will depend on which set of questions you consider (see Figure 4.1).

In the realm of research, a problem space for deciding on the research topic for your dissertation would include questions around

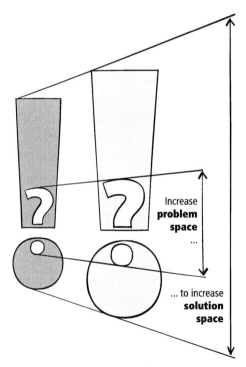

FIGURE 4.1 Increase the problem space to increase the solution space

what a "novel" contribution is in your field; how much risk you want to take with a cutting edge topic; whether you like working with data at a computer, in a lab, or in the field; whether your advisor will be easier to work with if you choose a particular topic, etc. Each of these is an important question to explore, but you can't answer all of these at once, and it's unlikely you need to answer all of them to move forward.

Stepping back to consider your problem space can help you determine what area of a broad field you'd like to focus on for a research project. In one of our classes, Rajiv was struggling to feel ownership over his PhD research, as he had been hired to work on a large grant and everything he did felt predefined. He sketched out the story of his advisor's project – essentially drawing the whole problem space – and then sketched in detail the area of that space he was working on. By seeing these two drawings in relation to each other, Rajiv was able to start refining his specific research questions and feel that he was making a concrete contribution to the field, albeit within the context of a larger project.

Stopping to broaden a problem space can also help you find new solutions to problems in your research process. Maria was the lab manager for Richard's lab – the low-productivity lab introduced at the start of the chapter. After the lab meeting when Richard shared his concern that the research team had not produced enough papers in the last year, Maria (and her colleagues) left the meeting feeling depressed, as they felt they were working hard with nothing to show for it. However, when Richard raised the concern again a couple of months later, Maria was fresh from a class with our team. Rather than rush to solving the "productivity" problem, Maria decided to first observe the problem space and gain some empathy and understanding for what the problem was really about. She met with the lab students and staff to brainstorm what might be underlying their slow progress and then had everyone track how they were spending their time over a week. She found that despite the high number of total hours they were putting in, they were collectively spending almost 80 percent of their workweeks on administrative tasks, and so only had a few hours to actually do research or write papers. At the next meeting, she proposed that Richard consider hiring an administrative assistant to free up the researchers' time for research. Persuaded by the empirical data from Maria and the rest of his team, Richard agreed. This solution would never have been possible if Maria just focused on Richard's initial view of the problem (i.e., we all need to simply work more) instead of stopping to explore what the underlying issue actually was.

Rarely does the exploration of the problem space point to as obvious a path as Maria identified. Thus, once you've broadened your problem to investigate the problem space, you need to figure out how to proceed. This entails two distinct tasks: finding the problem you want to address and then framing it in a way that makes it most tractable. Problem finding is figuring out which of the many possible things in the problem space is the real problem you need to solve (or at least which needs to be addressed first). Problem framing is asking which scale or angle of that problem you can or want to address.

Finding: Which Problem Should You Start With?

Despite the name, *problem finding* does not mean we're asking you to look for or create problems. It instead is the task of narrowing down your problem space to figure out which of the potential questions you might ask is closest to the root cause of the problem. Importantly, this is rarely the first problem you saw. Instead, that one is just the most obvious – there are often many other problems underlying or related to the obvious one. By looking at the larger problem space, you can see better what the problem's components are and where you might start. This is critically important when working with ill-structured problems (which is a lot of what you'll face in research), as they lack a clear starting point and can feel overwhelming.[17] Problem finding will help you determine which questions are perhaps easiest or most immediate to address, or which questions cut most directly to the heart of your dilemma. Starting with what Warren Berger calls "a more beautiful question" can "begin to shift the way [you] perceive or think about something – and that might serve as a catalyst to bring about change."[18]

A poignant example of the power of your starting question comes from Embrace Innovations, a social enterprise that originated in a class at the Stanford d.school.[19] They wanted to develop a more affordable incubator for hospitals in developing countries because (as they initially understood the problem) babies were dying because poor hospitals couldn't afford incubators. However, upon visiting Nepal, they realized this characterization didn't match the problem they saw in practice. The hospitals in Kathmandu had plenty of incubators, but there were very few babies to use them. In asking people why the incubators were empty, they realized that many premature births took place in rural areas, and few of these babies were able to make the journey into the city where the incubators were. The team realized that the real problem was that incubators were not portable and transportation for newborns was difficult. With this new view of the problem, they eventually developed a product that looks like a baby sleeping bag: a low-cost, portable way to keep babies warm without electricity. While developing a low-cost incubator would also have been beneficial (and in fact another team working in the same problem space did design one), by exploring the problem space and their starting assumptions, the Embrace team was able to find a more immediately impactful problem and thus a better solution.

In the research context, an important example of problem finding comes from sustainability scientist Pamela Matson and colleagues' work on agriculture in the Yaqui Valley, Mexico.[20] The team was interested in finding ways to improve crop yields while reducing how much fertilizer farmers had to use. While the conventional wisdom at the time was that more fertilizer necessarily led to higher yields, that didn't appear to be true in the Yaqui Valley: farmers had been increasing fertilizer applications, but without resultant increases in yields. So, the team decided to talk to farmers and observe them in the field. They found that it wasn't the amount of fertilizer that mattered in determining yields, but the relative timing of when fertilizer was applied and when irrigation started (which affected rate of loss of fertilizer to the environment). By spending time to explore the broad problem – "What influences the relationship between yields and fertilizer use in this location?" – they found a specific framing of the problem that would lead to helpful solutions.

If you don't pick the right problem to solve, solving that problem won't help you move forward or fix whatever underlying malaise you're feeling. Sometimes asking a useful question requires taking a broader view, challenging assumptions, and questioning the question you began with.[21] For example, when Kevin was midway through his PhD process, he felt burnt out and frustrated by his research. His initial reaction was that his problem was work–life balance and he decided to start engaging in more self-care activities like yoga. However, while this solution helped with the burnout, it didn't change his overall stress levels. Upon further consideration, he realized the bigger challenge was frustration that he lacked a direction for his research. Yoga didn't help him narrow down a dissertation topic, so he remained worried (if perhaps more Zen) about not knowing what he was doing. By not finding the right problem to solve – or more specifically not recognizing that there were two distinct problems that needed separate attention – Kevin ended up solving one problem while exacerbating another.

Framing: What Perspective Will Help You Solve the Problem?

Once you have identified which problem is most salient within the broad problem space, *problem framing* will help you explore different ways of viewing or naming the same problem to make it more tractable to solve. You can think of a framing as a perspective by which to view the problem. For example, in the early years of industrial agriculture, picking tomatoes by machine proved to be really difficult. The tomatoes were delicate, and machines couldn't be designed that could successfully pluck a tomato and hold it gently enough to not bruise it. Then, in the 1950s, University of California, Davis scientists Jack Hanna and Coby Lorenzen decided to frame the problem differently. Instead of asking how to improve the machine to pick tomatoes more gently, they asked whether they could breed tomatoes with a thicker skin that wouldn't bruise as easily. This new framing opened up numerous potential solutions, while the other had been a dead end.[22]

Just as which problem you decide to solve leads you to consider a particular set of solutions, so does your framing. In the tomato story, while the idea of building a thicker-skinned tomato was revolutionary at the time, that framing diverted the agricultural industry from other possible solutions that would lead to the tasty, thin-skinned heirloom tomatoes that are so prized today!

In your research, framing is a powerful tool to develop a novel research question or to choose the scope of your work. A senior scholar told us he uses wild perspectives to develop new research questions for studying land-use change: "If there's a conservation issue that was always approached from the viewpoint of the conservationist, what if I look at it from the viewpoint of the wildebeest? You try creatively to look at the issue in a way that hasn't been investigated." Similarly, your discipline or field may tend to look at research topics through a particular lens; by backing up to question these assumptions and consider other perspectives, you can find new, important questions to contribute to a well-studied field.

Likewise, when Amanda was figuring out her dissertation topic, she knew she was interested in how policy makers used information technology in their decision-making processes. But exactly which facet of that broad topic should she tackle? She used a tool called *Powers of ten* (see Exercise 4.4) to explicitly imagine what a research question might look like if she zoomed in or out to different units of analysis. At one end of the spectrum was a high-level analysis comparing across agencies: What technologies do government agencies use when making management decisions? At the other end was a close psychological study of an individual: What cognitive processes occur when a decision maker uses a decision-support tool? She was then able to use these possible topic framings to imagine the different methods that would be needed to study each unit of analysis. Exploring these multiple scales allowed Amanda to recognize she was most interested in group-level analysis: her eventual dissertation traced how a particular decision support software influenced group learning and decision making in a coastal-management planning process.[23] (In the years since finishing her PhD, other scales in the Powers of ten framing have reappeared in Amanda's research agenda.)

You can similarly use the idea of framing to enter a process-related problem in a way that feels more approachable or that has more diverse potential solutions. For instance, it's easy to feel stuck on a paper if you frame your problem as, "How will I possibly finish this conference paper in a month?" as that can feel overwhelming and you may have no idea of where to start. A quick time reframe – "What can I do to move this paper forward in the next thirty minutes?" – can open up a lot of possibilities (for example, write an outline, combine all the project notes into a single file, or figure out what analyses I need to do) and comes with the added bonus of feeling much less daunting than needing to finish the whole paper.

It's also important to consider the framing that you use to communicate your research to colleagues or students. Brian, a chemical engineer, was hired in the final days of a grant to rapidly build a scientific instrument to create nanofibers. When he started the project, his boss told him that the challenge was that they needed to make really thin fibers out of a specific polymer. So, Brian focused his energy on designing and building a tool that would use high voltages to spin extremely thin fibers. A month later Brian approached his boss with a completed instrument, but also with great confusion; while exploring the literature he had learned that the entire project had been accomplished before. His boss then explained the bigger scope of the research: that the polymer was the final achievement of a previous lab member, but they were actually working toward spinning a different material (with different properties from the polymer) to create fibers to make a fuel cell. Brian was incredibly frustrated; he felt like he had wasted his time and expertise designing a device to solve a previous step while leaving the biggest problem unsolved. If he had been told from the start that the project goal was to build a better material for a fuel cell – which is essentially the bigger problem space this research was operating in – he would have had many more ideas on how to go about addressing that problem. While it can be tempting to give a student or colleague a very well-defined task, by sharing the problem space and your reasoning for why you selected the problem framing you did, you give them the opportunity to share their perspectives on the problem space and help you direct your research in a new and interesting way. (And when you find yourself in a situation like Brian, where you've been given a problem to solve, your time might be better spent if you ask how your assigned task fits into the bigger problem space.)

APPROACHES TO FIND AND FRAME PROBLEMS

Adopt a Beginner's Mind

Finding and framing problems effectively requires keeping an open mind about what the right problem might be.[24] Sometimes core issues have nothing to do with the first problem you identified; other times the most tractable problem seems basic compared to the thing you were initially worried about. The goal of using a beginner's mind is to get out of your own way and approach the problem with fresh eyes: curious and mindful about the problem space, how problems within it interact, and how your own desires and the needs of other people intersect.

Every problem, even the easiest one, comes with a long list of implicit assumptions attached. By racing into solution mode, you take those assumptions as given and build a solution based on them. Approaching the problem with a curious and open mind can help you see what assumptions you're carrying and make them explicit. This allows you to explore whether they are actually true and discard any that are not valid.

In Chapters 2 and 3, you already started to practice the tools of mindfulness and identifying emotions – tools that contribute to approaching a problem space with a beginner's mind. By using mindfulness, you start to uncover *what* you are thinking about the problem. Then, just like a four-year-old inquiring about why the world works the way it does, repeatedly asking *why* you are thinking or feeling whatever it is you are thinking or feeling (see Exercises 3.5 and 4.1) can help uncover hidden assumptions and identify layers of related problems within your problem space. In other words, you want to get to the heart of what's really going on.

Crystal, a second-year PhD student, was frustrated because she knew she needed to spend more time thinking about big picture questions (like what topic to study for her dissertation) but constantly found herself losing hours focused on small detail tasks (like fixing computer code). This dynamic stressed her out. During one of our classes, Crystal's partner helped her dig into this frustration by repeatedly asking why:

- "When you sit down at your desk, why do you pick up a smaller task?"
- *"It feels easier, more manageable."*
- "Why do you think it feels easier?"
- *"The big picture is scary – I need to show my advisor progress and be smart. The smaller level details I can control."*

Then they switched to a different perspective on the problem:

- "Are there any times when you don't get sucked into details?"
- *"Yes, when I work at home."*
- "Why?"
- *"I love my desk at home. It's clean and pleasing. I like order a lot."*
- "So, do you think that big problems might feel too messy, whereas small details can be 'fixed' or 'put away'"?
- *"Yeah, I think that might be part of it!"*

In this conversation, by continually asking why, Crystal's partner was able to help her uncover some deeper emotions (e.g., fear of the big picture) and some potential causes of that fear. These ideas start to result in more tractable problems than her initial problem statement ("I need to force myself to think about the big picture every day.") For instance, Crystal could focus on finding ways to break her long-term research into discrete, more manageable tasks that could be finished and put away. (As a note, in this conversation it would have been easy for Crystal's partner to start suggesting solutions, but he was careful to stay in problem-finding mode.)

Finally, because the curiosity of a beginner's mind helps avoid the danger of getting stuck in one way of understanding a problem, it can be particularly important for problems that you encounter over and over again. Almost everyone has these – problems that you encounter regularly (and have never solved) and thus reflexively jump to the same view of the problem. Dave Evans and Bill Burnett call these anchor problems.[25] For instance:

- I need a day without any meetings before I can write.
- I need my advisor's approval before I can start any part of my research.
- I'll only be successful if I get a tenure-track job.

Reading these from the outside, you can see there are a number of assumptions built in to each of these problem framings – many of which are not necessarily true. So, when your thinking is fixed and not open, you need a way to help yourself see your problems from a new perspective or you won't be able to solve them. In these cases of habitual problems, or if a problem is really important to you or close to your heart, you may need to ask a friend or colleague for their perspective to help you see the assumptions you are making. (Or, alternatively, you might start with a smaller, easier, more tractable piece of the problem space.)

Consider Multiple Perspectives

The process of framing a problem essentially represents looking at your problem from multiple perspectives (Figure 4.2). One concrete approach is to write down several different lenses through which you could look at the problem. These could be the perspectives of different stakeholders (e.g., an advisor, a funding agency, or a family member), different mental models (e.g., a devil's advocate versus an optimist), or different lengths of time. Then, draw or write what the problem would look like from each perspective. What assumptions are you making

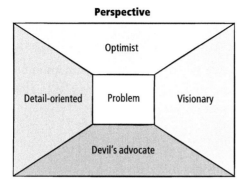

FIGURE 4.2 View a problem from multiple perspectives

about the problem? Would someone looking at your problem from these other perspectives make the same assumptions, or would they view it differently?

Use Solutions to Work Backward to the Problem Framing

While it's important to keep an open mind and be open to many possible solutions, there are times when solutions are simply more obvious than problem statements. You can actually make use of your brain's tendency to jump to solutions in order to identify underlying problems and the assumptions you make about them.

Here's an example. Within a problem space, a solution might arise first: for instance, a need, expressed as, "I need to publish more." If you stopped there, it would be a fairly limiting "problem-solving" process. But you can use this tendency as a tool to push yourself to identify the larger underlying problem you are implicitly assuming that solution is going to address. Dig deeper and ask: "Why do I need to publish more?" or "What am I assuming I would gain from publishing more?" This will help you see the deeper needs or desires behind the solution you identified, which help point you toward the problem you're implicitly identifying. In this case, deeper needs might be fear about the future ("I need to be competitive on the job market"), a desire to get research out to those who need it ("I need to reach a wider audience"), or a worry about letting collaborators down ("I need people to like working with me"). From the same apparent solution, you could uncover these three very different problems. And, each of these problems opens up a wide variety of other solutions, from finding ways to publicize your existing research to asking colleagues what else they look for in a collaborator.

How Do You Know You've Found the "Right" Problem?

We've been talking throughout this chapter about finding and framing the "right" problem. But how might you know when you've identified the right problem? Well, it depends on the situation and it's a bit of a "you know it when you see it" situation. But a few clues that you've found a useful problem statement are:

- **Root cause:** Sometimes it means finding the root cause of an issue. For example, someone might think he's struggling with learning statistics when the deeper problem is that he's unhappy doing a mathematics degree. In this case, solutions aimed at finding a better way to learn statistics will not make this person feel better as he'll still be doing research he fundamentally does not enjoy.
- **Immediacy:** Other times there is one problem that has to be solved first before another can be addressed. For example, the problem that someone cares about might be the paper they need to write. But if their computer hard drive just crashed, then most solutions addressed at writing the paper will be useless until they have a working computer again.
- **Tractability:** Sometimes there is a problem that is most feasible or tractable to solve first, or that solving it will create confidence, motivation, or otherwise change the emotional situation in order to make you more equipped to solve another problem (especially the root problem). For instance, someone might know they need to find a new PhD advisor, but for logistical reasons they can't do so until next semester. But maybe there's a problem they can solve in the meantime that would make their life more balanced and happier, like redesigning their course load.
- **Emotional response:** Your emotions can provide a clue as to where to start in your problem solving. A particular statement of the problem might resonate as something that you know in your gut that you need to address. (Note,

however, that an overwhelming emotional reaction can also suggest that the problem is hitting too close to home to solve right away or by yourself. In that case, you might try biting off a piece of it, or enlisting a friend to help. We'll talk about this more in Chapter 8.) Or a particular problem framing might inspire you to start digging in to solve it right away. If you can't wait to start brainstorming ideas in response to a problem statement, that is usually a sign you have found a generative problem framing.

Hopefully these give you some hints about choosing a problem statement. But if you still aren't sure, know that there isn't a perfect answer. Choose a statement of your problem and experiment with the exercises in Chapter 5 anyway. The real value of problem finding and framing is in the process and the intention of examining the problem space. Maybe you'll discover it wasn't the "right" problem, after all. Pay attention to your thoughts and feelings and learn from them. That's more information than you have right now, and you will be that much closer to reframing a different statement of the problem that you will be excited to move forward with. Ultimately, a problem statement is a tool for iteration. You can think of it like a scientific model: The problem framing you define might well be imperfect but what matters is whether it serves as a useful representation of the problem. If you find it doesn't do that job well enough, you'll always have the opportunity to cycle back and restate the problem in a more useful form later.

What Do You Do with a Problem Once You've Found It?

Once you've found the problem that feels like the right one to solve, it's time to work toward solving it. In order to do so, it helps to have a concrete statement of your problem and framing – in other words, to be precise and explicit about where you've chosen to start. Designers often use what's called a *needs statement*.[26] Write a description of the person or people whose problem it is, plus the underlying need you've identified. If you can capture any emotions you uncovered in your exploration, all the better. And even if the problem is one that you're facing yourself, write it in third person, as this helps you take a somewhat more objective stance. For instance:

- An overworked department chair needs to reconnect with her research.
- A shy PhD student needs confidence to question his critical advisor.
- A medical student needs to make genuine connections with underserved urban youth.
- A first-year demography PhD student needs to find the best statistical tool for spatial autocorrelation.
- An enthusiastic postdoc needs ways to prioritize when everything feels urgent.
- Richard and Maria's lab group needs to spend less time on administrative tasks.
- A busy researcher needs time for spontaneous, fruitful interactions.
- An overworked PhD student needs a way to unwind without feeling guilty.

You'll use this statement as the basis for generating solutions (Chapter 5).

Try to frame the problem so there's not a solution built in.[27] Consider, for instance, "A busy PhD student needs an inspiring work-space" versus "A busy PhD student needs to feel inspired." With the first you've limited yourself to solutions that affect the space where the student works, whereas in the second you have a much broader scope of possible solutions. What's the right size of problem to tackle? You want something that is broad enough that there's more than one possible solution, but that has concrete enough boundaries that it's specific to the particular person and problem you've identified.

A tractable statement of the problem is an important starting point. But just as we encouraged you to explore a range of problem framings, we also are going to encourage you to explore a range of solutions to the problem before choosing one. That's where we're going in the next chapter – to iteratively solve these problems you've found and framed.

SUMMARY

In this chapter, we've argued for you to lean into ambiguity, rather than trying to resolve uncertain or unfamiliar situations as quickly as possible. When problems arise, you don't know how they're going to be resolved, but if you take the time to expand your problem space, you expand your ability to solve your problem effectively. Just like that light shining on the sidewalk and obscuring the lost keys sitting just outside the cone of light, the problem you see determines your solution space. If you choose your problem intentionally rather than falling into the first one you perceive, you make it that much more likely that you will actually find your keys.

Finally, always remember that if you don't like the problem framing you choose first, you can always go back and try another statement of the problem!

EXERCISES

Try It

4.1 **Five why's:** Articulate a problem you are facing. Then successively ask why. Asking why can take on many different meanings: Why does the problem exist? Why are people behaving a certain way? Why don't we know the answer to this yet? Why is this important? Asking and answering why forces you to reframe what the problem is. If you repeat this procedure and keep asking why you may just uncover some new – and perhaps deeper – problem framings. (See Crystal's example above.) One of these framings may be more interesting or meaningful than the problem you originally set out to solve. We sometimes call this the preschooler exercise because children are outstanding at this. They don't have as many preconceptions about the world and are innately curious. When faced with something they don't comprehend, they ask why repeatedly until they develop a new understanding. Definitely channel your inner preschooler for this exercise. (If you have worked through Chapter 3, you may notice that this uses the same format as Exercise 3.5 but has a different goal.)[28]

4.2 **Multiple perspectives:** Take the same problem and write it with three distinct framings. For instance, how would the problem look from different people's perspectives? How would an optimist view your problem? How would a pessimist describe it? From a purely factual perspective, what is happening? From an emotional perspective, what is happening? How would the problem look if you described it today, next month, or next year? Spend ten minutes brainstorming solutions to each statement. How did the different statements shine different light on the problem?

4.3 **Practice ambiguity tolerance:** When a new problem arises, deliberately avoid coming up with any solutions for at least a day. Sleep on it. Let the problem marinate for twenty-four hours or longer. Spend time exploring the problem space and exploring problem framings. How does it feel to wait instead of moving straight toward a solution?

Practices

4.4 **Powers of ten:** This exercise helps you examine a problem on larger and larger scales, and then examine it on smaller and smaller scales. (The name comes from a quirky, retro video by Charles and Ray Eames from 1977 that shows a picnic on the lakeshore in Chicago at various orders of magnitude.)[29] For example, if you want to reimagine the mission of your research lab, a way to scale out would be to think about how the lab relates to the rest of the department. Then scale out further: How does your lab relate to the rest of campus? How does it relate to your disciplinary field? The wider world? You can scale the other way as well. How do subgroups within the lab relate to the lab as a whole? How does each individual relate to the lab? Scale can happen along a number of dimensions. Perhaps you want to frame the potential impact of a study you are planning to run. Think about what the impact of the findings could be over a year, two years, five years, twenty years, etc. Choose a problem you are currently facing and write it down. Scale up three orders of magnitude and then scale down three orders of magnitude. Often, exploring the challenge at different scales helps broaden your overall perspective; you might decide the problem is more tractable at a smaller scale or will have more impact if solved at a larger scale.[30]

4.5 **Why/how laddering:** This is an extension of the *Five why's* technique that allows you to understand problems by examining them in both an abstract and concrete way. When faced with a problem you can ask two questions: *Why does that problem exist?* and *How does it manifest itself?* The "why" frames the abstract. The "how" frames the concrete (see Figure 4.3). For each answer you generate, repeat the same questions (why and how) to see additional dimensions of the problem. You can alternate asking why and how or choose one and ask it repeatedly.[31]

4.6 **Assumption storming:** List out all the assumptions you have about the sources of a problem or the potential solutions to that problem. Pick two

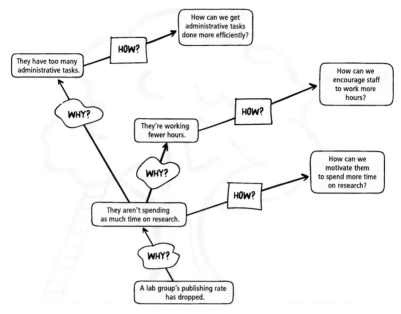

FIGURE 4.3 An example of why/how laddering using Richard and Maria's story

or three key assumptions and consider: Are these key assumptions true? What if they weren't? You may have to investigate them further.[32]

Reflect

4.7 Make a list of situations in your work and personal life where you routinely experience some level of ambiguity. Next, reorder the list, placing situations where ambiguity causes you the most amount of stress at the top. Why is ambiguity more uncomfortable in some situations than in others?

4.8 How do you generally solve problems? Do you typically take them on in isolation or talk through them with other people? Do you tend to analyze every aspect or go with your gut? Would you rather focus on one thing at a time or deal with everything at once? Try responding to these prompts for three to five problems you are facing now. Include big problems and small problems. Think about research challenges and personal struggles. How do your responses change (or not)?

5   Iterate and Experiment

Ingrid was not sleeping well. She was terrified that any day now her PhD advisor would email her to ask about her progress on the prospectus she was supposed to be producing. Since she was staying up so late each night as her mind raced, she found it hard to get up in the mornings. She kept hitting snooze on her alarm clock. Besides, the longer she stayed in bed, the longer she could delay the moment when she sat down at her desk to face the empty document file that should have turned into a finished product by last week. She knew she was struggling to write, but she didn't know what to do differently. She had checked every book on academic writing out of her university's library. She now found herself spending more time reading these books looking for advice than actually trying to write. Trying to write was simply too overwhelming.

Ingrid's difficulty writing is a particularly extreme example. But her basic assumption – that she needed to go directly from not knowing how to address an issue to a fully formed solution – is all too common. As time went by without progress, Ingrid was putting tremendous pressure on herself to reach the high standard of a finished product in a short period of time. Stress can sometimes be motivating in the right doses and settings (e.g., the night before a revise-and-resubmit deadline),[1] but more often the stress of performance anxiety actually impedes performance.[2]

If you are like most researchers, you like to get things right. Academic culture tends to encourage setting high standards for yourself and putting lots of pressure on yourself to meet those standards. For many scholars, the pursuit of excellence is accompanied by a strong desire not to mess up or be wrong.[3] Given the widespread desire for excellence and urge to avoid making mistakes in front of peers, we're going to suggest something that will probably sound radical: What if you think of mistakes as a helpful tool? Can you imagine what it might feel like to be comfortable with failing as a necessary step on the path to the outcomes you are trying to achieve? Fear of failure, fear of criticism, performance anxiety, and perfectionism,[4] all serve as emotional barriers or blocks to creativity.[5] And the process of learning from what doesn't work has been shown to be an important source of insight.[6]

In contrast to seeking a polished final product all at once – and in tandem, avoiding being wrong at all costs – this chapter encourages you to cultivate the intentional use of small failures to gradually produce the excellence you desire. Designers call this cycle of experimentation *prototyping*. In this usage, prototyping extends beyond the physical products or software the word is often associated with to mean a mindset of incremental iteration that moves research forward step by step (Figure 5.1).[7] If you like, you can think of this as a personal version of the theory testing and refutation cycle that moves science forward.[8] Scholarly knowledge moves in iterative cycles of what could be loosely considered as failure: A theory is advanced, and then other scholars try to disprove the theory, and then finally a theory like plate tectonics or homeostasis comes along that no one can disprove and it becomes accepted as a fact (though it is technically still a theory). We think of prototyping and iteration in research as playing a similar role. It helps you refine your thinking from the abundant but rough ideas you generate initially to the few refined ideas you distribute to the world.

The whole point of prototyping is to fail incrementally early in the process, enabling you to learn from and build on each version. You expect each iteration to be incomplete, so you aren't attached to each iteration the way you would be if you expected it to be the end of the process. You never thought of that version as a finished product, only as a necessary step that was going to teach you something you needed

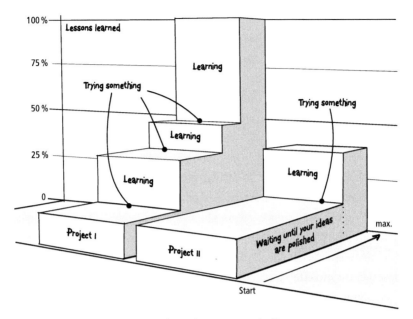

FIGURE 5.1 Learning through incremental effort

to learn to create the next version. The goal is to invest just enough energy into each prototype to learn what you need to create the next one. If prototype #3 is going to need revision anyway, then #3 should take only as much time and energy as absolutely necessary to allow you to learn what you need to create #4. And thus your thinking advances in manageable but steady steps.

    If you can embrace this power of incremental learning, three important things happen. First, you change the process of developing ideas into a continual cycle of trying something new in marginal ways and learning from it, which means the effort to develop any given prototype is much less than trying to create a polished finished product all at once. Second, you leave your inner critic shouting into the wind as you transform your relationship to your ideas; you no longer need to put pressure on yourself to make prototype #3 or #4 perfect. Any given idea is no longer a finished product you are putting into the world, on which your success is being judged. Each version is simply the most recent prototype in a long string of prototypes that you expect to tweak before you reach the idea you will finally declare "finished." (We'll warn you, though: work like this for too long and eventually even something as final as the book manuscript you deliver to your publisher starts to be viewed as only a more polished prototype in a continual, unending cycle of learning and iteration!) Finally, if you are paralyzed with no idea how to move forward (or conversely, unsure which of many ideas to pursue), you can lower the stakes of simply trying something and thus reduce the performance anxiety that so often plays a role in paralysis.

The power of experimentation we have just described rests on a dual foundation. First, iterative idea development draws on the cognitive and behavioral power of moving between convergent and divergent thinking. Second, when you practice prototyping as a behavior, it helps cultivate an attitude of comfort with small failures, which seems to influence your affective relationship to your research and particularly how you perceive the experience of receiving critical feedback.

DIVERGENT AND CONVERGENT: TWO COMPLEMENTARY MODES OF THOUGHT

Divergent thinking is wide, lateral, expansive thinking that generates a larger set of options, while convergent thinking results in narrowing choices based on evaluative criteria (Figure 5.2). Divergent thinking is associated with "the ability to shift between mental categories and perspectives ... and facilitates broad scanning ability and the generation of disparate, loosely associated ideas";[9] it helps you generate new ideas.[10] Convergent thinking is associated with "the use of wide mental categories" that allow "individuals to see similarities, patterns, and relations between apparently diverse pieces of information";[11] it helps you "identify one correct or conventional answer."[12] Paired together, divergent and convergent thinking help you generate innovative ideas and solutions.[13]

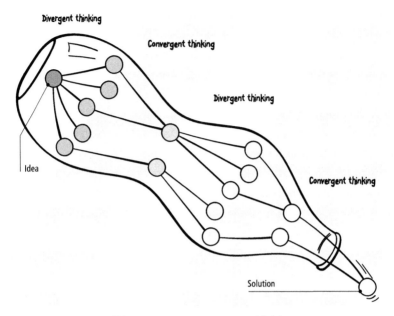

FIGURE 5.2 Divergent versus convergent thinking

Divergent Thinking: Generate Abundant Ideas

Divergent thinking was originally described by psychologist J. P. Guilford in the mid-twentieth century.[14] Guilford was interested in the component parts of creative thought and recognized that the ability he termed *divergent production* was a core part of what made people creative. While more recent measures of divergent thinking have clarified that it is a reliable indicator of creativity rather than being synonymous with it, tests of divergent thinking remain a common way of measuring overall creativity, emphasizing the link between divergent thinking and the process of generating new ideas.[15] More recent neuroscience investigations into divergent thinking suggest that successful idea generation requires the brain to shut off neural pathways that are responsible for "commonplace ideas and common associations, while at the same time allowing for activation of a network that promotes more remote associate connections ...

Thus [one important facet of] creativity may reside in the balance between an associative network allowing free flow of ideas … and an executive control network supporting the inhibition of irrelevant ideas."[16]

Divergent thinking has four distinct but related components: fluency, originality, flexibility, and elaboration.[17] Fluency refers to the sheer number of ideas someone can generate; greater fluency means having many ideas in a short period of time. Originality is the ability to generate novel ideas. Flexibility is the skill of generating ideas that cross conceptual categories. Elaboration is the ability to generate related ideas in a similar vein.[18]

The process of iteration starts with developing many more ideas than you will eventually carry through to fruition. This approach – of starting deliberately with multiple ideas – has several advantages. First, from a purely numbers perspective, the more ideas you generate, the higher the chances you have statistically for one of them to be world-changing.[19] More developed skills of originality, flexibility, and elaboration also result in higher-quality ideas.[20]

Second, starting deliberately with multiple ideas helps you avoid getting too invested in any single idea and stay open to surprising new insights.[21] This insight can be used deliberately when making research design decisions. The second year of a PhD, at least in the American system, is the time to narrow one's interests and define a specific research topic. During Nicola's PhD, she ended the spring of the first year on track, with a defined topic: evaluating the effects of drought management policies. Unfortunately, during the summer, she realized that it really wasn't a topic that would excite her enough to do good work for a full five years, so she returned to school in the fall without a topic and basically back at square one. Instead of worry, however, she decided to spend the fall exploring multiple potential research directions. The plan for this exploration was relatively simple. Nicola read the literature on each topic to get a sense of the types of gaps that existed and where her research might fit in. She brainstormed potential research questions – generating lists for each research topic – and also the type of research methods and field sites that she could use to answer the questions that sparked an interest. She discussed all three questions with her mentors and interviewed practitioners to see what sorts of useful information they would glean if she were to carry forward any of the directions. In other words, she did what any sensible PhD student might do to pick a research question. The difference is that she did it religiously with three questions rather than just one.

As it turned out, Nicola selected a research direction that wasn't included in the three initial topics she explored that autumn. During that quarter, she heard a thought-provoking talk about dam removal, chatted with a few faculty who worked on the topic, and realized that it was a direction that would allow her to tackle many of the questions she had been grappling with since her master's thesis. Being in the process of conscious exploration allowed Nicola to be open to new possibilities, since she was invested but not fully attached to the topics she was exploring.

Becoming too attached to a single idea can have more drastic consequences of path dependence as well. When Jake, a computer science postdoc, attended one of our classes, he was agonizing over deciding between two job offers at technology companies. One was a nearly ideal job, but located across the country, far from his family and girlfriend. The other was in the right location for his personal commitments but involved making significant professional concessions. Through the process of brainstorming about his challenge with other class participants, Jake realized that he had narrowed his focus to deciding between these two job offers and had forgotten that there were additional career options that might be available, even if they took more time and work to achieve. Creativity scholars call this "premature closure": there were divergent paths of idea generation Jake could have taken but he had prematurely (and in this case, mistakenly) decided they were not fruitful paths to pursue.[22]

Divergent thinking is also useful for addressing research process challenges. Scott was a materials science student who took one of our classes. His biggest challenge was his advisor, who provided excellent mentoring – except that months often went by as Scott struggled to schedule meetings with her. Determined to move his work forward and graduate on time, Scott tried to solve the problems he encountered in the lab on his own. One day he met another professor at a seminar and started meeting regularly with that professor. But he could not shake his feeling of guilt. Discussing the challenge with his partner during the class, he realized he was framing those meetings as "cheating" on his advisor. Scott turned this insight into the start of a divergent thinking process. By generating a list of ideas about different aspects of the problem ("How might I get the level of support I need? How might I work more effectively with my busy professor? How might I reframe the feeling of 'cheating'?"), Scott explored divergent paths to move forward and reported that the process of creating the multiple options ultimately made him feel less stuck.

Convergent Mode: Test Ideas through Incremental Action

In contrast to divergent thinking, convergent thinking seeks to eliminate ambiguity and answer clearly defined questions.[23] Where divergent thinking relies on lateral associations, convergent thinking relies on logical, analytical assessment drawn from one's existing knowledge base.[24] Convergent thinking is central to the cognitive processes involved in evaluating the quality of ideas generated through divergent thinking. Specific convergent thinking processes at this stage include recognizing promising lines of attack on a problem, seeing limits, being aware of weaknesses, assessing feasibility, and recognizing a solution. Convergent thinking provides a corrective to ensure that the novelty generated by divergent thinking translates into feasible, quality solutions to a problem, not just novelty for novelty's sake.[25]

One concrete way to make use of the power of convergent thinking is to choose one or more ideas and explicitly test out how well they work. An experimental prototyping process will help you refine one or more of the divergent ideas you generated into a solution you want to implement or present to the world. An important distinction here is testing your ideas by actually trying them out – by *doing* – rather than spending too much time thinking about or planning how you will implement them. Many academics and researchers are accustomed to thinking and planning for a long time before taking any significant steps on a research project. An interdisciplinary team launching a new collaboration might spend six months to a year writing a grant application and waiting to hear if they have received funding. Similarly, in many fields, PhD students spend months to a year or more perfecting (and defending) a dissertation proposal before they start collecting any data. While we agree that strategic planning can be important for success and all of us on the author team certainly rely on planning in our research lives, an experimental mindset says you can learn whether or not an idea works more quickly if you actually try out some aspect of it, rather than just think about it.

Testing ideas in action helps you save yourself work because you can change course with low investment. When Sebastian was working on his PhD, he drew a mindmap of literature domains he was using and how he understood them relating to one another. He posted it on the wall in the graduate student office so he could discuss it easily with his fellow students. When an assistant professor in the department stopped by for another reason, the map caught her eye. In a five-minute-long conversation, she made valuable suggestions, pointing out that he should include another domain, which until that moment Sebastian had not known even existed. By literally posting the current state of his thinking on the wall for everyone to see, Sebastian allowed the professor to immediately identify gaps and enabled himself to quickly expand his literature review.

As this story also suggests, one quick and easy way of testing your ideas that works well for abstract content is using visual thinking. Since visual thinking is the physical manifestation of connections you are making in your brain, it allows you to concretely see implicit assumptions you might be making. Hugo wrote us a few months after attending our class to report that the most important change he had made since attending was to stock his office with Post-it notes and brightly colored pens. He had found that practicing visual thinking let him experience the power of taking his thoughts out of his head and getting them into a visible format that could be played with and responded to – either for himself or by others. He turned to these new tools when he found himself struggling to translate the vague ideas in his head into a slide deck for an important invited talk at an international meeting. By using colors for different concepts and space on a tabletop to organize the relationships between the ideas, Hugo was able to work tangibly with his content and quickly home in on a new narrative structure. He was very pleased with the presentation he eventually gave and in his email he gave much of the credit to the techniques he had used for getting his ideas into a visual format.

USING CYCLES OF CONVERGENT AND DIVERGENT THINKING TO ITERATE AND EXPERIMENT

Successful iteration requires moving between convergent and divergent modes. As Arthur Cropley summarizes, "creative thinking seems to involve two components: generation of novelty (via divergent thinking) and evaluation of the novelty (via convergent thinking)."[26] An iterative, experimental problem-solving process goes through stages of divergent thinking – brainstorming, gathering as many potential solutions as possible – and convergent thinking – evaluating ideas with logic, then choosing one or a subset of these ideas to iteratively prototype and test, to see what works and what you can learn about your problem (see Figure 5.1). In a study that asked subjects to think aloud while completing a divergent thinking task, Pradip Khandwalla found that this iterative synergy between generating and assessing ideas happens at the task level as well as at the overall project level.[27] Divergent thinking provides the engine of creative power and convergent thinking provides the steering, preventing the associations generated by divergent thought from becoming ridiculous or unacceptably risky.[28] By cycling through convergent and divergent thinking, you combine the creative power of the divergent mode with the analytic power of the convergent mode.

Without this cycling between divergent and convergent thinking, creativity is hard to accomplish. Having too many ideas without a way to evaluate their quality is counterproductive, as is critical evaluation of nascent ideas. In the introductory story, Ingrid was approaching her writing struggle in a closed, convergent mode. She had become so focused on finding the right answer to her writing problem that she was shutting down the curious, divergent kind of thinking that could have helped her. One approach that would have likely helped Ingrid write her prospectus more efficiently would have been to generate a long list of possible solutions to dissolve her writer's block. Assuming (for the sake of argument, since Ingrid hadn't framed her specific problem as in Chapter 4) that her challenge was being critical of whether or not her ideas were contributing to the literature when she tried to write, potential solutions might have included freewriting a given number of words every day without judgment, writing sentences with a generic reminder to herself to add a citation and then going back later to fill them in, spending time at the end of a writing session to capture ideas and effort she was proud of, or finding a writing tutor to work with. After generating a list of these and other ideas, she could have chosen one or more ideas to experiment with, giving herself a path forward from the paralysis.

One way to systematize iteration in research projects is what we call adaptive management research design. Adaptive management is an approach to environmental management where uncertainty is planned for at the beginning of a project.[29] You can use the same idea to design a research project by planning upfront for when and how iteration will happen. Essentially, you create a structure identifying what you need to learn and how you will learn it at certain points. That structure can then be incorporated into grant applications and described as part of your method in papers. Depending on the project, you might plan for both divergent and/or convergent phases of your project. For example, you might plan to generate a list of survey questions once you have identified key concepts from your literature review, plan to test an interview protocol or survey with a small subset of subjects and revise it based on what you learn,[30] or conduct a study first with a local population to refine your research interventions before launching an expensive international field study.[31] You may be already using this kind of prearranged iteration in your methods, but not thinking of it as a prototype. By looking for opportunities for adaptive management research design, you may find more opportunities for using iteration as a tool.

This process – divergently generating a list of ideas and then evaluating and testing those ideas with evaluative thinking – is at the heart of creative work. By consciously practicing the steps and noticing how they work together in your idea creation and refinement, you will develop an increasingly sophisticated understanding of your own metacognitive process.

Step 1: Generate Many Ideas

The first step is to brainstorm as many solutions to your problem as possible. While you are likely familiar with the general idea of brainstorming, the details of how a brainstorm is structured are important in determining how effective it is.

One key is to start with a well-framed problem. At the end of Chapter 4, we discussed writing your problem statement as a needs statement: *A stuck graduate student (like Ingrid) needs strategies to write efficiently. A lab group needs to spend less time on administrative tasks. A busy researcher needs time for spontaneous, fruitful interactions. An overworked department chair needs to reconnect with her research.* (If you need a reminder, please refer to that chapter.)

To transform a needs statement into the prompt for idea generation, you can rephrase it into a "How might we ... ?" or "How might I ... ?" question: *How might we help a stuck graduate student like Ingrid write without judgment?* Or if Ingrid herself were asking the question: *How might I write without comparing myself to the literature!* Developed over years by commercial product designers, this specific phrasing is generative, encouraging you to move into divergent thinking mode.[32] (As a note, you can also run a brainstorm with any concisely worded question.)

Idea generation can be done individually or as a group. Sometimes you might brainstorm individually first and then with a group or vice versa. Incorporating both individual and group brainstorming can be especially helpful to ensure you get input from more introverted group members.[33] To brainstorm individually, set a timer for yourself, and come up with as many ideas as possible for how you might address your question in that time. Your goal is capture everything – write down or draw every idea you have, no matter how silly or wild.

For certain kinds of research challenges, we particularly encourage brainstorming with a partner or group. It can be easy to become overly attached to our own problems, which can make it harder to switch into divergent thinking mode.[34] You may already have a solution in mind and therefore not brainstorm well; involving others will force you to look beyond your preconceptions. For other problems, you may not have a solution in mind, but you may be so emotionally attached to solving the problem that you're frozen or unable to think creatively. In that case, other people will be able to look at your problem more objectively and likely offer a wider range of solutions.

Importantly, when you are in the divergent stage of idea development, you may need to work to deliberately turn off your convergent, evaluative thinking powers. Your job at the moment is not to cull "bad," "impractical," or even "impossible" ideas. You are explicitly staying in divergent mode, capturing and building on every idea without evaluating it.[35] You'll have plenty of time to sort, evaluate, and refine your ideas into potential solutions a bit later in your iterative process. While it may feel unfamiliar at first, entering this nonjudgmental, generative mode gets easier with practice. If you're brainstorming as part of a group, try to invite other individuals who can be intentionally optimistic and nonjudgmental.

The group brainstorms you have likely participated in – the kind you most likely picture when you hear the word, with people standing around a whiteboard or in a conference room shouting out ideas – get their basic structure from four Rules of Brainstorming put forward by Alex Osborn in 1957:

"1. Judicial judgment is ruled out. Criticism of ideas must be withheld until later.
2. "Free-wheeling" is welcomed. The wilder the idea, the better; it is easier to tame down than to think up.
3. Quantity is wanted. The greater the number of ideas, the more the likelihood of winners.
4. Combination and improvement are sought. In addition to contributing ideas of their own, participants should suggest how ideas of others can be turned into better ideas; or how two or more ideas can be joined into still another idea."[36]

In recent years, there has been a well-publicized debate about how well these group brainstorms work.[37] Critics cite studies that show people come up with more ideas individually than in a group setting,[38] that ideas generated individually may be more novel,[39] and that group brainstorming may encourage freeriding and social anxiety.[40] Brainstorming advocates who have observed how brainstorming functions in professional settings where brainstorming is used frequently respond that such studies are generally done with subjects (often college students) in randomly assigned groups (rather than in teams that know one another), using untrained brainstorm facilitators and inexperienced participants.[41] Stanford d.school cofounder Bob Sutton offers the analogy that this is like drawing conclusions about the sexual lives of experienced couples by studying what virgins do their first time.[42] Much less research exists on how brainstorming affects professional teams with established relationships. One study examining how accountants investigating fraud used brainstorming concluded that high-quality brainstorming improves teams' decision-making outcomes, but that the quality of brainstorming observed in practice (as measured on a twenty-one-point scale of best practices) was highly uneven among firms studied.[43] While individual items on the scale these researchers developed are specific to the financial fraud context, their three categories of attendance and communication (i.e., who you invite), structure and timing (i.e., how you organize the session), and team effort (i.e., participant motivation) would likely translate into other contexts. What this debate makes clear is that not all group brainstorms are created equal. The details of how a brainstorm is structured matter.[44]

Researchers who study brainstorming effectiveness offer several best practices for structuring a group brainstorm:[45]

- Consider assigning homework to group participants beforehand. For instance, you could ask everyone to come with one question for the group to consider and ten ideas to answer that question. This allows the team to benefit from the creativity of individual brainstorming as well as the creative synergies of the group thinking together.
- Set clear ground rules. The Osborn rules provide a starting point for this. However, one study suggests that posting "Brainstorming Suggestions" rather than "Brainstorming Rules" results in greater creativity.[46] Apparently most people's minds are unconsciously more comfortable when something is a guideline; imposing "rules" takes cognitive energy away from the divergent thinking task at hand.
- Cultivate the right environment. This is your job as the facilitator or convener of a brainstorm. Emphasize a positive, upbeat tone that makes group members feel safe to offer out-of-the box ideas and stress that the time for evaluating ideas is later on. Think beforehand about the size of the group and who you are inviting. For larger groups or more important brainstorming sessions, you might want to think carefully about details like the way the room is laid out or if you want to play music.
- Use "yes, and."[47] If you're working with a partner or group, try to build off one another's ideas: *We could reward Ingrid for writing each morning. Yes, and what if we pay her for every word?*

Another powerful brainstorming tool is introducing constraints. If you notice yourself or your teammates slowing down on generating new ideas during a brainstorm, you might try using a *constraint* – some criterion that all your new ideas must match. For instance, all ideas must cost $1 million, or be implementable in ten minutes, or be white, or happen outdoors, or involve magic. Requiring ideas to adhere to certain characteristics actually makes it easier for your brain to think of new ideas.[48] In our classes, we often present participants with a series of constraints to try (one at a time). While these constraints may initially seem trivial or even ridiculous (the magic one always gets nervous laughs!), they can lead to solutions you would otherwise not reach. One team was brainstorming ways to make sure that everyone involved in a multi-institutional research partnership studying links between poverty and disaster resilience had the same expectations about the project. During a brainstorming round during which every idea had to cost at least $1 million dollars, Lena was thinking about ways to bring the team together to meet. "Fly to the hometown of each Principle Investigator," she said. "Have meetings in each city we are studying," responded one of her collaborators, building on her idea. Given that the entire grant amount was less than $1 million, this constraint felt silly to this team at first. But this idea to have meetings in each city they were studying actually became something feasible and exciting: what if they hosted their kick-off meeting and each of their three subsequent annual team meetings not at one of their institutions, but at one of their field sites? The brainstorming constraint thus inspired the team to hold annual meetings that integrated study participants.

Finally, it's important to note that you can get frustrating brainstorms if you start with an ineffective problem framing or a certain point of view of the problem built in. You met Jake earlier in the chapter; he's the computer science postdoc who was trying to choose between two technology jobs: an ideal job far away from his girlfriend or a far-from-ideal job in an optimal location. When Jake tried to brainstorm by himself about choosing between the two job offers, he struggled. It took others helping him reframe his question from, "How might I best choose between these two job offers?" to, "How might I find a job that meets both my personal and professional needs?" for him to be able to effectively brainstorm a range of creative solutions to the challenge he was facing.

Step 2: Converge on One Solution

Once you have a long list of ideas you have generated, you'll need to decide which idea or ideas you want to move forward through experimentation. This is when you consciously switch from divergent to convergent thinking mode; if you are selecting as a team be sure to make this switch explicit to all team members. Depending on the importance of the problem and your timeframe, sometimes this idea evaluation step can be as simple as a gut feeling about which are the particularly promising or exciting ideas. Other times it can help to use specific criteria and rate ideas according to those criteria. The criteria you choose will be affected, too, by the specific problem. However, one helpful approach is to have one criterion for creativity (e.g., Which ideas are most innovative or groundbreaking?), one for feasibility (e.g., What is most likely to succeed? What is easiest to do? What can be accomplished fastest?), and one that considers how the idea might be received by the relevant audience (e.g., Which idea is most likely to excite a reviewer, grant officer, or hiring committee?). When brainstorming with groups, colored sticker dots can be used to let a group vote on which options meet the chosen criteria. (The idea that gets the most votes is not necessarily the winner. Think of this as a way to elicit ideas the team is most excited about and a good way to organize a discussion about which ideas to explore first.)

Some of our students have struggled to choose one or a few ideas to prototype because they felt like they were giving up on valuable ideas they wanted to keep. If you find yourself paralyzed by an abundance of ideas, acknowledge that this is a good problem to have and find a way to capture the ideas so you can come back to them later if or when you desire. Take a photo of the whiteboard you used to brainstorm. Or start an ongoing electronic or physical file for "Someday Ideas" to save the exciting ideas that you don't have the capacity to explore right now.

Step 3: Build a Concrete Representation of Your Idea (a Prototype)

Once you've made your selection, it's time to try the idea out quickly with a prototype. For engineers, designers, and software developers, a prototype is an incomplete representation of an idea that helps answer a question or teaches you something that helps you move forward.[49] Prototypes come in a variety of levels of refinement. As taught at the Stanford d.school, a prototype is a learning tool that you can build very quickly (often in as few as ten to fifteen minutes, though some prototypes will take a few days or a week) and test out without investing much effort, relative to the effort of creating the finished product.

The prototype itself is a tangible thing you can actually build or draw or write or do to try out your idea. Rather than daydreaming about what a conversation with your advisor might look like, actually write a script and try speaking the words with a friend playing the advisor's part. Rather than hesitate about redesigning your lab website because it will take too much time, draw a few sketches of what new pages could look like or set up a shadow site within your web server without making it live.

In our classes, we ask students to choose three ideas from the brainstorm (maybe using the criteria above) and quickly sketch what three or four prototypes would look like for each to keep them from getting too attached to any given idea. We encourage you to try the same. Maybe you spend twenty minutes or so on these sketches, or less if the problem is a minor one. From there, you can select the most promising or exciting or easiest to implement to start with.

We recognize that the idea of a research prototype might seem abstract. This is one of the more challenging concepts for our students to grasp. Table 5.1 lists some examples of what a research prototype might look like that we've seen and used frequently. We divide them into common types and offer examples for both process and content challenges. As a caveat, though, these are only examples; our students are

Table 5.1 *Examples of prototypes in research*

Type	Description	Examples
Abstract or outline	A rough version of an abstract, an outline, or a paper draft. You can prototype content, organization, or both.	• Make a one-page summary of a paper. Write the research question, a one-sentence (each) summary of your motivation, methods, results, and "so what" takeaways. • Use Post-its or a whiteboard to visualize a few versions of a paper or presentation structure.
Skit or conversation	A practice version of a conversion or the script for how an important dialogue might proceed. You can use the prototype to prepare what you will say or how you will react to what the other may say.	• Before an interview, print photos of each member of the search committee. Have a conversation with them about your research and how it interacts with theirs. • Create a short pitch that captures the essence of a presentation. Record it on video and show it to a few people to get feedback on the key messages you are hoping to communicate.
Drawing or visualization	A visual representation of a concept. You can prototype an abstract set of ideas or a concrete piece of visual content (such as a figure for a manuscript or a rough draft of key PowerPoint slides).	• Map your literature review as a Venn diagram. What are the big ideas in the field? (How) do they overlap? Where are there gaps? • To develop your research methods for a project, draw the figures you envision for your eventual paper. What data do you need to collect to produce those figures?

Table 5.1 *(cont.)*

Type	Description	Examples
Build something	A physical artifact that tangibly represents your ideas. This might be a scale model, a representation of abstract ideas made concrete through objects, or a traditional prototype like engineers build that allows you to explore the form something should take.	• Make a diorama of your dream office. Play with ways to capture features of the diorama in real life. • Write ten fun activities on popsicle sticks and put them in a jar on your desk. When you need an energy boost, pick out a stick and spend a few minutes doing that activity.
Change in habit or routine	A deliberate change in your daily schedule or customary behaviors. This also includes changes in how you interact with technology. Here, the activity is the prototype, and the spirit of trying and curiosity is what matters.	• Get up thirty minutes early to write in the morning every day this week. • Install software on your computer to pause your email so you do not continually receive new messages.

continually surprising and impressing us with the many ways they find to iterate and experiment with their ideas. Also, more prototype examples for how to prototype specific challenges appear in Chapters 9 and 10.

Say that Ingrid had decided to implement one or more of the prototypes we suggested earlier (see also Figure 5.3). Freewriting each morning is a change in a usual habit. The prototype and simply taking the action of writing merge, but the important part is the attitude of curiosity and learning one brings to it. Ingrid might have decided that for the next three days she was going to freewrite for twenty minutes when she first sat down at her desk. To capture her learning, she could keep a pad of paper next to her desk and note any observations about

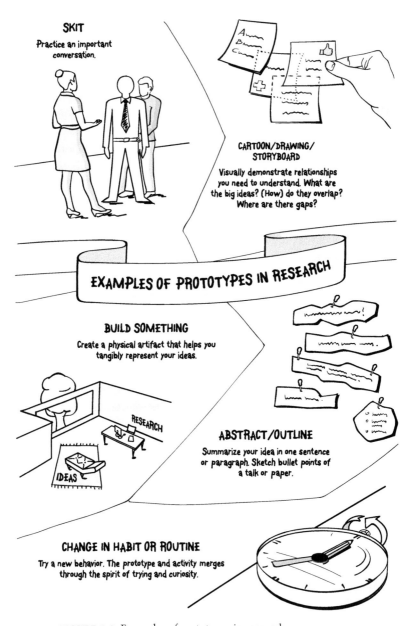

FIGURE 5.3 Examples of prototypes in research

how doing this made working on her prospectus later in the day easier or harder. She could capture ideas for what she might need to do differently; perhaps after three days she would decide that she liked freewriting but she would prefer to set a word limit rather than a time limit.

One of the keys to successful prototyping is to act before you have time to think. (Yes, we meant to say it that way!) Most researchers are very good at thinking. And analytic thinking is certainly a vital part of the research process. But when ideas are new and not yet formed, thinking about them too much is paradoxically often not the most effective way to move them into the world. Manish Saggar, lead author of a study on the neuroscience of creativity, describes this bluntly: "The more you think about it, the more you mess it up."[50]

The cycle of prototyping depends fundamentally on incremental changes. The only way to learn from incremental change is by taking action. The Stanford d.school calls this a "bias towards action;" we have described it to our students as a default that might seem unfamiliar at first but that will develop over time.[51] It requires trusting the iteration process even when you are not sure where it is going.

If you don't know what to try, that is the moment to simply try something. You might not produce something very good. You almost certainly will not produce something of finished quality. But in the prototyping mindset, learning how you can make the current version better is exactly what you are expecting and aiming to do. By trying something – trying anything – you break the inertia and give yourself or others something to respond to.

One technique that can be helpful if you're stuck and don't know what "something" to do is to ask this question: "What can I do in the next hour that would help me progress toward solving this problem in some way?" Similarly: "I'm going out to dinner; what can I do before then?" Or, for some problems, "today" or "this week" might be more appropriate. The exact timeframe doesn't matter. The point is to spur yourself into action. Essentially, you are using time as a constraint to spur idea generation. Generate at least three and ideally five or more answers to this question. Then choose one and immediately implement it.

Step 4: Test the Prototype

Now that you have a prototype – a rough abstract for your paper, a sketch of your figure, a plan to experiment with your daily habits, a tinfoil and pipe cleaner experimental setup like our students build out of "treasure" (see Exercise 5.2) – it is time to test it out. In testing your prototype, try to have a clear idea of what it is that you are trying to learn.

For many prototypes, especially for research process challenges, you are designing something for yourself, which means you are going to be your own tester as well. For Ingrid, the strategies she might have tried to write without judgment were only going to be meaningfully evaluated by her. For every strategy she tried – freewriting in the morning, capturing her writing accomplishments at the end of a session, or whatever else she came up with – she would have set aside a few minutes to reflect on how it went. She might have asked whether the experiment helped her write more, whether she felt less stressed, and what she learned about her problem that influenced what she might try next.

In some cases, the difference between doing something the way you normally do it and "prototyping" might be as simple as the attitude or spirit you bring to it; thinking of it as a prototype can help you be less attached.[52] For example, Ingrid could start freewriting every morning without considering it a prototype. But without calling it a prototype, she might fall into the trap of trying to implement it as a new rule for herself. Making rules for yourself can sometimes cause an unintended internal backlash because of the level of willpower required to implement such a rule. It's like the personal schedule version of yo-yo dieting, in which people who go on a strict diet ("I will eat this way forever") are actually more likely to gain weight over time.[53] When a schedule change is instead framed as a prototype ("I'll try this for a week and see what happens"), there is less pressure and thus less chance of internal backlash.[54]

Other times, testing your prototype will involve bringing in other people, either because you are creating a solution that is ultimately designed for them or because you need their input to help you understand your own reactions. Sharing ideas iteratively with a peer has been shown to result in more creative ideas and produce better results.[55] In Chapter 8, we'll discuss the importance of identifying people who are receptive to different levels of refinement, from the kernel of an idea to polished content. For now, though, we'll just point out that as you're testing your prototype, you'll want to make sure you're getting feedback from people who understand that what you're showing them is by design not perfect nor complete.

One final caution. It is possible to do *too much* testing. Ideally, you keep asking for feedback on different versions until you stop learning. If you catch yourself looking for someone to praise your ideas or do your iterative work for you rather than help you understand better how to develop your thinking, it's time to move on. You can generally avoid this by starting with a list of assumptions you are trying to learn about. When you've gotten feedback about those assumptions, you can consider the idea developed – or else ask yourself whether it's time to go back and start prototyping a different idea.

Step 5 to Infinity: Reflect, Iterate Again, Repeat

Once you've tested your prototype (and hopefully started to learn what it was that you were aiming to understand when you began), the iteration begins. At this point, it becomes a process of choosing your own adventure based on what you've learned and what questions are still outstanding. Sometimes you'll want to modify your prototype or build another prototype and then test it further and continue to refine your solution. Sometimes you realize this solution isn't terribly promising and you need to return to brainstorming mode and generate more ideas. Sometimes you learn something that changes your whole view of the problem and you need to go all the way back to reframe the problem again. In any case, we encourage you to avoid deciding that an idea or prototype is done too soon – there's often much that can be learned at each stage.

As you become more comfortable with this process and with being mindful of your research process, you'll learn to make these decisions about where to go next somewhat more intuitively. As you learn, though, Table 5.2 has some guiding suggestions that will help you figure out where to go next.

Table 5.2 *You've finished a prototype ... now what?*

You might try redefining the problem if ...	You might try brainstorming additional solutions if ...	You might want to build another prototype if ...
• you found a new problem that needs to be solved in order to solve the one you thought you were solving. • you brainstormed and none of the solutions seem quite right or they are uninspiring. • you learn something that makes the problem scope seem bigger. • you become so overwhelmed that you have to redefine the problem to be smaller or you'll go crazy.	• someone makes a suggestion that opens a door to many new possibilities. • you find yourself asking a question that begins with, "How could I ...?" or "How might we ...?" • someone offers a critique and you need to find ways to overcome the critique. • you know what's causing the problem and you need to figure out how to get around the known cause.	• you need to learn about another aspect of the solution. • you're still excited about this solution and want to make it better. • the solution seems close, but not quite there. • there are important audiences with whom you haven't yet tested the idea.

HOW ITERATION CHANGES THE EXPERIENCE
OF RESEARCH

Besides helping you move your research forward, an iterative research approach also changes the emotional experience of developing ideas. A focus on developing the perfect research output can lead you to focus on protecting yourself from criticism and proving to others that you are smart or creative, rather than trying to learn. Like Ingrid, so frozen by worry about whether or not she was doing it right that she couldn't write anything at all, this can be paralyzing. But if you anticipate that the first draft of the paper will get torn apart by your friendly reviewer and build space for that criticism and learning early on, you short-circuit the process of putting pressure on yourself. You start to trust that the best ideas will eventually be winnowed through experimentation. In other words, it can help you work more effectively with the possibility of failure.

While failure is defined differently depending on context, it is often perceived as a negative.[56] Mark Cannon and Amy Edmondson define failure as "negative surprises" or disappointments experienced in problem solving. These surprises might be experienced by individuals or teams, as in the cases these researchers studied; they might be small instances or have large implications. But what makes them examples of failure is that they have "unique psychological and [sometimes interpersonal] challenges associated with learning from them."[57]

At the most basic level, the psychological challenge of failure comes from a basic human desire to be well thought of by others and an implicit assumption that letting others know about imperfections or errors will undermine how others see you.[58] As a result, "most people have a natural aversion to disclosing or even publicly acknowledging failure ... [P]eople instinctively ignore or disassociate themselves from their own failures."[59] Besides this aversion to others' negative judgment, fear of failure is also influenced by people's basic psychological desires to believe they have control over what happens to them and to view themselves in a positive light. When you view yourself as having failed in even small ways, it can become difficult to maintain these beliefs and at the same time realistically recognize your mistakes.[60]

However, as the old cliché reminds us, it wouldn't be called research if it was easy or we knew the answer. By its nature, mastering the process of research means becoming comfortable being perpetually stuck in a multitude of small ways and moving forward anyway, in small stages, toward a destination you can't know for sure in advance where it is or if your idea of how to get there is going to work.[61] Stories of successful researchers emphasize that incremental learning is part of how they achieved the high regard in which they are currently held. For instance, Nobel laureate Elizabeth Blackburn spent decades iteratively developing the evidence linking telomere length, stress, and aging.[62] And as mathematician Andrew Wiles states, "I really think it's bad to have too good a memory if you want to be a mathematician. You need a slightly bad memory because you need to forget the way you approached [a problem] the previous time because it's a bit like evolution, DNA. You need to make a little mistake in the way you did it before so that you do something slightly different and then that's what actually enables you to get round [the problem]. So if you remembered all the failed attempts before, you wouldn't try them again. But because I have a slightly bad memory I'll probably try essentially the same thing again and then I realise I was just missing this one little thing I needed to do."[63] As this quote emphasizes, once you adopt this attitude, you might even start to view errors as a form of serendipity. While this process of becoming comfortable with moving forward in small stages may not always be comfortable learning, it is rarely paralyzing.

Adopting an iterative approach changes your relationship to each individual idea. Each idea no longer represents something you are putting into the world on which your ego, identity, and self-worth depend.[64] It's no longer "the solution," but simply a tool to help you learn more as you work toward the ("best for now," "best I got to before the deadline") solution. The process of moving between convergent and divergent thinking can also help shift from an attitude of scarcity to an attitude of abundance, which can help you be less attached to the success of any given project. Each idea or paper you start doesn't need to be groundbreaking, and it becomes acceptable to give up on an idea, because you learn to trust that there are many more where that one came from.

In order to make this shift, it helps to work with rather than against your innate stress responses. Fear of failure can trigger emotional responses that live deep in the brain. Using failure productively requires working with rather than against your neural circuitry. In a series of studies, neuroscientists evaluated the benefits of cognitive versus emotional responses to failure (thinking about the failure versus reflecting on the emotional experience of failing). They found that paying attention to one's emotional response helped participants learn from mistakes, while people who only thought about the error from an analytical perspective were more likely to act in a self-preservation mode and repeat the mistake again.[65]

SUMMARY

While scholars rightly tend to focus on finding the right answer, moving forward in the face of a sticky, ill-defined research challenge can often be more efficiently achieved through an experimental process of incremental learning. This chapter focused on the concrete behaviors that underlie successful iteration: moving between convergent and divergent thinking and prototyping, that is, taking a small, concrete, low-stakes action and then using the learning from that action to design the next action. Iteration can also transform the affective experience of practicing research, as you remove the need to know exactly how a project is going to end when you begin it. Instead, all you need to do is figure out how to design the next iteration and then trust that eventually you will iterate your way to success.

EXERCISES

Try It

5.1 **Brainstorm with constraints:** If you are feeling stuck generating new ideas
to solve a problem, try rapid-fire brainstorming using constraints –
requirements for each idea generated. (You can do this either individually
or in a group.) You can use one of our favorite warm-up prompts if you'd
like to be sillier ("A graduate student needs a way to get free food from an
event he was not invited to") or generate your own statement for
a challenge you're actually having. (Just a note of caution, we recommend
practicing with something not too high stakes at first.) You will
brainstorm in four successive two-minute rounds. The goal is to come up
with as many ideas to solve the problem as you can. Each round has
a different constraint. Some constraints work better than others on
a given problem. Try using a few from this list:

- All ideas must rely on Science Fiction technology.
- All ideas must be free.
- All ideas must cost $1 million.
- How would Disney solve this problem?
- All ideas must be zero waste.

For bonus points, try generating your own constraint for a last round.

5.2 **Build to think:** Researchers tend to be fairly abstract in generating and
testing ideas. Try using everyday objects to build a concrete, tangible
research prototype. In our classes, we provide an assortment of
treasures – craft sticks, paper, foil, tape, pipe cleaners, Play-Doh,
stickers, costumes, etc. – for students to build prototypes. We give our
students twenty minutes maximum to turn these elementary-school-
esque materials into a representation of an idea – and then we put
them on the spot and ask them to present their idea to someone else.
We invite you to recreate this experience in your own home or office.
Spend five minutes gathering a few supplies. Then spend fifteen
minutes building a physical manifestation of one of the ideas you
came up with in Exercise 5.1. (For treasure prototypes, the wilder the
idea, the better.) When you've finished, show the idea to someone and
ask them for feedback.

5.3 **Failure résumé:** Create a failure résumé by listing off failures you've had over the course of your life.[66] Include failures from childhood to now. Your résumé should include personal and professional failures. Feel free to play around with the format and style. But be sure to include what you learned from each failure, just like an effective résumé conveys what you accomplished at each job. You could also try doing this exercise in pairs. Each person creates the résumé alone. Then take turns role-playing a job interview. One person is the employer and the other is the applicant. Use the failure résumé as an argument for why you should get the job in the same way you would use a normal résumé. The only difference is, the selection criteria in this case is how well you convince your partner that you learned from your failures.

Practice

5.4 **Make three/choose one:** When you select ideas, get in the habit of generating at least three ideas before you choose one. For instance, when you make a prototype, come up with three ways you might prototype a potential solution, and then choose one to actually implement. The process of generating multiple ideas helps keep you from getting too attached to any single idea.[67]

5.5 **Highway to hell:** Sometimes switching a problem on its head can help you generate ideas. Instead of focusing on the solution, try to make the situation worse. Instead of saying, "How can I finish my conference paper by Thursday?" ask yourself first, "How can I make sure I get nothing done until Thursday?" Then, from those "dramatized" or "worst case" ideas, try to develop positive ideas. This can be quite fun to do, especially if you work with someone else.

5.6 **Bouquet of prototypes:** Try different types of prototypes for a given project. Look at Table 5.1 and draw ways you could prototype your idea with as many of these as possible. Then implement at least three of them. After each prototype, ask: "What did I learn? What is still unclear? How might I change the prototype to help myself answer that? What else do I need to learn to move forward?"

5.7 **Conversation table:** Sometimes you can create a prototype simply by use of an extended metaphor. For example, if you're developing a research question, imagine the literature you're contributing to as a conversation over dinner at a table. What is the topic that is being discussed, who is sitting at the table to talk about this, what kind of opinions or perspectives do they have, and what kind of alliances or oppositions do they have? Are just researchers sitting at the table, or are there corporations, governmental bodies, or policy makers? What stake does each have in this issue? What kind of conversation is it: a dialogue, a consultation, or a heated argument? Try drawing the table to gain insights about the current debate. Make sure to visualize where you are sitting at the table and what kind of contribution you wish to make.

Reflect

5.8   What are behaviors you usually exhibit when you get stuck? Do you tend to do the same thing regardless of the situation or does your response vary depending on the context? What types of situations are most likely to get you stuck?

5.9   In your day-to-day research, when do you use divergent thinking and when do you use convergent thinking? Some people naturally use one or the other more often (in general or in the face of certain types of problems). What do you tend to do, and what triggers you to diverge or converge?

5.10   What have you learned from "failures" or challenges on your research projects (either currently or in the past)? Is there a way you could have prototyped those challenges to have learned what you needed to know more efficiently?

SECTION II   Cultivate Conditions That Support Creativity

In Section I, we explored four foundational creative abilities: being mindful and aware of your thoughts and behaviors; using self-awareness and empathy to learn from emotions; exploring your problem space to frame the right problem; and using a cycle of iteration and experimentation to develop solutions. These are things you can do to directly generate more creative ideas and solve problems.

In Section II, we introduce three additional abilities, which you can think of as support structures that enable you to create the conditions for your optimal creativity. Think about your creativity as a garden. If the four foundational abilities are particular types of flowers that you're cultivating, the support structures are the soil, water, nutrients, and care that help your flowers bloom. If you add the right ingredients, the support structures can help you be more mindful or tolerant of ambiguity, boosting your creativity. But just like acidic or waterlogged soil can dampen your flowers' growth, the wrong conditions can also curtail your creative abilities. The overall point is that creativity doesn't happen without care, maintenance, and feeding. And sometimes focusing on these external support structures can be easier than trying to build the other abilities directly. As Mihaly Csikszentmihalyi wrote, "It is easier to enhance creativity by changing conditions in the environment than by trying to make people think more creatively."[1]

So, what are these support structures? First, we explore the role of language and stories. Storytelling is one way to identify and change your habits and behaviors. By consciously noticing and shaping the language you use when speaking about yourself and about your research, you are able to actively claim an identity as a creatively confident researcher.

Second, we explore building and managing your energy for your research and creativity. By understanding how your energy fluctuates over the day, distinguishing different types of energy (physical, cognitive, and emotional), and exploring how different activities, interactions, and spaces enhance or degrade your experience of energy, you are able to structure your day-to-day work in a way that matches your energy to the type of creative work you seek to accomplish.

Finally, we discuss using other people to boost your research. While many researchers tend to work with limited sets of people, building a diverse network for input into your research is a powerful means to enhance your own creativity. A feedback network can serve both to enhance your research process through helping you manage energy and respond to the emotional demands of research and to support the development of innovative content through iterative feedback on all stages of ideas.

Just like Chapters 2 through 5, the chapters in Section II include exercises (*Try Its, Practices, and Reflects*) for you to experiment with each ability. As we've repeated throughout the book, we encourage you to take the time to play with some of these exercises and play with your creativity. By consciously cultivating the creative support structures, you'll generate the conditions for better use of the creative abilities in your research and life.

6   Choose Your Language and Stories

LANGUAGE REFLECTS AND SHAPES YOUR UNDERSTANDING OF THE WORLD

Dave was a first-year PhD student who dreaded meeting with his mentor. Whenever Dave did force himself to schedule a meeting, he started to worry. He spent hours looking for one good idea to bring to the meeting, but he found himself rejecting idea after idea as insufficiently novel. When he attended one of our classes and discussed his struggles with a partner, he realized he was convinced that everything worth doing in his field had been done. He was unconsciously approaching meetings with his advisor with a crippling internal script: that his ideas weren't valuable enough to bring up because they were not original enough. As a result of this story, he was putting so much pressure on himself to meet an impossibly high standard that he was becoming overwhelmed and making it impossible for his mentor to respond to – let alone help him develop – any of the ideas that he did have.

Like Dave, all humans make sense of the world through language.[1] The words you choose, the metaphors you use, the visual imagery you draw on, and the stories you form with those words shape the way you perceive and interpret events that happen around you. Humans understand the world by categorizing things and experiences,[2] and the categories people have at their disposal are shaped by the languages they speak.[3] For instance, speakers of languages that use a single word for blue and green cannot distinguish between a green and a blue object,[4] and cultures that have multiple words for blue see more shades of blue than those with only one word.[5]

Beyond the individual words we use, humans tend to link multiple events into a causal chain to create a narrative.[6] This seems to be linked to certain mental capacities to capture, process, and store information,[7] as well as to mark the passage of time.[8] By organizing events in relation to others in the sequence of one's life, stories serve to shape and convey a person's understanding of what occurred when. Children first develop the ability to tell stories at the age of three or four years, the same age from which they retain their first lasting memories, suggesting that the ability to narrate events helps create a structure on which to order memory.[9] And until children can form narratives, they do not have a sense of history.[10] In the broadest sense, then, stories give us a sense of who we are by holding our memories of the past in easily accessible form. As Ronald Berger and Richard Quinney explain, "narrative . . . is about imbuing 'life events with a temporal and logical order,' about establishing continuity between the past, present and as yet unrealized future."[11]

In this chapter, we explore ways to use language and storytelling to author new creative patterns in your thinking and behavior. We define a story broadly as "a particular person's representation of the facts of a matter," emphasizing that there is generally more than one way to frame any given situation.[12] In this chapter (and throughout the book), we use the term *story* to refer to the phrases, scripts, framings, and narratives that you use to describe your world.[13] While narrative theorists and literary scholars draw careful distinctions between these various concepts, each describes ways humans use language to articulate what they experience.[14] Whether a simple script of, "Everything interesting has already been studied," or a more complex sequence with causal linkages ("I think better because I freewrite every morning"), the language you use has a larger set of associations and meaning embedded in it. By becoming aware of the language you use and stories you tell, you gain insight into how you understand the world and uncover implicit assumptions you might be making. You can then use this insight to consider whether your understanding and assumptions are supporting your goals.

In this chapter, we first encourage you to examine the under-lying language you use and evaluate how well it serves the creative abilities you have been developing in Section I. Then we encourage you to explore what new patterns you might wish to develop and how new stories might support them. By consciously crafting a narrative of creativity, you support your development of creative confidence and your identity as a creative scholar.

One important clarification is in order here. In research, story-telling is most frequently discussed in terms of science communication. This is storytelling in its role as a tool for communicating with others and perhaps influencing *their* thinking or behavior. This is an important application of storytelling, but one that has received extensive and expert treatment elsewhere.[15] In this chapter we are focusing on using language and storytelling to influence *your own* understanding.

THE DUAL ROLES OF LANGUAGE AND STORIES: UNDERSTAND AND CREATE

Through language, you continuously reflect and reinforce the current state of your understanding of events, their causes, and ultimately how you perceive your place in the world. Paying attention to these stories allows you to access a window into your own (often implicit) understanding. Thus examining the language you use and the stories you tell can play two roles. First is a diagnostic role, helping you understand the process of your research, your emotions, or the nature of a problem you are facing. Second is a creative role, allowing you to actively shape behaviors, thoughts, and emotions by paying attention to the language and stories that are contributing to them.

One place many readers may be familiar with intentional use of language and stories is therapy, which explores an individual's narra-tives to understand (and hopefully resolve) mental health difficulties or current life challenges. One common therapy approach, cognitive behavioral therapy (CBT), teaches patients to examine unconscious (and unhelpful) assumptions and thought patterns. Patients learn to become aware of the assumptions they make automatically, link those thoughts to feelings and behavior, identify where there might be biases or other distortions in their assumptions, and replace the habitual thoughts or assumptions with new patterns.[16] Another therapy approach that makes even more explicit use of storytelling is narrative therapy.[17] In contract to CBT's focus on discrete thoughts and assumptions, narrative therapy not only uses storytelling to heal, but explicitly conceives the act of narrating as mediating the relationship between the self and the world.

While therapy is a particular setting that relies on the relationship between the therapist and client, you can make use of the broader insight from clinical psychology that the stories you tell about your own life have real-world influence.[18] While emotion is generally understood to be automatically processed, as we described it in Chapter 3, at least one cognitive science study has found evidence that the words you associate with emotional categories provide important contextual cues for interpreting ambiguous emotional situations. The authors emphasize that even for young children, "emotion words anchor and direct a child's acquisition of emotion categories and play a central role in the process of seeing a face as angry, afraid or sad."[19] As an example of stories shaping identity, when individuals who have grown up in countries outside their passport country are asked how they understand nationality, they generally describe themselves as belonging to a global culture; this story shapes how these individuals interact within the cultures they inhabit.[20]

The stories other people tell about a person – including their assumptions and expectations – also can have real consequences. The expectations that teachers hold about their students in low-income areas, for instance, have been shown to influence student performance.[21] A study of how doctors described patients in medical records found that the choice of language and details used influenced the quality of the follow-up care those same patients did or did not receive from other doctors who subsequently treated the same patients and read the records of previous treatment. For instance, a simple change from a skeptical, "He appears to be in distress," to, "He is in obvious distress," made a big difference in how the patient's later doctors responded.[22]

However, the cognitive patterns shaped by the language you use and the stories you tell are not fixed.[23] The brain is highly malleable,[24] and you can train your brain to build new patterns, including consciously writing new stories.[25] Thus, storytelling can also be a conscious tool, shaping new narratives when you decide a pattern is not working as well as it might be.

Intentionally bringing focus to things you want to change (rather than ruminating on things you wish were different) takes advantage of the brain's inherent plasticity.[26] Therapist Linda Graham describes how attention can help create new patterns: "focused attention causes neurons in the brain to fire; repeated focusing on the same object or experience causes repeated neural firings; and repeated neural firings create a new and stable neural structure. When we focus our attention on cultivating a particular pattern of behavior, a character trait, or attitude or lens for filtering our experience, we incline the mind toward that objective. We notice more readily the desired trait or behavior, register it more fully in our consciousness, and direct mental activity toward it ... the repeated focus on that intention begins to build new brain structure and circuitry that support us in achieving the intention ... We turn a neural goat path into a freeway."[27] By intentionally noticing your linguistic patterns and practicing new patterns, you can use storytelling as a tool to help shift assumptions, habits, or attitudes you wish to change.

TELL NEW STORIES TO CREATE CHANGE

Understand the Assumptions, Attitudes, or Beliefs That Your Current Stories Reflect

The first step to creating new stories is becoming aware of the language you currently use and the stories you already tell yourself. Through the *Reflect* exercises at the end of each chapter, we have already been asking you to become aware of some of your attitudes and patterns. Now we encourage you to bring those same attitudes of mindful self-awareness to the underlying stories. You might think of this as "Mindfulness Part Two." For instance, you might notice the words you choose, the metaphors you use, and the visual imagery you draw on. You might note the emotional tone of the stories. (It may be helpful to go back to the various *Reflect* exercises you have already completed and see if anything jumps out at you in the writing or drawing you have already done.) Three particular instances where you might look for patterns are in the language and stories you use to describe yourself, how you describe your habits, and how you discuss your relationships with others.

You might find that you use certain language to describe yourself either in actual conversations or in your internal dialogue (Exercise 6.1). Do you identify yourself as someone who can or can't do certain things? Or who has or lacks certain skills or mental capabilities? Has this changed over time? You might have a story about failure, perhaps that you are someone who simply does not fail, or that you exceed expectations in everything you do. Or you might have an assumption that research or writing is hard for you, perhaps harder than for others. When thinking about the stories you use to describe yourself, you might also think about your usual answers to questions like, "What do you work on?" or your "go-to" stories, the ones you've told so many times you almost have the words memorized. What do these stories say about you? A final way to get at your implicit stories about yourself is to pay attention to how you react when someone else describes you in a certain way, or introduces you, or perhaps criticizes you. These reactions might suggest how congruent your inner narrative is with other, external identities you present to the world or that others give to you.

How you talk about your habits and behaviors can also be a source of stories to pay attention to. You might have patterns related to time. For many researchers, their prevailing story about time is one of scarcity and being busy. Or you might have an assumption that weekends are for surfing and not for science, as one PhD student we know did; this story was so core to his identity that he did not work weekends until the final quarter of his degree. You might have assumptions about fixed barriers, for instance, that you can't write on days you teach or when your kids are home. (We are not saying that these may not be valid conclusions resulting from learned experience. We are simply pointing out that it can be helpful to consciously notice what language you currently use when thinking about your research.)

Finally, you also have stories you tell about your relationships with other people. For instance, if you're a PhD advisor, how do you talk about your advisee? Are they smart? Diligent? Creative? Do you say that you work well together, or are they shy or needy? When you describe your work as part of a team, what things do you portray your team as doing well, and what things are presented as struggles? Has this changed over time? In each of the stories about your relationships, what is the role that you play, and what is the role of other people? Are you usually the good guy, or do you identify ways that you hold other people back?

Research using big data to examine a large corpus of fiction from Project Gutenberg has shown that there are common structures that appear again and again across contexts and types of stories.[28] While this study examined fictional stories, understanding these archetypal story arcs can be a concrete tool for helping you understand assumptions in the stories you hold about your own life. Following Kurt Vonnegut, who defined a story's emotional arc as how it maps on two axis (Beginning–End on the x-axis and Low Fortune–High Fortune on the y-axis), the authors present six basic shapes of emotional arcs. Considering these arcs can help you identify assumptions or patterns in your own life. You can also take this literary approach to identifying narratives you hold further. For instance, you might explore who the protagonist and antagonist are in your story. Is there a villain? What is the source of the conflict and which character needs to resolve it – you or someone else? Was your first assumption about who needed to take action correct?

Methods to Consciously Create New Stories

Once you have greater awareness of the language you currently use and the stories you presently tell yourself, you have the opportunity to

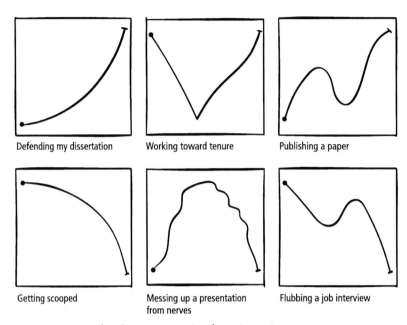

Defending my dissertation   Working toward tenure   Publishing a paper

Getting scooped   Messing up a presentation from nerves   Flubbing a job interview

FIGURE 6.1 Common emotional arcs in stories

rethink any stories that might not be serving your research goals as well as they could. Novelist Salman Rushdie captured this idea poignantly: "Those who do not have power over the story that dominates their lives, power to retell it, to rethink it, deconstruct it, joke about it, and change it as times change, truly are powerless."[29] Are there stories you are telling that might be standing in the way of your research productivity, overall well-being, and/or creative confidence? Assuming there is at least one story you'd like to rewrite (which there certainly is for everyone on the author team), you have a number of tools at your disposal to start taking advantage of your brain's plasticity to incorporate the new story you'd like to live. For instance, Adam's recognition that his approach to research needed to change after he had children (Chapter 3) was reinforced by shifting the narrative he told about research. You'll recall that his pre-children work ethic was supported by his story: "I can work through any problem that comes my way." By recognizing the limitations of this story and consciously updating it, he reframed his story to say, "When I work, I recognize and respect my needs and the needs of my family."

Writing, drawing, and being cognizant of everyday speech provide three concrete means for updating narratives.

Writing

Putting words on paper allows you to gain distance from the content, which can allow you to see stories and patterns more easily. The power of written storytelling is recognized in a diverse range of settings, from helping immigrant women express the challenges of assimilating in New Zealand culture,[30] to allowing trauma patients to communicate thoughts or events that may be too painful to express in speech,[31] to supporting university students' goal setting.[32] Among others, psychologist Timothy Wilson argues for an approach that goes beyond storytelling to what he terms "story-editing."[33] Story-editing asks people to examine a range of possible causes or reinterpret (their own or others') behavior in order to create new, more effective narratives in their lives. Wilson explains, "Writing forces people to reconstrue whatever is troubling them and find new meaning in it," leading to what another researcher of expressive writing, James Pennebaker, describes as "getting people to come to terms with who they are [and] where they want to go."[34]

We have been asking you to reflect in writing throughout the book. As you explore story-editing, we suggest using writing to consider possible alternate causes or new reinterpretations of your current behavior. You can then write in a more forward-looking, intention-setting way about changes you would like to make. By putting your intended new attitudes, behaviors, and framings on paper, you are rewiring the implicit understandings that shape your actions.

Drawing or Other Visual Media

As we've had you do throughout the book, you might prefer to approach this story-editing expression in a more visual way: by drawing the new stories, attitudes, behaviors, or assumptions you are trying to change. Or perhaps another medium appeals more to you, such as collages out of colored paper, or clay sculptures, or bold paints. Like expressive writing, self-expression through visual means is commonly used in therapy settings, though generally to tell stories about past events.[35] Creative expression through art provides a way to "externalize and objectify experience so that it becomes possible to reflect upon it."[36]

In Everyday Speech

Besides the time you might set aside for writing or drawing as you craft new stories, you also have the opportunity to tell new stories each time you mention the topic of your new story in your everyday speech. This involves mentally catching yourself when the topic comes up (either internally or in conversation) and replacing the old story with the new. For example, if someone asks how you are and you hear your automatic response of "super busy," you might consider if there is another answer: "deep in an exciting exploration of literature about science and creativity," or "busy but energized because I am teaching my first solo course." Each time you verbally reinforce the idea that you are "super busy," you are knitting those neuron pathways tighter together. So, paying attention to how you talk about your research moment-to-moment allows you to consciously decide which pathways you want to strengthen.

ENHANCE THE CREATIVE ABILITIES WITH STORYTELLING

In previous chapters, we've introduced (and hopefully you have practiced!) four creative abilities and specific techniques for using them. But these abilities will not truly become ingrained until you internally identify yourself as someone who has that trait.[37] In other words, you have to make your internal narrative catch up with the external behaviors you are learning. Linking behavior change to identity allows you to make use of the same motivational mechanisms that are frequently used in behavior change interventions. For instance, changing the framing from a behavior you perform (i.e., "I vote") to an identity you hold (i.e., "I am a voter") invokes people's positive self-concepts and has been shown to increase voter motivation.[38]

How Storytelling Amplifies Mindfulness of Your Process

From the beginning of the book, we have emphasized the importance of becoming mindful and, particularly, the importance of becoming mindful of the process of your research as well as the content that you study. The stories you tell about research reflect your metacognitive understanding of what research is and how you relate to it.[39]

When we interviewed Stanford faculty about their research process, we found that at some point in their careers most of them had left behind the story that it is possible to truly "be stuck" in research. When we asked them what they did when they got stuck, they basically defined their experiences outside the definition of "stuck." A humanities scholar talked about feeling something that was "not writer's block but [that] does make me pace around the house for a couple of days before I figure out how to do it." An anthropologist described how much he learned from finding out that his method was culturally inappropriate – while in the field, with his tenure clock ticking, halfway around the world.[40] These faculty narratives stand in stark contrast to the graduate students we have taught, many of whom have an implicit prevailing story that research is a constant series of obstacles and getting stuck and unstuck. The underlying experience of challenges and what it takes to resolve them might be nearly identical, but the narrative used to frame and interpret it is different.

By examining the story you tell about your research process on particular projects and throughout your career trajectory, you will come to see how your use of language might be influencing you. Examining the underlying story forces you to reflect on your process so you can become more aware of it and ultimately able to make conscious choices about how you wish to proceed. Telling honest stories of your process in the right settings gives you the chance to see them in a more objective light and learn from them, and eventually to use them as a tool for mentoring your students (see Chapter 12). A public version of exploring the story of your research is when your research process becomes a research object in its own right, such as a paper you might write about an innovative course you developed or other ways your process is unique and of interest to the wider community.

How Storytelling Enables Emotional Intelligence

Developing deeper awareness of emotional stories helps you use emotions to prevent challenges as well as diagnose them. In identifying emotional stories, it can be particularly helpful to pay attention to your body as well as the words you use. Does your voice change when you describe something or use certain words? Does your chest tighten or your stomach become slightly nauseous?

For some of our students, simply acknowledging the role their emotions play in their research (Chapter 3) has represented a big shift in their prevailing narrative – they become more self-aware (and therefore more emotionally intelligent) scholars. Alternatively, you might have read or heard about *imposter syndrome*, which refers to the feeling that you have gotten away with something, or that you don't belong because you are not qualified in some way to be doing what you are doing.[41] This can be a powerful narrative, and acknowledging it can bring relief because it emphasizes that you are not the only one feeling inadequate. The way you describe yourself may also have emotional implications. For instance, a person who "does not fail" versus someone who "always does my best but doesn't need to be perfect" likely places different amounts of stress on themselves.

You might find it useful to consciously make emotions part of the story when you present yourself to others. For instance, saying, "When I found this paper saying no one had looked at my topic, I felt excited because it gave me confidence that I could fill a gap in the literature," communicates a deeper meaning to your advisor or colleague than just, "I found this paper."

How Storytelling Helps You Tolerate Ambiguity and Frame Problems

The stories we hold about ourselves and our abilities affect the types of problems we see. For many graduating PhD students, anything less than a tenure-track job is often seen as failure; this is a hard framing to overcome. And, the academy as a whole tells the story of "alternative academic careers" (non-faculty positions), which obscures the fact that the majority of PhDs go into them.[42] If you are trying to find a job you enjoy, you may need to reframe the narrative of success or normalcy being tied to a particular type of job.

By becoming aware of the language you are using and the stories you are telling, you become aware of the assumptions you are making about a problem space. You often need to step back from what you assume you know about a problem space and essentially wipe the slate as clean as possible of preexisting stories. You might try telling a story of the problem from a child's or beginner's point of view, assuming you know absolutely nothing and have tried nothing previously to solve the problem.

How Storytelling Assists Iteration and Experimentation

Eagerness to learn and willingness to fail are the first prerequisites for experimenting and iterating on a challenge. Many graduate students identify as people who "never fail"; rewriting this story can be a powerful tool to help you start testing ideas before you think the ideas are ready. Even senior researchers might relate to failure primarily through fear, as one of our colleagues confessed the week after she turned her tenure packet in. Her main response to the question about what she might do in her post-tenure career was, "I'm looking forward to being motivated by something other than fear."

The author team has found the story of research as a prototype to be a powerful one in our own work. If research is a continual iteration process, then crappy first drafts and critical feedback become an opportunity, or at least necessary parts of the process. We have found that living the prototyping story for long enough means that over time, we have developed a permanent sense of playing with our research practices, habits, and routines. For Sebastian, for example, thinking of research as a prototype frees his mind to start writing when facing a blank page, which used to be challenging for him. By having a structured way to remember that something "does not have to be perfect, it's only a 20 percent version to get feedback on," he lowers the bar. The lower expectations he sets for his initial effort creates mental space that helps him get words on paper more efficiently and emotional space that allows him to not be critical of himself in the process.

SUMMARY

Human beings understand the world through language. Becoming aware of the stories you currently tell about your research and yourself as a scholar provides you with a window into your implicit understanding of behaviors, attitudes, and emotions. If you identify unhelpful patterns in the language you use or the stories you tell, you can actively use the brain's plasticity to support your efforts to create new actions and beliefs. By focusing your attention on new stories through writing, drawing, and awareness of your daily speech, you can rewire your neurons into new, more optimal patterns.

EXERCISES

Try It

6.1 **Notice your language**: During your workday, notice the words you use to talk about yourself or your research. This can be in conversation with other people or your internal monologue. Carry a small notepad with you to capture specific phrases (or use your phone). After several days of tracking, notice if there are any common themes that emerge.

6.2 **Hero of your research journey**: Write or sketch your research story, with you as the main character. What are your characteristics? What are your superpowers as a researcher? What are your blind spots? How do you overcome adversity? Who are your allies? Who are your foes? What is the setting in which your character works? If you like, you can draw the movie poster for this story and decide which actors you would cast.

6.3 **Tell process stories**: What are your favorite stories about particular research projects – either your own or others'? (These are stories about how the research happened, not on the output of the research.) Why do you like them?

6.4 **Any given day:** Write the story of how you typically spend your days as a researcher. What do you do? Where do you go? What do you never do? What opportunities or struggles do you face?

Practice

6.5 **Research timeline:** Document your research journey on a timeline. Include activities, behaviors, relationships, and salient moments. Update your journey as your work evolves. Consider sharing this journey with a friend or colleague.

6.6 **Rewrite a story:** Choose one story to focus on. Notice when and how that story appears in your everyday speech. Commit to consciously rewriting how you tell that story when you talk to other people.

6.7 **Your research future:** Use expressive writing or drawing to envision your research future. Do this regularly, perhaps at the beginning of the month or the beginning of the semester. Describe who you want to become as a researcher, and how you want your research to evolve.

Reflect

6.8 What do you notice when you explicitly consider how your language and stories reflect your understanding of the world or yourself? In what ways do the stories you tell about your research shape your approach to your work?

6.9 What stories about research do you hear your colleagues, peers, mentors, and/or students talk about? Do you notice any links between their stories and their actions?

6.10 Can you map the stories you or other people tell onto the archetypal story structures (Figure 6.1)? Do you gain any additional insight by doing so?

7   Manage Your Energy

After she started her first faculty job, Rachel developed a terrible case of procrastination. She knew she needed to start turning her dissertation into a book, but the task felt daunting. Months went by without progress as she put off working on the book to take care of the things that felt more important on any given day: preparing for classes, meeting potential collaborators on campus, mentoring students. When she started to pay attention to her writing schedule, she realized that she always tried to work on her book – a task that was difficult and novel and required a lot of willpower – at times when her energy was low. She had regularly been sitting down to work on the book after teaching a seminar or during the wide-open block she had on Friday afternoons, which also happened to be when she was depleted from a full week. As a result, she made an important switch. She identified the windows during the week when her energy was the highest and started protecting that time to work on her book (not teach or do service). She noticed her workflow started to gain momentum, and whenever she started writing she was able to stay engaged and complete even the hardest thinking and revision tasks. Within just a few weeks of rearranging her schedule, she became more confident that she could finish the project and by the end of the year she had a solid manuscript to send to publishers.

Energy is defined as "the strength and vitality required for sustained physical or mental activity."[1] Energy is vitally important for your productivity, creativity, and enjoyment of your research. Different dimensions of energy have been shown to boost people's engagement with their work,[2] reduce psychological stress and burnout,[3] and lead to more creative ideas and outcomes.[4] Unfortunately, like Rachel, many researchers and other knowledge workers may not be immediately aware of their energy and its fluctuations, and instead work wherever and whenever they always have or whenever they perceive time to be most available. Indeed, people's habitual ways of "managing energy" (e.g., switching tasks, browsing the internet, or drinking another cup of coffee) are usually not that effective at increasing your focus, engagement, or creativity.[5]

Luckily, there are better ways to consciously manage your energy. Throughout this book, we've discussed the importance of bringing intentionality to what you do. Now, we will explore how being mindful of when and where you do particular tasks allows you to manage and enhance your energy, which supports you in being your most productive and most creative self. By exploring different types of energy, you can start to be more specific in understanding *how* you are tired, which helps you understand what you need to do to recharge. By becoming aware of your patterns of energy over time, you'll gain tools to match more or less cognitively demanding tasks to your energy levels. Finally, by exploring the people, places, and activities that change your subjective experience of energy, you'll start being able to design your research life to optimize how you spend your energy.

HOW TO USE ENERGY TO YOUR ADVANTAGE

At its most basic, human energy depends on physical stores of nutrients (especially glucose and adenosine triphosphate or ATP) contained in your cells. When you engage in any type of activity, you access some of these nutrients to fire your muscles, neurons, and other organs. In physics terms, drawing on human energy requires converting potential energy into kinetic energy.[6]

The kinetic energy required for different types of activities varies substantially. For instance, activities that require self-control, focus, and concentration or that force you to make a choice can deplete your stores of glucose and lead to mental fatigue over time.[7] At the same time, your subjective feeling of energy may change depending on the type of activity you're doing and how you're engaging in it.[8] For instance, even though exercise definitely requires physical exertion and burns calories (technically consuming energy in the process), people usually feel more energetic after a run.[9]

By understanding how your body uses energy for different types of activities, and how your subjective experience of energy changes based on internal and external characteristics, you can start to be more proactive in how you work with energy in your research and life.

Become Aware of Different Types of Energy

The first step to better energy management is self-awareness. By noticing your level of energy and learning to distinguish different types of energy, you'll build awareness that provides the basis for being smarter about your energy.

Throughout this chapter, we will distinguish three types of energy.[10] First, *physical energy* relates to your body's ability to engage physical activity; when you lack physical energy, you feel fatigue, expressed in your muscles and in the body. Second, *cognitive energy* relates to your mind's ability to focus, concentrate on challenging tasks, or think quickly or creatively; when you lack cognitive energy, you find yourself unable to focus, concentrate, or draw connections between concepts. Third, *emotional energy* (which is sometimes known as *subjective vitality*), relates to your emotions and your subjective experience of energy; when you lack emotional energy, you may feel agitated, irritable, or bored. To be precise, these three types of energy are "the energetic arousal that a person feels about investing effort (kinetic energy) into particular types of activities (physical, cognitive, or emotional)."[11]

At its most basic, building awareness of your energy means checking in throughout your day to notice how energetic you feel. When you check in, we encourage you to start distinguishing between the different types of energy (or tiredness) you're experiencing. For many people, it's easiest to start by noticing the state of your physical energy: Do you feel sleepy or energetic? Is there fatigue in your muscles or tiredness behind your eyes? But you will also want to check in about your mental and emotional energy, since it can sometimes be hard to distinguish when you are physically tired from times when your mental or emotional energy is low. Mental energy fluctuations often show up as fluctuations in concentration and focus: Are you able to concentrate on challenging tasks? Do you feel like you're capable of generating your best ideas? Are you rapidly connecting concepts or are you struggling to follow what colleagues in a meeting are saying? Emotional energy can similarly vary: Do you feel excited by the work that you're doing? Are you in a good mood?

You may also want to play with noticing the quality of your energy, which psychologists refer to as "arousal."[12] Specifically, there are two types of "high" energy arousals – calm energy and tension – and it can be easy to mistake tension for energy. When you are in a tense arousal state, it can feel like you're coiled up, ready to explode out of your skin. While this might feel energizing or motivating to work, it's a very different sensation than a calm energy state, when you feel enthusiastic, excited, and clear-headed. Recognizing this distinction is important for using energy to boost your creativity, as it affects the type of thinking you're poised to do. When you're in a calm arousal, you're in a good mood with an open, flexible mind and tend to be proactive; when you're in a tense arousal, it generally puts you in a negative mood with a closed, inflexible mind and a tendency to be reactive.[13]

Calm versus tense energy can apply to each of the three types of human energy. High physical energy means your body feels active and fit; high mental energy means your mind is open and flexible; and high emotional energy means you are in a good, excited mood. On the other hand, high physical tension means your neck and shoulders are tightened; high mental tension means your mind is inflexible and you have a narrowed perspective; and high emotional tension means you are concerned, impatient, and strict.[14] Just as you can check in to notice whether you feel energetic or tired (and what kind of energetic or tired you feel), you can also check in to see whether your high-energy state is tense or calm.

By learning to distinguish between the different types of energy, you can be more precise in determining what types of activities or rest will help reenergize you. Luckily, the same types of activities can help you shift from a low-energy to a high-energy state as will help you shift from tense to calm arousal. If you identify that you need to boost any particular type of energy, you can start by trying some of the activities in Table 7.1.[15]

While it might seem somewhat paradoxical, you can also use your knowledge of different types of energy to be more intentional about what you do during longer breaks from work (weekends or vacations). To do this, check in with what type of energy you feel you need to restore. In other words, when you have a break, the first question should not necessarily be where to go or what to do, but what

Table 7.1 *Activities to create calm energy*

Physical:

1 Ten-minute movement	e.g., walking, running, cycling
2 Small light snack	e.g., fruit, vegetable, yogurt
3 Relaxation technique	e.g., progressive muscle relaxation

Cognitive:

4 Raise awareness	e.g., asking yourself: "What am I actually doing? What do I want to achieve?"
5 Create short-term objective	e.g., getting something done in the next fifteen, thirty, or sixty minutes
6 Method "to act as if ..."	e.g., playing the role of the motivated person

Emotional:

7 Energizing social contact	e.g., phone call, coffee, lunch
8 Get something small done	e.g., replying to an email, filling out a document
9 Distract yourself	e.g., listening to music, doing something new

you need in terms of energy. By understanding what fell short during your work time, you can best design your break to recharge. If you are lacking physical energy because of feeling exhausted, look for ways to regenerate and replenish your physical energy. If you are lacking cognitive energy by feeling bored through routine work, look for a variety of activities and new inspiring stimuli.

Understand and Manage Your Energy Levels

Once you've started to become more conscious of your different types of energy, you can also start to notice patterns in how your energy levels fluctuate over time. A good starting point for increasing awareness of your energy levels is to actively map your energy (either in general, or of one of the three types) for several days. You could start intuitively, by thinking about your usual day: When do you wake up and go to sleep? When do you think you have more physical energy? When do you tend to be able to concentrate well on hard tasks? A more precise way, though, is to check in throughout your day and write down how energetic you feel (Exercise 7.1). One of our class participants wanted to draw the energy curve for his overall energy (physical, emotional, and mental treated as one aggregate) as precisely as possible. He put an alarm on his smartphone every hour to assess his energy level on scale from 1 to 7 and collected this data for one week. At the end of the week, he graphed his average energy curve and the variance around his energy at any time. (You don't have to get this detailed, though!) Finally, you may want to try drawing multiple energy curves, perhaps one for during the week and the other for the weekend, or one for your field season and one for when you are in the lab analyzing data.

Once you have your energy curve in place, you might play with trying to understand what the data are telling you about when your high- and low-energy times tend to be. Studies of people's waking energy patterns show that most people have several characteristic trends in their daily energy, though the timing of those trends varies from person to person.[16] To start, you should have a several-hour period during which you have your highest overall energy; Horne and Östberg, two of the pioneers of sleep and energy mapping, called this your "peak time."[17] You'll also probably have one especially low time for about one to two hours every day. You may also notice that you have a second "high time": a two to three hour increase in energy, but that may not reach the same levels as your peak time.[18]

Look at your energy curve and see if your days conform to these trends. You may notice that you have a strong two-peak-and-a-trough pattern that is fairly consistent in timing from day to day. Or you may notice that different days have very different energy. Perhaps your Mondays start off strong, but by Friday the amplitude of your peak has diminished. Or perhaps your different types of energy follow different trajectories. Perhaps your cognitive energy is highest in the morning, but you have ample physical energy for exercise in the afternoon or evening.

It can also be helpful to understand your chronotype – patterns of preferred wake and sleep times – as these can affect the timing of your high- and low-energy periods. While there's some debate over exactly how many chronotypes there are, many typologies break individuals into morning types (people who wake early and are most alert in the morning), evening types (individuals who prefer to sleep in and go to bed late and are most alert into the night), and indifferent types (those who don't have a strong preference either way; their peak times spread throughout the middle of the day).[19] Morning types have their prime time almost immediately after they wake up, while the evening types need a couple of hours to get into their prime time.

Once you've started to be more aware of your energy levels and when your high and low periods are, you can start to be smarter about allocating particular tasks to certain times during your day. Different types of work require different levels of energy and attention. For routine work – things like entering data into an Excel spreadsheet, routine meetings, or filling out travel reimbursement forms – some concentration is required but rather little brain work is necessary. In demanding work, higher levels of concentration and mental flexibility are required. This could include writing emails, grading student essays, or reading a paper. Finally, novel work like data analysis, planning a long-term project, or writing a paper takes high levels of thinking and effort.

Ideally, you want to match these different levels of work into your higher- and lower-energy times, focusing particularly on your cognitive energy. Try to allocate novel work into your peak time. Your cognitive capacity is the highest then, and you have the greatest emotional energy to deal with difficult tasks. If there is something you tend to procrastinate on or really don't want to do – e.g., writing that literature review you've been putting off for two weeks – the peak time is best to tackle those challenges too, since willpower declines as you become more tired.[20] As the peak time is so important, we suggest that you protect it "like a tiger," as one student described it. Second, you can allocate the demanding work to your second energy peak, if you had one, as you still have sufficient energy to deal with work that requires some cognitive and emotional effort. Or demanding work can be the next priority for peak time when novel tasks are complete. Last and definitely not least, try to allocate routine work into your low time. This way, you can still use low-energy times to be productive, but you won't spin your wheels trying to tackle something that requires a lot of brain work and emotional energy.

After one of our classes, Gabrielle, an anesthesiology postdoc, spent a week mapping out her energy, hour by hour, day by day, and then used this information to reorganize her workdays. She asked her labmates to move the daily meeting to 9:30 instead of 10:00 (which was right in the middle of her productivity peak), and she started checking her emails right after lunch (her worst time for productivity). After making these changes, she also noticed that by respecting her low time after lunch (accepting that she probably was not going to get much more done then except write emails), she made her second high time more productive later in the afternoon. Sustainable productivity does not come from having high energy all the time but from knowing when you are in which energy state and intentionally allocating the

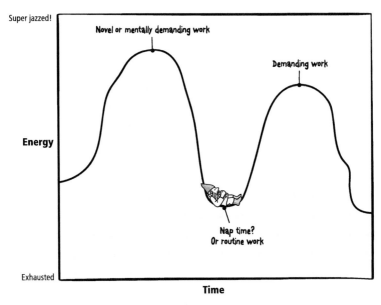

FIGURE 7.1 Allocating work to your energy curve

tasks at hand according to your energy level. Allocating different levels of work to your different time zones can have a huge effect on your creativity and productivity.

Another good way to use your low time is to take a power nap. In addition to increasing your energy during your high times, napping has the added benefit of putting your brain into particularly relaxed and creative mindset.[21] As you fall asleep, your brain waves ("alpha" waves) become slow and increase in amplitude, sending your mind into a relaxed, reflective state; when you wake up, your "theta" brain waves – even slower and larger amplitude – put you in a state of deep relaxation. Both stages are particularly good for generating ideas and creatively finding solutions for problems.[22] Indeed, many creative people, including Albert Einstein and Salvador Dalí, would deliberately short naps to enter this liminal state by holding a key, spoon, or other noisy object that would drop as soon as they fell asleep.[23]

Notice that your energy and work demands also fluctuate over longer time scales. You probably are familiar with the energy high at the beginning of a semester or the feeling of exhaustion that comes around midterms. Similarly, the energy available for and demanded by various research projects may ebb and flow as you transition between generating research questions, collecting and analyzing data, and sharing your results. Just as you can actively optimize your work to match your daily or weekly energy levels, you can try to match your energy and work demands over longer periods of time.

Explore the Sources and Sinks of Your Energy

Finally, recall that different types of activities change the subjective experience of your overall energy level, even though they are converting the same amounts of potential energy.[24] By developing awareness of the people, activities, and places that boost your energy or take your energy away, you can set up your life to feel optimally energetic.

Other people can boost your experience of energy, but they can also drain it.[25] In general, there are several factors that predict whether an interpersonal interaction will be energizing. First, emotions can be contagious; if someone else is in a good mood, you're likely to pick up their energy.[26] Second, interactions that are stimulating, such as when someone challenges you to think hard or makes you feel that your input is useful, can give you energy.[27] Third, balanced interactions where everyone involved gets to listen and talk to the same extent tend to be more energizing than those where one person dominates the conversation.[28] Think about which types of social interactions leave you feeling energized: Do they tend to be with large groups, or just one or two other people? How do other people's moods affect your energy? Are there particular people who always seem to leave you drained after a conversation?

Different types of activities also give or take away energy. Often, activities that are more self-directed, where you have higher autonomy over the task, and those that require your specific skills and competences tend to give you higher feelings of "vitality."[29] Notice what types of activities you're engaged in during the times that you feel particularly energized. You may also want to think about the nature of the tasks you're engaging in: Are they contributing to your physical, cognitive, or emotional energy? (A more structured way to do this exploration is Exercise 7.2, where you'll map out the people and activities that give and take energy for you.)

After thinking about what people and activities give you energy, you might brainstorm ways to get more of these energy-givers in your life. Likewise, try to find ways to reduce or remove the activities or interactions that drain your energy (or at least move them to times that you don't need to be at peak performance or in your most creative mode).

Additionally, the physical space where you work can affect your energy levels. Environmental psychologists have shown that ambient environmental conditions (light, temperature, noise, and ventilation), furniture and office layout, and employees' agency over and ability to influence decisions about their workspace can drastically affect employees' satisfaction with their workplaces, sense of belonging, and overall productivity.[30] Moreover, physical settings that contribute to positive moods – windows to the outside, aesthetically pleasing furniture, plants, pleasing odors or music – can support employee creativity.[31] The Stanford d.school has been conducting a long-term exploration of how the arrangement of classrooms and other spaces influences team creativity, which is detailed in the book *Make Space*, if you would like more inspiration.[32] In other words, characteristics of the space where you work can affect your mood, your ability to concentrate, and your overall energy.

Chen was a first-year PhD student who was assigned a desk in a shared office space with other students in his department. He was excited when he arrived, because his desk was facing the only window in the office and he knew he thrived on natural light. But after working there for a couple of weeks, he felt increasingly frustrated. The space got too hot in the middle of the day, making him feel lethargic. His office mates were very social; he loved the opportunity to practice his English and the companionship, but it felt like almost every hour two or more people would start a new conversation, and to make progress he needed to concentrate on his work for extended periods of time. And worst of all, the room seemed to give him allergies, so he was congested and sneezing by midmorning, which sapped his energy to work.

While your habitual workspace might not have as obvious effects on your physical, cognitive, and/or emotional energy as Chen's, it is worth assessing where you work and what characteristics of the space seem to give you energy or drain your energy. Then you can use this information to redesign your existing space to be more energizing. For instance, Chen asked his advisor to ask the building manager about the ventilation system; it turned out the air filter into his office was missing, so there was a quick fix to his dust allergies. You might also play with adding light sources or shades or decorating your space to make it feel like your own. Sometimes, though, you might need to find additional spaces to support your work. Rather than asking his office mates to be quiet, Chen started reserving a cubicle in the campus library for times that he knew he needed quiet to focus.

Finally, you may find new ways of adding new energy into the system. We've focused so far on increasing the awareness of your energy levels and strategies to be smarter about your energy, in essence treating energy as a problem of allocating a scarce fixed resource. However, you can also use specific strategies to add new energy to the system. At the core of gaining new energy is to get good-quality sleep, eat well, make time for physical exercise, and use methods for relaxation. There is extensive research on each of these, which we are not delving into here, but we encourage you to take good care of your body to help make sure that you have available the most energy (and therefore the most creative cognitive capacity) that you can.

HOW ENERGY ENHANCES THE CREATIVE ABILITIES

While making yourself more energetic can have a wonderful overall effect on your productivity and well-being, it also directly supports each of the other creative abilities we've discussed throughout the book.

Mindfulness

Energy and mindfulness interact in several ways. First, checking in with your different states of energy during the day uses the same skills of intention and awareness used in mindfulness, so becoming aware of your energy helps you practice mindfulness more generally. At the same time, managing your energy more proactively boosts your cognitive energy, helping you concentrate and pay better attention to your thoughts and behaviors.

Emotional Intelligence

Being emotionally intelligent means that you need to be aware of the emotions you're feeling, be compassionate toward yourself for feeling those emotions, and be empathetic to the needs and desires of other people. To do this, it helps to be in a more calm, curious state (and therefore to have higher energetic arousal). At the same time, your emotional state also affects your energy level, especially your emotional energy. If you are angry, sad, or anxious, it's going to distract from your ability to focus and potentially make you tense. Thus, managing your energy is important for working in a more emotionally intelligent way, and being emotionally self-aware is important for noticing when you might need to adjust your activities or location to help boost your energy.

Problem Finding and Framing

For the task of problem finding and framing, it helps to be in a state of calm energy, when your mind is flexible and open to new perspectives. Tackling this activity when you are tense or tired is much more challenging and potentially frustrating. Conversely, your state of energy at the time a new problem arises can affect your tendency to be either open and curious or to rush to a resolution. If you have high calm energy, you are in a more open, proactive state, and thus more likely to pause and explore your problem space. Conversely, if you are tense, you are more likely to have tunnel vision and see only a single perspective on the problem. This means that when you encounter a new problem, you may want to pause and check in on your energy before you start thinking about solutions or how to frame the problem.

Iteration and Experimentation

As with the other creative abilities, your ability to iterate and experiment toward a solution is enhanced by being in a curious, calm, alert state. When you need to brainstorm or prototype, try to either schedule these activities into your higher energy times or do one or two activities from Table 7.1 as a quick energy boost before you start.

For times when you want to engage in divergent thinking, you might also want to capitalize on the alpha brain waves generated when you are going to sleep or waking up. Try keeping a notebook by your bed to capture wild ideas you might have as you fall asleep or building naps into your day to access this thinking state.

Language and Stories

Storytelling is an excellent approach to uncover the internal beliefs you have about energy. Think about what stories you hold about energy (in general and specific to you). Are you an energetic or lazy person (or energetic or lazy in particular contexts)? What do you believe about the sources of energy? Is energy infinite? Does it get depleted every day, or until you eat, sleep, go for a run, listen to music, or leave work? What language do you use to talk about energy ("I'm burnt out," "I'm on fire," "I can't keep my eyes open")? See if identifying these stories seems helpful for your more conscious use of energy.

Additionally, as you start to restructure your day-to-day research to better match your energy cycles, you might want to use storytelling to reinforce the new habits that you're developing. Come up with new stories that match the identity you're creating: "I write in the morning because that's when I'm most alert"; "As soon as I feel my mind wandering, I get up to take a walk around the building"; "I work with, not against, my natural energy cycles." See how these stories feel to try on and notice if they help you stick with the new behaviors you're cultivating.

SUMMARY

Energy is a fundamental part of being a productive researcher, yet researchers don't necessarily work in ways that reflect or enhance available energy. In this chapter, we've encouraged you to become more aware of your energy, including becoming cognizant of different types of energy and of trends in your energy over time, and to use that knowledge to work smarter. Working with your energy can also help you boost your creative abilities, by helping you cultivate the mental and emotional state that best supports you to be emotionally intelligent, to find and frame problems, and to ideate and experiment.

EXERCISES

Try It

7.1 **Energy curve:** Map your energy over time. In this map, the x-axis is time and the y-axis ranges from positive energy above the x-axis to negative energy below the x-axis (see Figure 7.1). Begin by plotting daily events and their associated energy. Do this for at least a week. Notice when your high- and low-energy times are.

7.2 **Sources and sinks:** List all the activities you perform during the course of a normal day. It might be easier to choose a specific day to start with. Then, add those activities that you might not do regularly but which are still important. Next to each activity write down if it gives you energy or if it takes energy away. The goal is not to eliminate things that take energy (they can be important) but to become aware of the balance between the two. Perhaps you can affect your overall energy by finding a better order of activities to engage in.

7.3 **Space prototype:** Try working in different spaces. Pick an activity, e.g., reading or writing. Over the course of a week spend at least thirty minutes each day doing that activity in a different space. Reflect on how that felt. Were you more productive? Did you think about things differently? It can be easy to assume that your current default locations are the best for you, but we encourage you to test your assumptions empirically.

Practice

7.4 **Match energy and tasks:** Set aside different times of day to do different kinds of thinking. Try to link your highest energy times to tasks that need more mental attention. For instance, many people like writing first thing in morning, which helps to create a flow state linked to a particular time of day and to the location where they write. Or create "themes" for the week, for instance, schedule as many meetings as possible on Thursdays and leave all administrative tasks to end of week on Fridays. This has the added benefit of creating a habit, linking the time and the activity. (Remember also that these are prototypes – if a schedule you've set is not working, think about what you learned and change it!)

7.5 **Energy boost:** If you feel low energy it might be time to take a walk around outside. Bring a friend if that helps you. As scholars going back hundreds of years knew, this can be a valuable way to recharge your energy levels and it might help you incubate some creative ideas to challenging problems.[33]

7.6 **Your ideal workspace:** Design your space to support different energy levels. Some spaces work great for sitting alone and reflecting, while others are better for small teams to meet or generate new ideas. Think about the wide range of activities you engage in during the course of your research. Consider ways that you can make your space flexible enough to transform to support each activity. Or if you don't have that much control over your personal space, try to collect a go-to network of public spaces that you can move through that support your activities.

Reflect

7.7 How well do your work processes function day-to-day? Do you tend to have decent energy and motivation for your work? Or do you usually feel tired or drained? Are there certain settings where you feel like you have more energy?

7.8 Do you work better alone or with others? With quiet, music, or ambient noise? Have fun: If you had unlimited money and resources and could design your perfect work environment, what would it look like?

8   Make Your Research a Team Sport

INTRODUCTION: INPUT FROM OTHER PEOPLE IS A GIFT

Patrick had just started a prestigious postdoc at a new university. He knew he should be excited – he had before him two years of working with a top expert in organic chemistry on a project that would help explain the years of experimental data he had collected during his PhD. But he wasn't. He was lonely. His mentor was traveling the world; the other professors he reached out to brushed him off as not knowing enough since he had a PhD in biology rather than chemistry, and he didn't know where to start in establishing collaborations with other junior scholars. This made him variably frustrated, angry, and sad, and definitely detracted from his being able to dive wholeheartedly into his research.

You may have felt like Patrick – as if you are in a bubble of research, thinking about it day and night with not many other people to bounce ideas off or share your excitement with. You might feel that you are the only person excited about your research topic, or at least the only one excited enough to dedicate years of your life to it.

Like Patrick, many researchers tend to work in isolation, whether by default or design. The isolated entity can be an individual, but it can also be a mentor–student pair, a lab group, or a team convened for a specific project. The individual or team usually develops ideas internally, with little sharing outside this core group until ideas are well-developed and polished. Even within research teams, rough ideas tend to be shared more frequently with other researchers at the same stage (e.g., graduate students), with time to polish the ideas before they are shared with a faculty member or other people up the hierarchy; it's generally rare for a faculty member to seek input on a new research idea from a first-year PhD student. As a result, sharing your research often becomes the task of performing for others – convincing them that you have a good idea, are smart, are ready to defend your dissertation, or should receive funding – with little emphasis on receiving feedback to help make the ideas better before they are ready for prime time.

In this chapter, we argue for a reframe: that as a researcher you need a diverse team of allies to help you on the path to learning and iteration. When we say "team," we follow Amy Edmonson and colleagues' concept of *teaming* to mean the people you interact with about your research process or content – not necessarily a formal group.[1] This could be one other person or a larger group of individuals, and it could be a regular interaction or infrequent meetings. Used wisely, other people can amplify your power and energy, boosting your creativity and productivity and providing emotional support. Whether or not you are part of a lab, if you act like you have a research team you will be more productive and less lonely. And for those of you who are in a lab or research group, you'll probably find that you will benefit by bringing in a more diverse network to supplement this formal community.

The Value of Teaming for Creativity

While society tends to laud the individual creative genius – the writer, the painter, the entrepreneur – creativity is a sociocultural process, and most great works and innovative breakthroughs are the result of a team. Jazz musicians make great music through structured improvisation in a group; book writers benefit from working with agents and editors, and great actors and directors work collaboratively together in rehearsals to make a truly memorable play.[2]

Specifically, bringing together multiple people – ideally people from diverse perspectives or backgrounds – has repeatedly been shown to enhance creativity. When you have multiple people working together, it enables cross-fertilization of their respective knowledge and ideas, leading to the generation of more and more unique ideas than you could generate alone.[3] And bringing in other people early to your research helps you identify more or less promising ideas, enabling you to drop the less promising ones before you put in too much effort.[4]

In other words, working with other people – including people outside your discipline and perhaps even non-academics – can help you generate more diverse and creative ideas, find or create the energy and momentum you need to work, and access the support you need to help you through the mental and emotional challenges of research. Working with a team also gives you the opportunity for seeking early and ongoing input into the content and process of your research. Learning to give and get input will help you at all stages of the research cycle, from problem framing, to iteration, to prototyping/testing. It will help you refine ideas as you learn to communicate your needs clearly, and it will help you learn to be ever more mindful of your process and your emotions.

Finally, strong support networks are also important for overall well-being. According to numerous studies, having strong relationships is critical in predicting overall health and how long you live, while loneliness is associated with obesity, heart disease, and other health problems (not to mention discontent).[5] Strong relationships with colleagues can be an important part of one's overall support network.

HOW A RESEARCH NETWORK SUPPORTS YOUR CREATIVITY

Building a collection of diverse individuals who you can draw on for feedback and support has numerous potential benefits for your research, as it helps to amplify each of the creativity abilities we've discussed in the book.

Mindfulness

Learning how to ask for feedback – identifying what type of input you need and when – helps you learn to be more explicitly conscious of your research process. Identifying your feedback needs (which we discuss in detail later in this chapter) means that you have to be aware of when you're stuck and whether you'll be best able to move forward if you find someone to help reframe a problem, help you brainstorm research questions, or just lend an ear and reassure you that your idea isn't crazy. Developing this awareness is a skill that takes practice, but asking, "What's going on, and how might someone else view what I'm doing, thinking, or feeling?" can help deepen and broaden the awareness you bring to your research process.

Emotional Intelligence

Giving and getting feedback on half-baked ideas can be an important source of empathy and self-compassion, particularly when sharing with people at the same career stage. When you share your questions and struggles with a group, you very quickly realize that many other people have faced very similar struggles. In our classes, we have regularly seen students be transformed by learning that they are a part of a shared enterprise and are not alone in what they face. We teach students from many different fields, and we are consistently reminded how similar PhD struggles are, regardless of a student's department. This realization also helps our students develop self-compassion when they come up against a new problem or feel inadequate in their ideas or research.

The benefit of sharing common struggles isn't just for PhD students. Postdocs, junior faculty, early-career scholars, and senior scholars can all benefit from the sense of camaraderie that comes from sharing your experience – both good and bad – in the research world. When Nicola was a postdoc, she attended a training event with a group of postdocs and senior researchers from around the USA. During an informal lunch break, several postdocs started chatting about imposter syndrome.[6] One of the senior researchers asked, "What's imposter syndrome?" After someone defined it for him, he – a respected member of the National Academy of Sciences – said, "Oh yeah, I feel like that all the time." Afterward, several of the postdocs commented how refreshing and empowering it was to hear that even someone as established as that scholar didn't always feel confident.

Other people are also valuable for helping you see when a problem you're facing has an emotional core that you might be blind to, and they can help you identify what emotions you're feeling. For instance, when Jorge – the student from Mexico studying earthquakes we introduced in Chapter 3 – was struggling to decide whether to change his dissertation topic, faculty mentors helped him identify that the strong emotions he was having (frustration and anger about his family's struggles trying to get aid from the government) suggested a more systemic problem that could turn into a research topic about government performance.

Problem Finding and Framing

When you're going through the process of exploring a problem space and finding the problem you want to solve, other people can help you identify blind spots you may have and help you see the problem in a new light. First, when you are really deep in a problem, it can be hard to step back and critically appraise whether your current framing or approach is a helpful one. Having somebody look at it from a fresh perspective can help you move in new, unexpected directions and progress your project. This can be particularly beneficial if you are really committed to a particular framing of a problem (e.g., the anchor problems we discussed in Chapter 4).

The second benefit of seeking feedback is that other people are often better at identifying possible emotional aspects of a problem. Because emotions are often a signal that you're nearing the root cause of a problem, finding them is important for making sure you solve the problem that will actually address the challenges you're facing. In Chapter 4, we talked about Crystal digging into her frustration about always getting sucked into small tasks. We reproduced the dialogue she and her partner had that led her to a new understanding of the problem. Her partner was key in uncovering these insights – helping her see where she had unconscious assumptions about the problem or its causes.

Iteration and Experimentation

Solving problems through iterative cycles of generating and testing ideas is a key place to bring other people into your research. It creates the opportunity to come up with ideas that you might not have on your own. Recall that the more ideas you have, the more likely it is that one of them will be a gem. Each person is individually constrained in the types of ideas and perspectives they bring to bear on a problem. If you work with one or more other people, you add their aggregated ideas and perspectives to your own, increasing the number of ideas that you have at your disposal.

For collaborative or team-based settings, you can get particularly creative ideas if you actively generate ideas together, rather than each contribute ideas individually. Every time Lisa, a political scientist, sees one of her coauthors at a conference, they always make time to grab a beer or coffee and brainstorm. They chat about their individual projects and interesting talks they heard at the conference. Then they switch consciously into divergent thinking mode and riff on new questions to ask or new ways to use data the other person has already collected. They always leave the conference with four or five concrete ideas for new papers. While they don't write all of them, this process of setting aside time to jointly generate ideas results in projects that neither Lisa nor her coauthor would come up with individually.

When it comes to prototyping and testing ideas, other people can help you flag potential problems before you invest too much time or energy into a particular direction or solution. As we discussed in Chapter 5, failing early is an important tool to move ideas forward quickly. Because other people have different perspectives on the world and can therefore see things that you can't, sharing early stage ideas with others gives you the chance to learn quickly whether and/or how to revise or discard them. It also gives you the chance to learn about things that have been tried before, so you can incorporate that knowledge as you iterate.

Language and Stories

Working with other people can boost your skills in using storytelling as a tool. Continuing on the theme of other people bringing new perspectives to your work, a trusted person can help you uncover internal narratives you have about how you work and perhaps help you shift them to be more constructive. You can also be explicit in seeking out people who think differently than you, for instance, bringing in someone who is a visual thinker if you tend to like words, or vice versa.

You might find stories appearing in your relationships with others that are more or less effective. When you hold a different narrative than someone else you work with, it can create tension. For instance, a new assistant professor probably views their research agenda somewhat differently than other faculty in their department, or two advisors might hold different expectations for a jointly advised PhD student. Understanding these stories can help you work more effectively together. Teams also develop shared language to describe the world and tell collective stories. These can be as simple as how the team names itself, but also extend to how a group describes its purpose or the behavior of its members (e.g., expectations that Liz will always be late or an expectation that the team is made up of quantitative social scientists). Team stories often reflect unstated or informal team norms and expectations.

You can also use the skill of storytelling to help you proactively work with other people. As you think about who you might go to for feedback, consider the narratives you might have about the people you could ask. How many times have you thought, "Oh no, he's too busy, there's no way he would read a paper draft," or, "Her research interests don't overlap enough with mine, so she probably won't give helpful feedback?" Do you know this to be true, or is this just a story you have about this person? Or do you hold a narrative about yourself that you're independent, or introverted, or just a first-year student, or any other number of reasons why you shouldn't or can't or don't ask other people for input? You can use the skills we discussed in Chapter 6 to actively reframe these stories: emphasizing that you do have a diverse network and are some-body who leverages that network to help you do more creative research.

Energy

Other people can be great when you need an energy boost. This can take a lot of different forms. You might meet a friend or colleague for a quick walk around campus when you hit a slump, help someone else with a problem or question they have, or meet over coffee and share your ideas. Engaging with other people can also reinvigorate your energy for your research. During one of our classes, participants exchanged visualizations of their dissertation projects. One PhD student told us afterward, "I've been working on my dissertation for two years, and it's become dull. It was so cool to see how excited my partner was about my topic; it completely reenergized me!"

While these can be spontaneous interactions, there are also benefits from intentionally scheduling time with other people into your day. Sarah, a linguistics professor, likes to schedule meetings in the afternoon, when she knows she'll be lower energy. This saves her peak time in the morning for focused research tasks and also helps her be a bit more energetic and productive when she would otherwise be tired. Additionally, there is a lot of research demonstrating that you can stay more motivated to work (or exercise, or quit smoking) if you have made a public commitment to another person.[7] Writing groups, in which you have a scheduled meeting where you show up and write with other people, can be a great way to leverage other people to help sustain your energy.[8]

On the other hand, there are plenty of people who will quickly sap your energy for research, whether because of their pessimism about the department or because of their enthusiasm for talking at length about your mutual rock climbing hobby. If you have people like this in your department or life, think carefully about when you interact with them so you don't drain your prime working times.

You can also consider the effect of space on the quality of interpersonal interactions when you work with other people and how that might affect your creativity. Think about the dynamic of a room when there is a clear division between a presenter or panel at the front and the audience; if you're trying to encourage shared discussion, you probably want a space that has fewer separations between those in the presenter and audience roles. Similarly, consider who "owns" the space when you meet: How would a meeting between a PhD student and their advisor change if they met at the student's desk versus in a shared lab space versus in the advisor's office? You might intentionally set up a room to encourage the type of thinking you want in the meeting. Setting up a room for everyone to stand around a whiteboard is great to get people into an open, idea-generating mindset, while you might want a more quiet space with comfortable seating if you're trying to work through data analysis together.

HOW TO BUILD AN EFFECTIVE RESEARCH NETWORK

The Demand Side: Identifying Your Needs

As a project progresses, people benefit in different ways from social interactions. Research shows that creators benefit most from input when the social network they draw on matches their needs, whether that need is help with generating ideas, championing the idea, or implementing it.[9] Thus, working effectively with other people actually starts with figuring out where you are in the progression of your research and what types of input you need. For the economically minded, you can think of this as the demand side of a feedback equation. Draw on your own mindfulness and self-awareness to understand what you need from others so that you can effectively ask for the kind of feedback or support that will be most useful.

Your input needs for a given project at a given point in time likely have a number of dimensions you might want to consider:

- **Feedback or support:** At the moment, do you need feedback (input to move your research process or content forward) or just support (e.g., an energy boost, an ear to listen, a shoulder to cry on) or maybe both?

- **Process versus content**: Do you want input into *how* to move an idea forward, or are you looking for input into what is working or not working about the *content* of the idea itself?
- **Project design stage**: What phase of idea development are you in and what kind of feedback would most help you move your idea forward? When you are trying to define a problem, it might be that what you need is someone's input about how you've scoped the problem and their questions about what you might be missing. When you're in the divergent stage of iteration, you might need someone to push you in lateral directions and help you think of crazy ideas you might not have considered or to see where you are imagining constraints that don't exist. When you're in the convergent stage of prototyping, you might need detailed feedback about the pros or cons of a given idea that helps you evaluate whether to keep working on that solution or to go back to your brainstormed list and try another one. And sometimes, especially at the stage of identifying emotions and framing problems, but also all the way through, you might just need someone to listen and reflect your own concerns, feelings, and thoughts back to you – essentially someone to be a mirror so you can become more aware and mindful of what is going on emotionally or cognitively for you. In these cases, their value is less based on the actual feedback they offer and more on the way their attentive listening helps you generate feedback and self-awareness.
- **Your emotional state and resilience in regard to the project**: What level of critique are you ready for right now? Sometimes what you need might be an honest assessment from someone else of whether the idea is worth pursuing or not, but if you are particularly attached to an idea, you might not yet be ready to hear very detailed criticism. You may instead benefit most from high-level general feedback that doesn't feel too threatening.
- **Your iteration timeline**: How long do you have to respond to the feedback you are requesting? Can you realistically rewrite the whole paper if that's what someone suggests you should do, or are you facing an imminent submission deadline in two days that will require a more modest revision? In one vivid example, Antonio was preparing a prestigious fellowship application and shared a draft of the application with his mentor. Unfortunately, he received extensive feedback only the day before it was due; the document was metaphorically dripping with red ink. Trying to respond to the well-intended criticisms at short notice crushed his

confidence, leading Antonio to submit an application of which he wasn't proud. If he had had more time to both adjust emotionally to the feedback and incorporate it, it would have helped, but in this case receiving feedback when he did actually had a negative impact on his work.

- **Your capacity to reciprocate**: One final thing to think about as you evaluate the input you need is your own capacity to give input. Just like being invited to dinner at a friend's house brings with it the social expectation that you'll invite them to something in the future, when you ask for feedback from people you are often implicitly promising that you will return the favor of giving feedback in the future. If you are at a point in your research career when things are going well and you have sufficient bandwidth, there are lots of advantages to building this kind of reciprocal network with peers. But if you are in the last year of a dissertation and working two jobs to pay for school, you might jeopardize relationships if you ask for input without being able to reciprocate (or specifying that you probably won't be able to reciprocate, at least in the short term). Thus depending on your current capacity to give feedback, you might make different decisions about asking peers versus those whose jobs or relationship to you contains an expectation to give feedback without the need to reciprocate (e.g., advisor, writing center tutor, or copy editor).

The Supply Side: Cultivate a Network Who Can Provide Support at Every Stage

Once you've clearly identified what you need in terms of feedback or support (the demand side), you need to identify who is best suited to approach for input for a given project at a given time (the supply side). As your input needs will vary widely by project, idea-development stage, and over time, you will want to cultivate a diverse network of people who can meet your diverse set of needs.

To identify the person or people to approach to provide feedback for a given idea at a given stage, you need to evaluate who you know with the emotional and cognitive skills to meet the needs we have just identified. If you need empathic listening, who has stellar active-listening skills? If you are going to want multiple rounds of feedback, who has time available for iteration? If you're feeling particularly vulnerable, who tends to frame their feedback in a more constructive versus harsh way?

As you build your network, you might look for people who fit these commonly sought needs:

- **Early-stage, divergent content feedback**: You need people who can provide early feedback on unpolished, half-baked ideas – the rough outline for a grant proposal or paper, a list of potential research questions, a sketch of a new lab instrument. These people are there to respond critically to early versions, allowing you to learn and generate new ideas, and they tend to be individuals who are comfortable working with rough ideas.
- **Late-stage, convergent content feedback**: You'll also want more targeted feedback when you have more developed ideas – people to help you refine your methodology or identify gaps in a literature review. This tends to be an area where many scholars are most comfortable and is the type of critique most common in many lab groups or seminars.
- **Preparing research for dissemination**: You may need people who can help with the final-stage polishing process. If wordsmithing presentations, copy editing manuscripts, or formatting figures is your strong suit, great. If not, find someone whose it is. This is a place you can often find university-wide resources (e.g., a writing center) or even hire professional assistance if need be.
- **Process feedback**: While many advisors and researchers are comfortable providing critique about the content of research, they may not be as familiar with thinking about and providing feedback about process. You might need to seek out people who can help you figure out how to move your ideas forward and get unstuck – which is very different than telling you from their point of view what's good or bad about your current situation.
- **Emotional support**: Finally, while you can get a sense of camaraderie or relief from good process or content feedback, you want to make sure there are people you can draw on for emotional support, a listening session, or an energy boost.

Different people in your network have distinct roles to play; your job is to identify what their creative, analytic, and emotional strengths are and tailor your input requests accordingly (Figure 8.1).

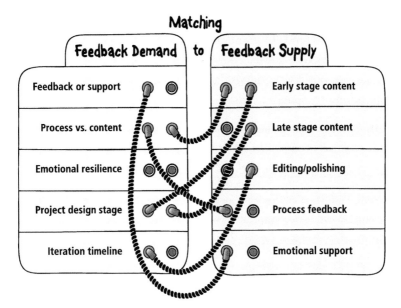

FIGURE 8.1 Matching feedback demand to feedback supply

For instance, Anja has a colleague who is excellent when she needs to figure out what theory might apply to a potential research question, but who would get completely bogged down in details if she asked about the big-picture framing of a project. Likewise, Adam has a colleague who he seeks out when facing a big decision (like whether to switch lines of research), as he knows this colleague is great at asking about the logic behind the decision and diving into personal considerations Adam might not have explored.

Once you've identified what input you need and who you're asking, you need to communicate what you need in such a way that the person you've identified will understand the request and provide what you need. The format of what you share will also help communicate where you are and what type of input you need. When you show something unfinished and rough, people see you are still very early in the process and you need help, so they tend to think of the big picture and help you refine your idea. On the other hand, when you show something that appears polished (even if the idea is still in its early stages), people switch into a critical mindset; they can only see mistakes and focus on details (which is not a particularly useful level of feedback when you are still trying to figure out whether the idea is even worth exploring further).[10] If you have an advisor or colleague who tends to nitpick on grammar, try sending them a paper draft as bullet points and see if it changes their focus to the content.

While we mentioned the norms of reciprocity, we encourage you not to overthink asking for feedback so much that you stop yourself from asking. In general, our students have found that people are a lot more willing to help than they thought. And keep in mind that someone's desire and their capacity to help at a given point in time are not necessarily the same thing. Often, the worst that can happen is your labmate says, "Sorry, I'm too busy." The one situation where you might be more cautious is when you're expending what sociologists call social capital to ask for feedback – say, when you ask a senior scholar in your field for a friendly review of a manuscript.[11] If this is someone you know well enough to ask for a review only once every couple of years, it behooves your career to be careful about the relationship and try to offer feedback in return when you're able.

Look for Diverse or Unexpected Teams and Sources of Feedback

Reading all this, you probably are already thinking about people in your feedback network and other people you could recruit to be more active participants. If you're like most researchers, it's likely that most of these top-of-mind people are colleagues; most of them likely do research similar to yours, and most of them are likely at similar career stages.

Here we want to challenge you to expand your view of your feedback network outside these "usual suspects," if you haven't already done so (see Exercise 8.6 to help you to flesh out this thinking). As we discussed above, research shows that the more diverse group of people you have to discuss your ideas with, the more diverse set of feedback you are going to get. People in disciplines, career stages, departments, or even professions outside your own may have very different framings of the world and suggest "wild ideas" that you and your more homogenous colleagues never would have generated. These people also are not attached to the theories or methods that might feel obvious or even sacred to you (whether or not you recognize it). Finally, the unfortunate reality is that too many departments and disciplines have unhealthy levels of competition. In a difficult employment climate, going further afield for feedback can be necessary for someone in a departmental culture where sharing ideas in development risks their being stolen.

Here are some ideas about where to look for diverse sources of feedback and support:

- Your cohort are people who are at a similar stage in their career, often in a similar department or discipline as you but not working on the same research topic. These individuals can be very helpful for emotional support, as well as process and content feedback. However, depending on your university or disciplinary culture, there may be some intra-cohort competition, which can flavor the type of ideas you'd want to share and their willingness to give you feedback.
- People from neighboring disciplines can be especially useful if they work on similar problems but think about them with different methods, framing assumptions, or under different conditions.
- People from other career stages can be especially helpful in terms of process feedback. After all, the PhD is explicitly designed with a faculty mentor built in, and many junior faculty are also assigned mentors by their universities – in both cases with the goal of helping people navigate their research and institution more effectively. But finding cross-stage support networks can be wonderfully helpful as researchers continue past graduate school, and especially for senior researchers (who tend to receive far less process feedback than their peers who are earlier in their careers).
- People from a completely different department can provide a fresh, welcome perspective of beginner's mind to your research. They are great for emotional support and process feedback. These people can also help with the big-picture framing of your research, which is necessary when you're

justifying the importance of your work. They force you to step back and explain why your research matters or make you aware of your implicit assumptions. Often, students from our classes will continue to meet in small, interdisciplinary groups for process feedback and help with brainstorming.

- University and/or departmental culture can drastically shape assumptions underlying how you do research, from what are considered valid research questions, to the types of methods you "should" use, to the types of people and places you study. Interacting across universities can offer new perspectives on strong divisions in your field, such as on the relative importance of theory and empirics.

- Spending time with a group of researchers who live or work in different parts of the country or the world can similarly bring a novel perspective to your work. Assumptions about research may be subtly absorbed from the surrounding community and change the experience of someone working in Montana versus Los Angeles versus Hong Kong.

- Outside of the academy, drawing on practitioners who use the products of your research, non-academics who work on similar problems as you, or researchers working outside of universities (i.e., individuals employed by a corporation, government agency, or nonprofit organization) can provide a new view on content-related questions.

- Finally, the cliché about telling your grandmother about your research contains quite a bit of wisdom. Framing your ideas in a way the "average citizen" can understand can help you clarify what it is that you're doing and why your research matters. You might talk about your research with your spouse's coworkers or during Thanksgiving dinner. You might find that the average person's reactions and seemingly obvious questions can help you better understand what you are doing, why it matters, and (especially) how to communicate why it's so important. And sometimes, serendipity will intervene. Someone might know someone or know something specialized that helps move your research forward. Or the interaction might spur an important question for you to consider in your research.

Drawing on a diverse network can result in unexpected insights. For instance, Peter, a geologist, was surprised to discover that physicists were studying the same class of materials that he was studying, just at much lower temperatures. Apart from the differences in jargon and

acronyms between the two fields, they were using the same spectro-
scopic data technique and had much they could share in terms of
workflow tips and data interpretation. He has since started building
connections with a physics lab on his campus. Maggie discovered the
power of non-specialist responses to her research during her dissertation defense. Her father, to his eternal pride, asked a question in the
public part of her defense about how her work on water and sanitation
in Tanzania might apply to challenges he faced as a hospital administrator in Colorado. Maggie's committee liked the question so much
that a good part of her closed-door defense focused on how her theories
and methods would apply to different infectious disease settings in the
developed and developing world. In a subsequent project, Maggie
worked with a colleague who studied health outcomes among home-
less patients in California to compare opportunities and challenges
across the two settings.

MODELS FOR WHAT YOUR NETWORK MIGHT LOOK
LIKE IN PRACTICE

There are a variety of different ways you can set up your network to get
the feedback and support you need (Figure 8.2). These range from very
informal – running into a colleague in the hall and asking, "I'm struggling with responding to this critical peer review comment. Do you
have any ideas?" – to very formal, like in a class or seminar. They also
range from one-time instances (requesting a friendly review on a journal
manuscript) to ongoing (a lab or dissertation group). Some of these you
might already be a part of, and some you might need to take initiative to
create yourself. We discuss a few common examples below.

On the more formal end of the spectrum, conferences, seminars,
workshop series, and classes can be structured for scholars to share in-
progress work with other people in the field or sister disciplines. For
instance, many PhD students take a research design class, which can
be designed for students to iterate their research projects through
several rounds of presentation or feedback, or to test what their

FIGURE 8.2 Varieties of feedback settings

research might look like if they used various methods. Likewise, brown bag seminars provide opportunities for junior and senior researchers alike to share their work. Sometimes these are just a presentation (great for getting feedback on your ideas) or they can include sharing the written work (great for moving a manuscript toward publication).

In these settings, you want to watch out for the tendency we discussed at the chapter outset – of sharing your research to demonstrate that you are intelligent or have good ideas (performing) versus sharing your research to seek input to make it better. Often, ongoing seminars or classes develop a culture that leans toward either tendency. A seminar might be oriented toward generative feedback and refining ideas. Presenting students might use the time for everything from brainstorming possible research methods, to refining a conference talk (with a focus on the presentation rather than the content), to thinking through the structure of their written dissertation. But in seminar series oriented toward sharing "polished" research, that sort of big feedback frame could feel foreign to attendees. Even in these settings, though, don't fall into the assumption that just because other people present their work as "finished," you have to do so as well. Instead, you can use them as opportunities for feedback if you clearly state what you need and explicitly ask the audience for that kind of feedback. For example, you could start or end your talk with, "This is a relatively new research project, and I would appreciate any ideas you have for additional analyses I might do with these data." Or you could end with a slide that states several questions (areas you want feedback on) for the audience. If this comes right before an audience Q and A, you can bet you'll cue people to address those areas in the discussion. For poster sessions, one postdoc we know likes to put a "feedback corner" on the edge of her posters as a place for passersby to collate any thoughts or ideas they might have on her work.

A lab or research group is likely a more familiar model for people to seek feedback. These are usually convened by a professor or senior scholar around shared content. As with a seminar series, lab groups also develop cultures of either presenting finished content or collaboratively refining ideas. If you're presenting in a lab group that tends toward detailed critique of polished research, try the techniques we mentioned of cueing questions to seed the type of feedback you want. Or ask for permission to share incomplete research, and give your advisor a copy of this book. Over time, you might find that the group leader becomes more open about lab members sharing early work and that your peers are more receptive to providing the types of feedback you seek. If you're the leader of this lab group, think about how you can help your participants get the feedback they need. Maybe you set ground rules for feedback in your group meetings (e.g., no side conversations, build on other people's ideas) or set aside times for generating versus critiquing ideas. Maybe before group members present, you meet with them and go through some problem finding or brainstorming exercises to identify areas they could use feedback on. Consider asking presenters to write clear questions for the group to discuss, including at least one content-related question and one pro-cess-related question.

A writing group, research group, or dissertation group is an ongoing small group established by researchers (often at a similar career stage) who want a place to talk about their work. While there are numerous models for these groups, they should meet regularly and provide time for members to discuss their research (both process and content).[12] Sometimes everyone shares what they've been working on (as a form of accountability), with time to ask questions about what to do next. Sometimes one person will share an ongoing piece of research (a paper draft, a presentation, etc.), and get detailed content feedback. In the groups that the authors have been a part of, the group also provides a safe space to get support and feedback on various challenges that arise, from negotiating health concerns with the university administration, to finding a job or planning a new research position.

Lastly, don't discount informal and fluid sharing of ideas, every-thing from sending papers to select colleagues to sharing ideas around the water cooler.

For most people, we recommend having multiple places where you can get the input you need. If you're part of a lab group, try to start structuring it so you can ask for early feedback or input on your process, and take the time to develop your informal network. If you are in a more solo research field, build a team, perhaps by attending a brown bag seminar series or starting a writing group. The most important piece of advice, though, is to find what works for you.

A NOTE FOR THE RELUCTANT OR SHY

We wanted to end with a note for those of you that feel overwhelmed by the idea of reaching outside of your comfort zone and either asking for early feedback or finding diverse people. If you are shy and/or worried about sounding stupid, we encourage you to push yourself to reach out anyhow. In the corporate world, employees who ask for feedback more often are rated as more creative by their employers (irrespective of whether they actually are by objective measures).[13] If you are worried about finding a big, diverse network, studies of team size, composition, and innovation often observe a U-shaped curve: You can realize big gains from adding one or two voices, but the marginal value of each additional person decreases and eventually declines once the group gets too large.[14] This is all to say, try it out. Some feedback is a whole lot better than no feedback, and you may even convince your advisor or colleagues that you have good ideas in the process!

SUMMARY

This chapter encourages you to use other people to boost your creativity. Working with a diverse team of allies helps you generate and refine ideas so they ultimately end up being more impactful. Learning to notice when you need feedback helps you become more aware of your research process. And sharing your research process can remind you that you are not alone in the challenges you're facing.

EXERCISES

Try It

8.1 **Seek feedback:** Take a project in its current state and find someone who can give you some minor feedback on it tomorrow. Think about what kind of input from someone else would help you move forward on the project. We know you probably don't feel ready, but practicing asking for early input before you feel ready is exactly the point.

8.2 **Process versus content:** Next time you go to a seminar, come up with at least one piece of content feedback and at least one piece of process feedback that you could give to the presenter. (Whether you choose to share both types of feedback with the presenter will depend on the norms of the seminar.)

8.3 **Diverse feedback:** Seek feedback about some aspect of your research from someone you never would have considered to have anything useful to say about it – perhaps a family member, someone in a different department, or someone at your spouse's work function.

Practice

8.4 **Plan for feedback:** Set a recurring personal deadline for you to ask for feedback. Whatever stage your project is in when the deadline comes around, figure out what feedback you would most benefit from and who you can ask. (One benefit of forming a writing or dissertation group is that this deadline is built in, and you have a committed audience of people to give you feedback.)

8.5 **Feedback formats:** If you want to practice with more formal feedback mechanisms or want a format to incorporate into your teams, you could try the following:

a Create a gallery walk.[15] Think of this as a poster session but with less refined artifacts. Place several pieces of work in progress on a whiteboard or a wall. Then spend fifteen minutes looking at each participant's work. Write feedback next to each item (on the whiteboard or on a Post-it note). After you have given feedback, start a larger discussion about your work as a whole.

b End working sessions with a debrief. One of the ones commonly used at the Stanford d.school is called "I like, I wish."[16] In this format all sentences begin with either "I like" or "I wish." It is a simple way for teams to get a sense of what various group members thought about an event or whatever is being debriefed.

c Use the PPCO formula.[17] Plus (P) stands for what you like about the research; Potential (P) stands for where you see more potential in the research; Concern (C) stands for concern you have regarding the research, and Overcome (O) stands for ideas of how to overcome the concern. The crux of this feedback method is that you start with two positive aspects of Plus and Potential and that with every Concern you provide you also have to offer at least one Overcome, otherwise you are not allowed to present a Concern. Combining Concern and Overcome in this way leads to especially constructive feedback sessions and attitudes.

8.6 **Map your support network:** Place yourself at the center. List people who fill each of the common input needs listed in Figure 8.1 as nodes in a large map. Are there any holes in your network? What part of your network do you rely the most on? How could your network be more diverse? Who could you invite to join it? Who could you add that would be unexpected? Imagine you were to map out the support network of the key people on your map. What roles do you play for them? Then look at the map of your network. Identify a gap and find someone who will fill that gap. Regularly revisit your map (e.g., once a semester) and continue to build your network.[18]

Reflect

8.7 When do you tend to seek feedback? Do you do it early on or more toward the end? Do you prefer the ideas you are testing to be highly resolved or rough? Why? What are your strengths and weaknesses in receiving feedback? What are your strengths and weaknesses when giving feedback?

8.8 Can you remember a time when you didn't get useful feedback? Can you identify any mismatch in expectations between your feedback needs and the other people's feedback strengths that might have contributed to the situation? How (or who) might you have asked differently?

8.9 What is the most satisfying team experience you have ever had? What role did you play on the team? What made that experience great? To what extent have you replicated that experience in subsequent work? Might there be elements of that experience you could bring into your current research?

SECTION III Bring the Abilities into Your Office or Lab

In Sections I and II, we introduced seven creative abilities: the things that creative people do (Figure 9.1). The first four focused on cognitive behavioral, and emotional skills that can apply directly to your research process, while the latter three serve as supports that enhance your overall creativity. Through the readings and exercises, you've hopefully started to understand what these abilities are, how they work, and how they intersect with your research. Section III provides another level of scaffolding in your exploration. While earlier chapters introduced the creative abilities as discrete things, Section III gives you tools to integrate the abilities in the day-to-day practice of research.

In Chapters 9 and 10, we'll provide examples of ways you might use the abilities to address common challenges that researchers face. Through these examples, you'll start to see the abilities as different tools you could apply to any problem. While these chapters do not include any specific exercises, we encourage you to try out some of the approaches we suggest. For instance, if you have a paper to write, you could try approaching writing as a prototype or exploring your emotions around writing (both of which are covered in detail in Chapter 10). Then, we provide a series of prompts for you to reflect on what you've learned after you've explored with these approaches. The conclusion to each chapter provides two alternate ways to think about integrating the abilities: as a sequence that moves through the abilities in a structured order, and as a series of lenses that illuminate different facets of a challenge.

If you are looking for a more guided approach to learning the abilities, Chapter 11 provides a thirty-day learning progression. We provide a series of readings, exercises, and reflection prompts for you

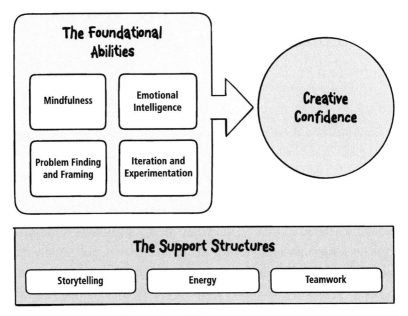

FIGURE 9.1 The creative abilities

to practice using each of the creative abilities. Mirroring the structure of our in-person curriculum, we ask you to choose a current challenge that you're facing in your research (this can be either process- or content-related), and then use this challenge as a springboard to apply the abilities.

Lastly, many of our readers are likely in roles where you are mentoring others. Chapter 12 provides suggestions on ways to develop the creative abilities of your students or mentees.

By engaging in this work – the guided examples of Chapters 9 and 10, the structured practice of Chapter 11, and/or helping others become more creative with Chapter 12 – you'll continue to develop your skills as a creative researcher. As you practice and develop your creative confidence, there are an infinite number of directions you might continue to explore. It truly is a choose-your-own adventure. With this freedom in mind, we conclude (Chapter 13) with key lessons we hope you will take away and suggestions for where you might go from there.

9   Integrate the Creative Abilities, Part I

INTRODUCTION

Chapters 2 through 8 introduced abilities exhibited by creative researchers along with stories and exercises for you to try applying the abilities in your own work. However, the abilities rarely operate in isolation, but instead interact and reinforce one another to build creative confidence.

So, what does this look like in practice? This chapter and Chapter 10 demonstrate how the abilities fit together in addressing real world research challenges. For each challenge, we describe in detail three abilities that we have seen to be particularly helpful for moving your thinking forward and/or solving the problem. We'll discuss several ways these abilities contrast with usual ways we, our students, and our colleagues have tried to solve the problems, and how they help cast a new light on the problem. While we focus on three abilities in particular, we will briefly summarize ways all seven abilities can play a role.

These two chapters are parallel in structure and content. However, this chapter focuses on challenges more salient to PhD students, while Chapter 10 focuses on challenges relevant to researchers at all career stages (with a tilt toward later stage PhD students, postdocs, and faculty). Specifically, the challenges addressed in this chapter are: (1) choosing a dissertation topic, (2) creating a good working relationship with your advisor or supervisor, and (3) managing time. For each, we describe potential approaches to combining the abilities in practice and provide concrete guidance and exercises to solve the challenge in a way that emphasizes creativity. In the text, we provide detail on how three abilities can help address each challenge.

A box at the end of each challenge section provides brief ideas for applying the remaining abilities to that challenge.

While this chapter and the next are roughly divided by career stage, we recommend reading both chapters because they build on one another. Chapter 9 provides a simpler, more clear-cut depiction of the challenges researchers face by treating process-related and content-related challenges separately. Chapter 10 addresses the more realistic situation: that process and content are often intertwined. The two chapters also present distinct ways of understanding how the abilities relate to one another. In Chapter 9, we treat the abilities as steps in a cycle, wherein each incorporates information yielded by the previous one. In Chapter 10, we present each ability as a lens through which you can explore different dimensions of a given research challenge. Finally, faculty and Principal Investigators might find concrete suggestions in Chapter 9 for working with their PhD students who are facing these challenges. Similarly, PhD students who have not yet reached the stage of writing a journal article or teaching an independent course will hopefully find inspiration for the future in Chapter 10.

We encourage you to read the chapter and try addressing one or more of the challenges in your own work. Explore what it's like to play with these ideas and claim a more creative approach to your research.

CHALLENGE 1: CHOOSING A THESIS AND/OR DISSERTATION TOPIC

One of the biggest milestones for many PhD students is finding a suitable topic for your thesis or dissertation. This is objectively hard: You have to find something that will contribute new knowledge to your field, be doable within a few years, and excite you enough to set up the research trajectory that you may continue for the rest of your life. In addition to the challenge of arriving at an interesting topic, the choice also entails confronting a number of emotional, logistical, and intellectual questions that vary from individual to individual, including your willingness to take risks; family, health, or financial considerations that dictate where and when you can work (or how long your dissertation can take); and what types of research activities you enjoy or loathe.

For this challenge, we encourage you to take a big picture look at the process of finding a dissertation topic and play with many different perspectives on the challenge. Exactly which perspectives you find most resonate with you will help you figure out which mix of abilities to employ in addressing it.

Also, even if you already have selected a dissertation topic, you can use these same strategies for finding or refining any new research project.

Approach 1: Considering Emotions

Thinking about emotions provides an important complement to the analytical tools you're likely already using: reading the literature to identify gaps, talking to your advisor and other people more advanced in the field, and refining a prospectus through research design classes or other formal coursework. Learning to pay attention to your human needs and embracing emotions as a source of insight can help you find a topic that in turn will help you feel like a whole person engaged in an intellectual pursuit. It should be a topic that keeps you energized for several years.

An important first step is to be compassionate with yourself about the process of choosing the dissertation. We have seen many students and colleagues stuck trying to find the perfect topic – the one that will be most marketable, get you into *Science* or *Nature*, or win you a dissertation award. Or you may be in a situation where you don't have that much freedom in choosing your topic (like if you are working on an advisor's grant). No matter what constraints you face, it can help to explicitly acknowledge that there is no one right dissertation, either for your field or for you. Find something that works and that you think you can be happy doing for two, five, or seven years. This requires being mindful of any expectations or assumptions you might have about the dissertation, letting go as much as possible, and learning to honor your feelings. You can start to explore these expectations through techniques like journaling or drawing. Spend ten or fifteen minutes to sketch or write (without censoring) about your expectations: for instance, what you think good research is and what you aspire to achieve with your dissertation.

The second step in using emotions to help guide your choice of dissertation topic is to expand the range of what you might want to consider and the criteria you use to choose. While specific questions will vary from individual to individual, some of the things you may want to explore are:

- Do you like using the methods you are proposing (e.g., fieldwork versus modelling versus labwork versus archives), and can you see yourself doing them for one to eight years? Do you like sitting at a computer all day, or would you rather be outside, working with people, or building things with your hands? What would your day-to-day life look like doing this research, and how does that make you feel?
- What types of people will you have to interact with (e.g., undergraduate lab assistants, the general public, policymakers, no one but your advisor)? How does that make you feel?
- Do you have family, health, or financial constraints that impact the type of research you can or want to do? Can you travel easily? Do you need to finish quickly? Will these constraints affect the type of work you'll be doing after your dissertation?
- Are you in a highly competitive field where a novel project is likely to get scooped, and are you emotionally willing to take that risk?
- What is your long-term career goal, and how will a particular type of dissertation contribute to that goal?

For example, Jennifer applied to PhD programs with the dream of working on a remote island in the South Pacific. When she got to school, she started learning about her advisor's life working on Madagascar (not the South Pacific, but close enough for Jennifer's dreams). He had taken his first research trip to Madagascar during his PhD and had since formed strong ties to the island and its people. He regularly advised the government on development policies, he traveled there with his wife and children every summer, and many of his closest friends were from Madagascar. Learning about his experience gave Jennifer some pause. On the one hand, she loved the idea of becoming intimately familiar with a place and its people. On the other hand, she saw her advisor living a split life – forced to teach in the USA to make a living but wanting to spend his time in Madagascar, which he had come to consider home. She realized she wasn't willing to make this commitment and decided to ask her advisor about the possibility of doing fieldwork in the USA.

When you start to ask these questions, you may already know the answer to some of them (whether explicitly or intuitively). For others, you'll probably need to experiment and learn more about the possible options to decide what works best for you. Which leads us to . . .

Approach 2: Prototyping

A prototyping mindset entails approaching your research topic iteratively through a process of divergence and convergence, recognizing where there are opportunities for you to learn more about what your research might look like, and treating every idea as a possible (but not final) solution – able to be adjusted or discarded with the goal of learning.

So, what can you prototype? Anything! But seriously, as we discuss here you can use iterative methods to refine your topic, as well as to answer any of the questions in the previous section about the kind of research you'd like to do that you don't yet know the answer to.

What does a research content prototype look like?

First, a class project can be a prototype for a dissertation chapter. Rather than just using class papers to check off a requirement, try to use them as an opportunity to learn more about your content or what the research itself would look like. For instance, you could start digging into the literature, or you may want to see what it's like to work with a particular dataset or use a particular analysis method. The benefit of this approach is that the class project doesn't need to be the scope of a full chapter, but – if you learn that indeed the dataset is promising – it could later evolve into part of your dissertation.

Second, use cycles of problem finding, brainstorming, and prototyping to narrow into a researchable, defendable dissertation topic. While you committed to the field you're working in when you were admitted to a doctoral program, you still have to decide the problem space within which your research will sit. If you're a sociologist, do you want to study labor, migration, or social movements? Within this problem space (let's say you choose migration) you must decide the general problem you're interested in: the interaction between global trade agreements and patterns of migration? Or the impact of immigration on local development patterns? Or the lived experience of migrants in new cities? Finally, you need to home in on the specific questions, study design, and methods you will use for your project. If you're looking at the interaction between global trade and migration, you might want to conduct a global-scale analysis, identifying whether countries that trade more goods with one another also tend to have more mutual migration. Or you might be interested in the local scale, seeing how individual migrants perceive patterns of globalization and how that affects their choice of whether and where to move. The first would likely entail a quasi-experimental, statistical design; the latter an embedded ethnographic approach. These two approaches would result in quite different experiences during the PhD for the two researchers who chose them.

So, how does this relate to prototyping? Each of these decisions – what problem space, what specific question, what methods – is something that can be prototyped. Within the problem space of migration, you could brainstorm hundreds of different topics (based off what you've read in the literature), and then write short abstracts for particularly promising ones to see which might have some meat on them. Or you could prototype outstanding process-related questions to refine your methods: "How might I know whether I have the stamina to conduct a large door-to-door survey?"

For example, when Ali was starting his PhD, he felt completely overwhelmed. He had so many ideas, but no clear vision of how the many pieces of his research might fit together into a coherent project. To make sense of the overwhelming possibilities, he sketched out several possible versions of his research trajectory, including how a conceptual paper he was working on might feed into future empirical work. Visualizing everything in one place helped Ali feel like he could find a straightforward plan for his dissertation, and he appreciated having "the physical evidence of [his] brain work" to show his supervisor for feedback.

As you prototype, you need to be very clear about what it is that you want to learn at each stage. This can help you identify prompts for brainstorming, select potential ideas to prototype, and decide when and from whom you want to seek feedback.

Approach 3: Using Teams for Ongoing Feedback

The final tool we encourage applying as you develop a research topic is seeking early and diverse feedback. While feedback is a critical part of helping you move prototypes forward, feedback is also critical (yet often underused) for the more analytical pieces of identifying your research topic.

Who might you want feedback from?

- **Your advisor:** While this one feels obvious, some PhD students have a tendency not to want to share ideas with their advisor until they are fully formed. For instance, you might hold off until you think you have read everything in a particular subject area so you can safely claim "no one's done this before," perhaps to combat against your advisor pointing out that you're not up to speed on the state of the field. However, we encourage you to bring your advisor into the conversation early. By telling them that you're interested in a particular topic and you think it might be promising, you make it possible for them to tell you who has written something in that space (saving you hours of library searches and skimming abstracts) or point to a colleague who might know more (giving you the opportunity to expand your network and meet new people). They also have a lot of experience developing and refining their own research projects, and so can sometimes tell you whether something might be a dead end.

- **Other researchers working in your field:** It's important to recognize that your advisor will rarely have all the information you need to inform your choice of topic. You might be working on a new topic for them, be working between disciplines, or drawing on a method they haven't used before. For example, when Dan was developing his dissertation topic, he was working on early Renaissance Germany – a topic none of his advisors (and indeed no one at his home university) had expertise in. To know whether his understanding of the literature and its gaps was accurate, he emailed several professors at other universities with a short abstract and the question whether this was a good topic. Despite this being a cold email, all three faculty responded positively (giving him and his committee the confidence to move forward) and recommended additional books that he hadn't yet come across. As an added bonus, he is still in regular touch with two of the faculty, and they might even be letter writers for his tenure case. Finally, even if your advisor is *the* expert on a topic, it's still worth getting feedback from other people, because different people might see things differently. Again, earlier input is better – when you can still change directions if needed.
- **Senior graduate students who do the type of research you're considering:** While faculty have a longer view on a field and its trajectory, students, postdocs, and recent graduates are often the people who are actually engaged in the day-to-day research. Senior graduate students and postdocs in your department or at other institutions can provide valuable input into the pros and cons of working in a particular area. They can share everything from what their day-to-day work looks like to what the job market prospects are. They also probably did a substantial literature review in the not too distant past, so can likely help point you to gaps in the literature.
- **Your spouse, partner, and children:** These are the people who will be supporting and depending on you while you research whatever topic you ultimately pick. As you refine your methods, you may want to check and see what they think about what your research will mean for your lifestyle. What do they want the next five-plus years of life to look like? Are they excited to buy a camper and spend a summer driving 3,000 miles around the country for you to do interviews, as one of our colleagues did with her husband and infant, or do they dread the prospect?

Seeking early feedback can help in a number of ways. First, other people can help you refine your ideas. Individually, there is a limit to the number of ideas and perspectives you can bring to a topic. If you work with other people, they can help you see what you've been rehashing in a new light, perhaps giving you some ideas for how to move forward.

Second, they can help you figure out what is truly a "new" contribution in a well-studied space and avoid black holes that might be less fruitful. Many fields suffer from a bias in which the published literature doesn't reflect everything that might have been attempted – only the interesting/statistically significant/etc. results make it into print. If you limit your search to the published literature and don't ask anyone about it, you may fall down a rabbit hole pursuing a research topic that others have already tried and abandoned.

Other Ways to Use the Abilities to Find a Dissertation Topic

Mindfulness: Pay attention to your day-to-day research life, and notice what you think and feel, both when you explore different research topics and/or work in different settings (e.g., conducting a literature review versus doing lab work).

Problem finding and framing: Try to explore multiple potential projects and consider multiple ways to frame each project before selecting one. What might the different framings reveal for your field? What might they mean for the type of research you would be conducting?

Language and stories: Try using story editing to claim the identity of someone working on your topic. When someone asks what you study, try on a concrete research topic ("I study the history of gender roles in dance," not "I'm thinking about studying gender roles in dance but still figuring it out") in a confident, know-what-you're-talking-about manner. Ask yourself, does this feel like an identity I want to have at happy hours and barbeques for the next six years?

Energy: As you explore different topics, notice your energy and excitement. Notice how the physical locations associated with different research methods or subjects appeal (or not).

CHALLENGE 2: CREATING A GOOD WORKING
RELATIONSHIP WITH YOUR ADVISOR (EVEN IF THEY
ARE NOT EASY TO WORK WITH)

Your relationship with your advisor is different from many other relationships in your life. It is likely more intimate than other supervisor–supervisee relationships you might have had in the working world. It is generally assumed to be lifelong. In the best cases, your advisor is a trusted mentor, colleague, and even friend who will continue to provide advice, recommendations, and assistance throughout your career. But as with any close relationship, you will likely encounter tension with your advisor and may not always get the support and guidance that you want.

So how might you use the creative problem-solving approaches to help you build a more effective advisor–advisee relationship?

Approach 1: Problem Framing

The first tool is to actively consider the problem frame that you use to define your relationship with your advisor. The goal, as always with problem framing, is to converge on a tractable problem. When you begin this process, especially in a moment of frustration, you might start with, "My advisor is terrible," as the problem statement. This is not a problem you can solve and is indeed the kind of problem that is likely to paralyze and overwhelm you.

One concrete way to start exploring your understanding of this problem is to use the *Five why's* technique presented in Exercise 4.1. By successively asking why, you start to identify the root causes of your own feelings, frustrations, and expectations. By asking why you feel that your advisor is terrible, you might come to understand that you are actually frustrated that you never get time to meet with them. Or that after you meet, you feel confused about what they expect you to accomplish before you can graduate. These are tractable problems, ones that you can approach your advisor to talk about and/or use as the basis for brainstorming and prototyping.

One way you can tell you have reached a tractable problem is that you are describing behavior, not personalities ("My advisor doesn't respond promptly when I have an urgent question," versus "My advisor hates me").[1] By focusing on behaviors, you identify traits that can be changed, helping to pinpoint the shifts you need in order to move forward. Note that changing a behavior can sometimes also resolve an emotional situation. For instance, getting more frequent feedback might help address your fear about not doing good enough work.

If you are experiencing a more explicit conflict with your advisor, it is easy to understand the problem as a zero-sum game. Either you are right and they are wrong, or else they are right and you are wrong. In almost all cases (with the caveat of truly abusive advisors, which we'll discuss in a minute), the conflict lives in the interaction between two people. It is a function of the intersection of their needs, wants, and expectations. And so, asking who is right is rarely the most useful way of viewing this problem. Instead, you might try reframing the conflict to the level of the relationship, focusing on the interaction between the two of you. Try asking the question: What needs to happen so I can work with this person? Sometimes this framing might point to behaviors that you or your advisor need to change. Other times it will point to underlying emotional issues that need to be resolved. Asking what you need in order to work (better) with your advisor is a broader problem framing that helps you think about all the needs you might have as a person, not just your academic mentoring needs.

Actively finding and framing your problem can also help you understand if you are in one of those rare but extremely unfortunate situations where your advisor is bullying, toxic, dishonest, or otherwise abusive. If you look at the situation and identify the core cause is that your advisor truly has no empathy or desire to meet your needs or is otherwise engaged in intolerable behavior (such as sexual harassment or intellectual dishonesty), then by all means, please get yourself out of that situation.[2] No one deserves that kind of advising experience.

The rest of this discussion assumes your conflict is of the more common variety, where different personalities, needs, expectations, incentives, and constraints are creating tension but your advisor is basically on your side.

Approach 2: Understanding Your Advisor's Emotions

Another way to deepen your understanding of the problem is to explore your advisor's needs, emotions, and motivations in the situation. This might be hard to do at first, especially if you are angry or anxious. But even if you can't truly feel empathetic, you can take a more instrumental view of this analysis: Your advisor's behavior is being shaped by their emotions, constraints, and expectations. If you can understand those underlying causes, you likely have a better chance of resolving a situation that may be causing you significant stress or discomfort.

How do you do this? Depending on the state of the relationship, you have a number of options. The ideal way is to have a conversation where you hear about your advisor's emotions and expectations directly from them. For reluctant advisors, a good way to do this can be to frame it as a conversation that your campus Graduate Student Affairs office (or this book!) encouraged you to have. Have a series of prepared questions, maybe even printed out, on expectations and needs: for research, for how often to meet, for career trajectories, anything. Stanford University's Vice Provost for Graduate Education has developed a worksheet on discussing Student–Advisor Expectations that can serve as a helpful starting point.[3] For instance, you might discuss expectations about how often to meet, who makes decisions about when and where to publish work, and what emotional or career-related support the advisor will (or will not) provide. Make sure this is a two-way conversation – your advisor will likely be much more open to share if you are frank about your expectations and needs. You can also prototype this conversation first with a trusted friend, partner, or labmate.

But talking directly to your advisor might be difficult or impossible, at least as a first step, as they may not be in tune with their emotional needs or there may be accumulated friction between you. In this case, you can use the exercise of walking in someone else's shoes from Chapter 3 to use empathy to explore their perspective. What motivates your advisor? What incentives or motivations might they have in this situation? How does your performance affect advancement in their career (e.g., does the university reward mentors whose students finish on time)? How might they feel about interactions with you? Your goal is to mindfully set your own feelings about the situation aside and bring a beginner's mind to understanding your advisor's needs and point of view. You could also talk to another professor you trust to help you imagine a faculty member's point of view.

Approach 3: Brainstorming

In conflict resolution practice, the understanding of each person's needs described in the previous section provides the foundation for generating solutions that can simultaneously meet both people's needs (i.e., "win–win" solutions).[4] You can do this divergent thinking step either with your advisor or on your own. Select a brainstorming prompt that explicitly asks, "How can I meet my need for X (from your problem framing) while also meeting my advisor's need for Y (from your understanding of their needs)?" For instance, you might ask, "How might I get feedback on my thesis while working around Professor Jones' travel schedule?" From there, use all the brainstorming tricks you learned in Chapter 5, focusing on staying in a divergent-thinking, idea-generating state of mind until you have a long list of possibilities. Then you can select one or more promising ideas and either agree to try it (if you and your advisor generated the list together) or bring a few best ideas as suggested solutions to your advisor (if you brainstormed by yourself or with peers).

A second brainstorm you might try is brainstorming how you might get some portion of the needs you identified in your problem framing met without involving your advisor at all. Obviously, there are certain things your advisor has to do (signing your thesis generally being the top of the list). But the advising relationship can take many forms. If your advisor spends long periods of time in Africa doing fieldwork, perhaps there is another professor in the department who can provide day-to-day feedback while you are collecting data.[5] And in cases where you have a less than optimal advisor but are too far along to switch, figuring out how to get needs met by others might mean the difference between finishing efficiently (or at all) and not.

Other Ways to Use the Abilities to Work Better with Your Advisor

Mindfulness: Notice the assumptions you have about your research process, your advisor's assumptions about your research process, and expectations you hold about the advising relationship.

Emotions: In addition to considering your advisor's emotions, don't forget to have compassion for yourself. It would be great if everyone all had ideal advisors, but it's important to recognize your needs and feelings.

Language and stories: In your problem finding, think explicitly about the narratives you hold about who you are as a researcher, who your advisor is as a mentor, and what you need from the relationship. Do you believe that you deserve your advisor's attention? Is your research "wasting" your advisor's time? If these narratives are unhelpful, how might you claim a new story?

Energy: How does meeting with your advisor affect your energy level? Do you feel motivated, overwhelmed, or drained afterward? Where do you meet with your advisor, and is there a way to change that space (or move to a new space) to make meetings more productive? How could you use space creatively to optimize your time with them? For instance, perhaps you could walk together between meetings across campus to extend your meeting time?

Teams and feedback: Use your network wisely. Ask other graduate students (including your advisor's other advisees) for ideas on how to work with your advisor, or to help you frame your problem or brainstorm solutions. Remember that when your emotions are high, other people can help you see the whole picture more objectively.

CHALLENGE 3: MANAGING TIME EFFECTIVELY

We probably don't have to tell you that time management can be challenging as a graduate student. The dissertation process itself is long and has a lot of moving parts. On top of that, you may still be taking classes. Your funding (if you are lucky to have it) likely requires a certain number of research assistant hours each week and/or serving as a teaching assistant. You may be working on other projects to gain experience or learn data analysis techniques. You may be serving your department, university, or discipline in a range of roles, each valuable in its own right and giving you valuable experience and exposure but also requiring more of your scarce and precious time. And then of course, there are the demands on you as a person: as a spouse or partner, as a parent, as a family member, as a friend. Perhaps you are a member of a church, a rowing club, or a bowling league. Perhaps you serve your community in a more personal volunteer capacity. You might need to supplement any university funding with an outside job. All told, this means you probably have a lot on your plate, and being as effective as possible with your time can help tremendously.

Approach 1: Becoming Aware of How You Actually Use Your Time

One key to feeling more in control of your time is to really understand where it goes. Mindfulness can help you become more conscious of your relationship to time and how you currently use it.

Noticing your relationship to time starts with noticing when you feel most busy and why. Where do you work well? When, why, and how do you procrastinate? How does being busy make you feel? For some people, it can be exhilarating, while others become paralyzed by stress. You might also reflect back on times when you have done your best work, whether in graduate school or before. How did you manage your schedule at those times? How was it similar or different to your current approach?

Becoming aware of how you currently use your time can often benefit from a quantitative, data-driven approach. People are notoriously bad at remembering how they spend their time. Time-use studies find that people who work at least twenty hours a week overestimate the amount of time they spend working by 20 to 50 percent (adding up to twenty-five hours' imagined work to their weeks!).[6] To overcome this, researchers who study time use try to capture activities as they happen, contacting their subjects at random intervals and asking the subjects to report exactly what they are doing.[7] You can take this approach with yourself. There are numerous time-tracking apps that can show you how you spend your computer time, including ones that track how many windows you have open or what websites you spend time on. Or, for a lower-tech option, you can set a regular timer and record what you are doing when it goes off. Remember not to judge at this stage. Your first task is to get an accurate picture of how you really spend your time – not how you think you spend it or should spend it. If you find yourself judging when the app says you spent two hours on Facebook when you thought you were writing, notice, accept, and learn from that judgment too.

Approach 2: Optimizing Your Energy

A second approach is to play with reframing your search for optimal "time management" to one of "energy management." One of the biggest challenges in using your time effectively is that time is a finite resource. In contrast, energy can (to a certain extent) be systematically expanded and regularly renewed through intentional behaviors. Thus, by actively building your energy and intentionally allocating activities to your high- and low-energy times, you can be more productive with the finite hours you have.[8]

First, try tracking your energy at the same time that you track time spent on your various activities (Exercise 7.1). What time of day are you highest energy, and what are you doing during that time? When do you feel completely drained, and what are you doing during that time? After observing yourself for a week or so, you may notice patterns (e.g., that you're always alert an hour after breakfast or when you have a meeting with collaborators). Next, try to schedule your week so that you match your higher-energy times to the more cognitively important tasks you have to do, or to alternate between activities that boost your energy or drain it (so that you don't have a day where all you do saps your energy).

Second, you might try intentionally building new stores of energy. If you don't sleep regularly or enough, try setting a strict bedtime for a week and observe how it affects your overall energy (and use of time).[9] Or make sure that you're eating healthy meals that release blood sugar over time.[10] You could also choose two activities that boost your energy (see Exercise 7.2) and then schedule yourself to do them every day.

Finally, come up with a few shorter exercises you can have in your back pocket when you need an energy boost. You might play with doing five or ten minutes of guided meditation or a relaxation, listening to a piece of music that you love, or going for a brisk walk outside. When your energy is low (but you still need to be productive), pull one of these out and recharge.

Approach 3: Exploring Language and Stories

Finally, conscious use of storytelling can complement your mindfulness exploration and energy management approach. Explore what stories you tell about your time and consider how you might consciously craft new stories to approach your time differently.

Amanda went to a small liberal arts college on the East Coast. The prevailing story that she and her classmates told one another was that they were very busy and working crazy hard all the time. They used to call it "misery poker." You tell someone you have a paper and presentation deadline and rugby practice, and then they answer that they have three papers and a debate tournament and a music show and being student council president. A third person might then chime in with an even more staggering workload and describe how it's going to take them all weekend to finish it. While the students did work hard, they also spent all four of Amanda's undergraduate years talking constantly about how busy they were.

Amanda only realized how much she had absorbed this prevailing story when she moved to New Zealand for her master's study. There,

Amanda found that no matter how busy she was, no one was interested in hearing about it. Her classmates and friends worked plenty hard but the stories they told each other were the exact opposite of misery poker. Indeed, they minimized how hard they worked or any difficulties they were having. Public discussions in the graduate student lounge were almost always positive, focused on the outdoor adventures students had been on the previous weekend or were planning for the next weekend. This cultural tendency meant that there was little space to discuss challenges or offer support even when someone was actually struggling. When one of the students in Amanda's department was in danger of not finishing his thesis by the deadline, he was not interested in talking about it or accepting help.

Neither of these extremes is a story we would recommend. But we offer them as examples of how the prevailing campus or department culture can shape the stories you unconsciously tell yourself and others about your work and your productivity. It's worth reflecting on these stories and whether they are the stories you want to be living. You might ask: What stories do you tell about your time? Are you "busy"? Do you strive for "work–life balance" or "work–life integration"?[11] Is either one possible in your department? How do you talk to others about your time? Is it scarce? Abundant? Well used?

Next, explore how these stories shape how you go about your day, week, and life. For instance, outside or extracurricular activities may be the ones that seem easiest to give up when you are busy or stressed or overwhelmed. Conversely, non-negotiable commitments or roles that relate to the core of who you are as a person (e.g., "I am a parent first, a scholar second," or "I run because it gives me energy and mental focus for everything else," or "I go to church every Sunday, period") are clearly recognized as essential to your identity and well-being.

For each of the stories that you identify, the next step is to be proactive. Use journaling and drawing to amplify the beneficial stories you already hold, and start reframing the prevailing narrative for less helpful ones.

Other Ways to Use the Abilities to Manage Time Effectively

Emotions: Build on the awareness you develop through mindfulness (observing what you actually do) and ask why you spend the time as you do. Are there feelings underlying the way you spend your time? If you spend less time on a task than you think you should, do you avoid it because it makes you feel anxious or worried? Or are you getting sucked into more pleasurable activities? Conversely, are you spending extra time on less important tasks in an effort to make them perfect or to avoid other tasks?

Problem finding and framing: A lot of researchers carry a "busy" narrative, so statements in this problem space often start with being overwhelmed or not having time. Use problem finding and framing to develop tractable problems tied to root causes. Often, time management and use habits or behaviors have roots in emotions or motivation.

Prototyping: A prototyping approach to time management changes it from a search for a perfect solution to a continual tweaking and experimenting process.[12] It removes the cycle of making a plan (usually by making a new rule, like: "No Facebook during writing time") and then facing the frustration and self-criticism that results when you inevitably break that rule. Prototyping instead asks, "What if I didn't check Facebook until I am done writing at noon?" When you approach a schedule modification as a prototype, it becomes a playful experimentation process, not something you have to achieve or win at, and thus no longer something that inspires an internal backlash when your willpower becomes fatigued.[13]

Teams and feedback: Many people use time in habitual, unconscious ways much of the time, meaning that it can be hard to see what you are doing. Other people can help you identify behavioral patterns or unconscious assumptions you are making. Try having a friend look at your calendar or time tracking sheets and see what patterns they observe.

CONCLUSION

While this chapter has introduced each ability individually as it applies to certain challenges, as you continue to explore the creative abilities, you'll begin to see that different abilities seem to flow naturally from one another. In general, it's usually best to start with a deep understanding of a problem space, in particular by being mindful about what's currently happening and how that affects the emotions of everyone involved (you or others). From there, you can begin to frame a more tractable problem, converging in from the broader problem space. This problem statement gives you a starting point for iterating between cycles of divergent/convergent thinking using brainstorming, prototyping, and testing (Figure 9.2). Throughout this process, working with a team and seeking feedback can help provide more insight than you have alone. You learn to recognize and reframe the stories you tell that may reinforce or reflect how you see problems and yourself. And managing your energy helps you match your energy levels with the type of creative thinking you're engaged in. This flow is what design thinking calls the design or innovation cycle.[14]

Over time, as you become more familiar and confident in the process (and mindful of your own process!), you can begin to choose different abilities to start from, depending on what you need.

REFLECT

If you tried any of the challenges, we encourage you to reflect on the following questions:

9.1   What was different about the way you would have normally approached the problem? What did you like about that difference? What didn't you like?
9.2   How did you choose which ability to apply to your problem? How did you move between the abilities (if you chose more than one)?
9.3   How did the abilities fit together?
9.4   Did you feel confident in your process? Did you feel creative? Why or why not?
9.5   If you did more than one challenge, what was similar or different across them?

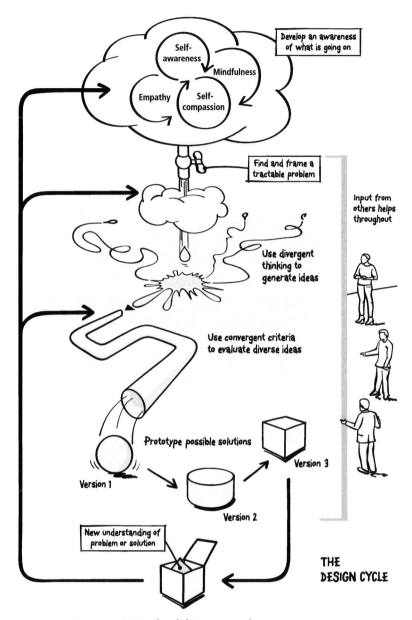

FIGURE 9.2 Using the abilities as a cycle

10 Integrate the Creative Abilities, Part II

This chapter, like Chapter 9, demonstrates in practice how to combine the abilities we've introduced throughout the book to address concrete challenges commonly faced by scholars, this time with a focus on challenges faced by more experienced researchers. This chapter follows an identical format to the previous chapter. We present three familiar challenges: (1) writing a paper, (2) developing a team project, and (3) designing a class. For each one, we suggest three key abilities that might shift your approach to the task in a more creative direction. We also include a box that suggests how the remaining abilities can help you with this task.

CHALLENGE 1: WRITING A PAPER

While many people reading this will have plenty of experience writing journal articles, take a moment to pause and consider the complex series of tasks required in getting a manuscript from initial idea to out-the-door.

First is deciding what to study or write and what contribution you want to make with your scholarship; this step aligns substantially with some of the considerations raised for choosing a research or dissertation topic (covered in Chapter 9). Next is conducting the research: developing the project, collecting and analyzing a paper's worth of data (which is often a sizeable task), and deciding when you have a proper "publishable unit" for a paper in your field. Then, in whatever written material you produce, you need to frame the importance of your topic within the existing literature, describe why your contribution is novel and important, describe what you did, convince readers of the rigor and analytical merit of your evidence or contribution clearly and succinctly, and address disagreements with existing literature or other scholars in a tactful and convincing way. Getting to that final product requires actually producing words on a page, revising (and sometimes throwing entire drafts out completely), knowing when and from whom to get feedback, and deciding when you are ready to submit. And in many fields, the manuscript is likely to be coauthored, requiring that you work with students and/or busy colleagues as you produce words or frame the contribution.

As experienced scholar writers know, scientific writing is a unique blend of analytical and creative thinking, and one that can vary greatly between projects. Some papers are quite easy to write, and others are like pulling teeth. And all researchers have unique processes – conscious or unconscious – for how and where they get their writing done.

In this challenge, we'll consider ways that the creative abilities can help you refine whatever process you use and improve your written content.

As a note, there has been a lot of great work on how to write (a lot, more concisely, in a more engaging manner, etc.).[1] Here we specifically address writing as it relates to the creative abilities.

Approach 1: Observing How You Write

A great entry point to writing more creatively, efficiently, and/or productively is watching your process and observing what is working (and not working) about what you're currently doing. Start actively reflecting on your writing process; your goal is to develop metacognitive awareness of what you currently do. This can be in a journal, on Post-its by your desk, or with a group. One of the best ways we've found to reflect is in a short memo/log at the end of each writing session, noting where you are, what time it is, what you did, and how you felt about it. As you reflect, try to think about writing as a process, rather than just as a product.

First, notice how the setting where you write affects your process.

- When do you write? Do you write in the morning before your family wakes up, try to squeeze in time between meetings or classes, or wait for school holidays? How does that approach seem to work?
- Are there particular times of day when you feel like you write most clearly?
- Where do you write? Do you write best in your office? In a coffee shop? In the library? What is it about these settings that helps or hinders your writing (noise versus quiet, other people, etc.)?

Second, notice how the types of writing tasks affect your process.

- What kinds of articles do you prefer to write (e.g., review articles, short research reports, or in-depth empirical work)? Do you find certain types of data easier or harder to report?
- What sections of the paper are hardest or easiest for you? In what order do you tend to draft the paper? Do you start with results, literature reviews, discussions, or figures?
- Do you prefer working on first drafts, which require searching for literature and generating ideas, or later drafts, which require refinement and convergence?
- What about different types of writing (e.g., writing a grant report versus a manuscript versus a department memo)?

Finally, try to be aware of how your mind works as you actually go about writing. Think about a paper you're currently working on. How do you decide what to do next as you proceed? When to turn back to the literature? Whether to start by writing the introduction, the methods, or the results? When to ask for feedback?

Approach 2: Prototyping through Trying and Feedback

Prototypes on Process

Once you've started to notice what works about your current writing approach and what areas you'd like to tweak, you can use prototyping and feedback to begin refining your process. You can prototype many different things about your writing process: where to write, how long to write, when to write, how to keep yourself accountable when you say you're going to write, how to nudge a slow coauthor to respond. What's important here is that you actually try things out and play with your process.

If you want to create the time to write first thing in the morning, for instance, brainstorm ways you can support yourself to do that. Maybe you've noticed that your problem is frequent drop-ins to your office. You could try taping a sign to your door that says: "Writing. Do not disturb." See if that reduces the number of unexpected visitors. Or you could try going to a library or café where coworkers can't find you. Maybe your problem is getting distracted by email, grading, or other work. You could try turning off your internet access or putting your pile of ungraded exams out of sight in a file cabinet. Then, as you try these things, see how they work. Were you able to write more successfully? Did you feel less distracted or more anxious? Does the sound level help or hinder your thinking? And remember that every prototype is just that – a prototype. So, if it doesn't work, think about ways to adapt it or be willing to drop it as a failed experiment and move on to another idea. Remember, by continually trying new things, you give yourself the chance to learn incrementally.

If you write with a coauthor or a team, you can also try ways to write more effectively with your group. For instance, when we started writing this book, Amanda and Nicola started with the approach of outlining each chapter in a Skype call, and then dividing up sections to write individually. We initially planned to write fairly complete first drafts before discussing them jointly, but after the first chapter we wrote we realized that approach wasn't working. Because by now we both have the habit of constantly treating our work process like a prototype, we had a short dialogue about what to do instead. We realized that we could write rough drafts of all the chapters more quickly if we didn't aim for "complete." We would be able to revise these zero drafts more effectively once we saw where the whole book was headed. Similarly, Nicola was taking on most of the "literature review" type sections and after two chapters realized that she was spending an inefficient amount of time tracking down relevant research. Instead of forging ahead as planned, we decided to set those aside (leaving them in outline form) and then hire a research assistant to help us with that work.

Prototypes on Content

Bringing a prototyping mindset to your work can also help you develop the content of what you write. This means treating all of the various steps along the way to a submitted manuscript as opportunities for learning and feedback. For instance, rather than using presentations (to a lab group, at a conference, or a guest lecture) to show everyone how airtight your argument/data/etc. are, think about ways to frame what you share as openings to get feedback to refine your analysis and how you present that analysis. There are many ways to bring prototyping into your writing pro-cess. For instance, writing a conference abstract can help you refine your argument and test whether an idea is of sufficient scope to be a stand-alone manuscript. Or, you might write three different conference abstracts and then choose one. Some scholars will sketch the types of figures they want to have in the final manuscript, and then think about what data they would need to collect to get to those figures. Others like to start outlining as soon as they have the germ of an idea for a paper. Forcing yourself to put ideas on a page is an easy way to test whether there is in fact a robust enough idea to consider pursuing or to determine whether it's something you'd like to keep working on.

As you continue to develop the paper, try using visual thinking to help you structure your argument. Sebastian uses Venn diagrams and arrows to draw the ways his contribution is related to existing knowledge, helping frame the introduction and literature reviews. Our colleague Mark, who recently published his first book, color-coded sections of each chapter to help him reorganize and reshuffle ideas in the revision process.

Another benefit of thinking of papers as prototypes is it can make it easier to let go of papers midstream rather than persisting out of habit. If you have lots of ideas that you are playing with, you're less attached to them and it's easier to accept when an idea doesn't work out.

Approach 3: Noticing Emotions

Another way to experiment with your writing process is noticing how emotions affect your relationship to your writing, whether in general or to a particular project. You may approach writing with baggage – being afraid of criticism (especially those terrible comments from Reviewer 2) or rejection. Or, you may be excited about starting a new manuscript, when there are lots of ideas swirling, but dread the process of editing and revising. Learning to observe and work with your emotions as they relate to your writing can be a real source of information about what works well and what might need to change about your process.

As we discussed in Chapter 3, start by tracking your emotions as you write. Notice (and log) how you feel when you sit down to write, and how you feel when you finish. Try to observe what patterns emerge. Do you have more resistance when you work on a particular type of project, or a particular phase of a project (first drafts versus figures versus editing)? What types of writing give you energy or drain your energy? For bonus points, you can also make how you feel something you write about with a quick freewrite at the start of your writing time.[2]

Noticing your emotions can point to possible problems or solutions. You may realize that a blank page triggers anxiety. In this case, you may realize that you need to start with a half full page (which can easily be accomplished by copying in text from another project, writing around it, and then knowing that you'll edit it out). Or unconscious worry about negative feedback might make it hard to start a project. In this case, you could try having a list of ideas you're excited about and remind yourself that you have these other promising ideas when you find yourself afraid of critical feedback.

For some people, writing may be a deeper, more pervasive challenge. If you are deeply afraid of writing – whether of being seen as a fraud, of communicating in your true voice, or of failing because your writing isn't good enough – you'll need to start by accepting that about yourself and having compassion about your fear. This can be a very difficult process. You may want to work with someone else, like a writing coach or therapist, to help you identify the underlying causes of your fear and find solutions.

Finally, in some disciplines, your emotions can also become part of the content that you write about. In autoethnography, scholars write about how collecting, analyzing, and revisiting their data makes them feel, as demonstrated by two of our colleagues. Scott Bollens, a planner who studies conflict in cities, drew on his feelings of vulnerability and fear to investigate what life was like in highly militarized Jerusalem and segregated Belfast.[3] Drawing on emotions to add insight to a topic is not only the domain of social scientists. Lauren Oakes' memoir of research on yellow cedar decline in Alaskan forests describes her personal struggle as an ecologist to reconcile grief and hope while researching the on-the-ground impacts of climate change.[4]

Other Ways to Use the Abilities to Enhance Your Writing

Problem finding and framing: When you feel stuck on a paper, take the time to step back and understand what the deeper root of your problem is. Is the block process-related (e.g., emotions, motivation), content-related (e.g., is there not enough data, is the argument not convincing?), or both (e.g., are you unsure about the overall value of the project?)?

Language and stories: Think about the stories you tell about your writing or your identity as a writer. Do you talk about writing as being hard or a chore? Do you consider yourself "a writer"? Why do you write? To get tenure? To communicate your findings with the people who need them? Because you have to? Because you enjoy the process of putting elegant words on paper? Think about ways to reinforce positive writing stories and reframe less helpful ones.

(cont.)

Energy: As you observe your writing, notice how the space where you write motivates or hinders you. Think about ways to change your space to motivate yourself to write when you don't want to. Or, build in five-minute energy boosters to start or finish a writing session, such as listening to your favorite song or taking a walk outside when you finish.

Teams and feedback: Get frequent feedback on your early writing prototypes. Figure out who you can share rough versus final drafts with. Think outside the box. Don't just ask colleagues – what about students? Or perhaps you can show a figure to your kids, or even have them help you draw it?

CHALLENGE 2: INITIATING A TEAM PROJECT

You probably know that developing a team project can be challenging. As we did with the task of writing a paper, let's step back and explicitly note the emotional and cognitive tasks that are involved when a new research collaboration is initiated. You can think of it overall as a challenge of organizing ideas, resources, and people (each with their own interests, hopes, and expectations) to come together at the same time. And the complexity only increases as the number of people, ideas, and/or resources grows.

People can come to a collaborative team organically or through invitation. Usually a research team is generated when one or more people has an idea. And depending on the size of the project, the convener recognizes the need to recruit others to realize that idea, which requires "selling" it. They may need to identify and get to know people they previously did not know to find the right expertise; this may mean connecting across disciplinary and/or institutional boundaries. And everyone who joins the young team comes into the group with prior experiences of working in teams (both positive and negative) as well as individual expectations, interests, needs, and personalities.

For most team research projects, ideas represent the core of the group's work. These ideas are often diverse, originating in different academic disciplines, on different sides of the research-to-practice boundary, from different geographical regions, or different institutions. And ideas are subtly shaped by the cultures from which they come. Integrating the best of these ideas often requires juxtaposing diverse cultures, which is not always a straightforward process.[5]

Building strong relationships between people and integrating their diverse ideas requires time, energy, and sometimes material items such as lab equipment. These resources are what power the team's collaboration. People need salary and research money. Team members must devote time both to develop ideas initially and then to work together to implement those ideas. The need to travel can require even more time, particularly when collaborating across institutions. Usually it falls to the team to organize resources to power its work. Yet the team may have to negotiate resource distribution to team members at a time when relationships in the team are new and untested.

Approach 1: Problem Finding and Framing

One key approach is to explicitly frame team formation as both a content problem and a process problem. Many research collaborations begin with content, often when a team is writing a grant proposal together or exploring potential areas of collaboration. One or more Principal Investigators has an idea for a project, identifies a research opportunity, and then invites other researchers to join the grant application. Since the focus is on the product of the grant (often with a looming deadline that is competing with other priorities for everyone's time) or other research output, the focus is necessarily on the content of who will be on the team and how the ideas and expertise of the team will fit together in terms of research questions, methods, products to be produced, etc. These are essential things to consider: how to jointly frame the research questions of a project to meet the interests of everyone on the team.

But it's equally important to remember that the team that will eventually conduct the research begins to form its identity and norms in the course of writing a grant. If you step back to explore the entire problem space of starting a successful research collaboration, you'll start to recognize that there are a variety of other considerations that don't just relate to the content of the research. These are process elements of the challenge of forming a team.

A process framing highlights the question: How might we best organize people and resources on our team to accomplish our (individual and joint) research goals? Try working with your team to generate a list of questions you might want to consider about the process. These might include:

- Who has responsibility for each aspect of the research?
- When and how will we keep one another informed about progress on our respective pieces?
- Do we need funding for planning phases, or is that time being donated?
- How will we identify gaps in our collective expertise and people to fill those gaps?
- How will we ensure the workload matches people's expectations and capacity?
- What types of research products or contributions will be most useful for each member of the team?
- How will we ensure people and institutions get credit for their contributions?
- Are there any upcoming life events that could affect a team member's work pace, and how might the team support those?

As with most problem-finding processes, you probably don't need to answer every question to have a productive team process. After expanding your problem space, be deliberate in selecting those queries whose solutions are most likely to help your team work well together. You might focus on questions that have caused problems for group members in the past or the ones that seem the easiest or hardest to answer, or perhaps you simply make a list and select randomly, discussing one per meeting for the first six months. Those questions that you select can then form the basis for group conversations or prototypes.

While many research teams eventually get to these questions (often once a project has been funded), we encourage you to start considering them as early as you start discussing content. Besides helping to create norms that can help the team function, the act of having discussions about work preferences, wants, and needs early in a team-formation process can be a tool for building the initial trust and empathy necessary for developing psychological safety. Psychological safety refers to "a shared belief that the team is safe for interpersonal risk taking."[6] Members' perception that the team is a safe place to be vulnerable has been shown to be important for team productivity, since this perception goes along with a willingness to engage in behaviors that are important for group learning like admitting mistakes or discussing problems.[7]

Finally, discussing your research process early on can also inform the content that you ultimately produce. It helps ensure that everyone understands their distinct contribution and how the roles of group members fit into the broader research plan. This holistic understanding can shape the methods or data sources you propose and could even change the types of grants your team chooses to apply for. It might even fundamentally change the project's level of ambition, if people talk openly about how much workload they're willing to take on.

Recognizing the benefits of proactively considering team process, the National Cancer Institute has generated a significant toolbox of resources to help those starting research collaborations address these kinds of questions with their colleagues. Resources include a collaboration "prenuptial" partner agreement.[8] There is also a diagnostic survey to help team leaders assess their team's motivation and satisfaction level.[9] This Team Science Toolkit is based on empirical findings generated out of a fertile research field called the science of team science, and we encourage you to seek it out if you are starting a large project.[10]

Approach 2: Language and Stories

An important part of forming a team, especially one that will persist for any length of time, is developing a collective or shared identity.

Paying attention to the language you use and the stories you tell can be a key tool for helping the team be intentional about its shared identity.

Content Stories

Developing a shared story about the content that your team will be producing can help your team work through the diverse and at times competing ideas, cultures, and visions that collaborative research necessarily entails. One way to generate this story is through a mission statement – a short narrative about what the team is doing, why, and how. These statements have two purposes. One, they communicate with the outside world. But perhaps more importantly, they build a common story within the team.

When Adam coached a large, interdisciplinary climate change research group early in their collaboration, he asked each team member to write an eight-word mission statement about the group's work, and to write a timeline for their work over the next year. The team members then shared these with the full group. By sharing these visions, the group could see where different collaborators were coming from in their research, where different members of the team thought they might get stuck, and where there were overlaps or differences of opinion in the group's shared vision.

Process Stories

Process stories also support the team-formation process. These are less likely to be published on a research website, but in more subtle ways they shape the way team members understand their role in the collaboration.

The first step is to notice what process language your team currently uses. Do you call yourselves a collaboration, a team, a working group, or a network? Are you coauthors or colleagues? Are students or postdocs referred to as "students," "coinvestigators," or "group members"?

Then you can reflect together: Do these stories match the relationships you envision? Do they match the needs and expectations of team members? For instance, if students are called "coinvestigators" but are not trusted to do independent work, that might be a place to address how the story and the reality are not matching. Similarly, if the collaboration is called a network, what does that mean to members? What are the responsibilities of network members?

Once you've started to build collective awareness of and reflection on your team stories, you can begin to consciously use your stories to build a shared vision of what the team is and what work you're doing. One team Sebastian coached spent the first ten minutes of every meeting sharing positive stories about the work they'd done, and it changed the overall attitude of participants to their work. Not only did the team start each meeting on a positive note, the team members began to look for positive stories throughout the week to be able to share them in the following week's meeting.

Approach 3: Managing Energy

Finally, when you work with a team, you can try applying the principles of managing your energy and space to help your team function.

For space, try to choose spaces to work according to the task at hand. For instance, if you're trying to generate ideas for a new research project, you might want a lively environment with a nice view. On the other hand, if you're working through a complex theoretical problem, you may want a sparse space with minimal distractions.

For energy, think about scheduling your meetings around your teammates' energy cycles. Have a discussion about your colleagues' preferred times to meet and how it relates to their energy cycles. Do they think best in the morning? Do they protect certain times of day for writing? Are they always sluggish after lunch? When you send out a scheduling poll, work around these preferred times if possible. For certain creative tasks, you'll want to try to find a time that matches everyone's most alert or energetic times, while more routine meetings might be OK during lower energy times. While this can be especially helpful for the early stages of a project, when you're establishing norms, it can also be great one or two years in, when people's excitement for the work may have started to wane.

There are also a number of ways to boost a team's energy during meetings when you notice it dropping. The team leader or facilitator plays a large role in setting the tone. For some groups and in some settings, a "stand up and stretch" break will feel edgy enough, but other teams will follow the lead of a brave facilitator who cranks up the music for a spontaneous, reenergizing dance party. For two or three people, you might try a goofy three-minute brainstorm to get everyone laughing (e.g., about how to get a toddler to eat broccoli, or about how to win a free trip to Mars). If you have a large group, one of our favorite energy boosts is a rock–paper–scissors tournament. First, everyone pairs off and plays rock–paper–scissors. Whoever wins two out of three is the champion, whoever loses becomes the winner's biggest fan and cheers them on as they find another opponent. Two winners then pair up and compete; again, the loser becomes the winner's biggest fan, and the winner goes on to find another opponent. Like any tournament, it whittles down to a face-off between two challengers and finally, you'll end with a great big room of cheering when everyone has become a fan of the grand champion.

Other Ways to Use the Abilities to Form a Team

Mindfulness: As a group, take time periodically to notice what is working well or not so well. Pay conscious attention to the automatic steps people are taking to move the project forward. Are some people contributing more than others? What group norms are being created? Are they norms you want to build into habits? You might also practice naming group dynamics for your team as you see them happening, for instance, "It seems like our energy as dropped off," or, "Great, I see us shifting from brainstorming to evaluating ideas and I just want to check we are ready for that." This role of monitoring a group's process is sometimes formally assigned to a facilitator, but it can often be helpful for collective understanding of process if team members share the same observations.

Emotions: Pay attention to individual and collective feelings and needs. Seek to understand when emotions are underlying someone's actions or responses. Take time to check in with one another at the

(cont.)

start of meetings so you understand the wider emotional context in which team members are operating. You can also try using the prompt, "How do you really feel?" (a deeper question than the standard, "How are you?") as a one-time icebreaker or regular opening to meetings.

Brainstorming: Use the problem statements you identified (both process and content) as the basis for a brainstorm. Brainstorming can be a useful way to move beyond preconceived expectations the leader or convening organization might have and can increase group buy-in.

Prototyping: Try treating everything your team does as a prototype. For content prototypes, you might work on a planning grant to test the viability of an idea. You could publish a conceptual paper or commentary to get early feedback on an idea through producing a relatively low-effort product before investing lots of energy collecting data. For process, even if your plan or grant said you'd meet biannually, notice whether that's working and change the plan if you need to meet more or less often. Or try prototyping a working relationship by doing a smaller project with new people before signing onto a five-year grant.

Feedback and teams: Create an explicit process for feedback in your teams. For instance, you could go around the room and share one strength and suggestion for improvement for each team member, or say what you like and what you'd change about your team process.

CHALLENGE 3: DESIGNING A CLASS

As with the other challenges we've covered in this chapter, designing a class requires that you engage in a diverse array of cognitive and emotional tasks. Depending on your institution and the type of class you're teaching, you may have more or less flexibility in deciding what you teach, when to teach it, and who your audience will be. However, whatever the context, designing a class means that you have to first fit the class into the broader goals of your department and institution (especially if the course is a prerequisite or part of a sequence). Then you decide what content you'll share and how you'll share it, including how to frame that content at the appropriate level for your audience. You also need to figure out how to deliver content, give students a way to practice it in a way that is pedagogically effective, create assignments, and assess them. You have to fit all of these activities into a schedule that will work for you and your students. And finally, you have the actual in-class engagement: interacting with students, managing their expectations and emotions, and managing your energy and enthusiasm. Designing a class also happens at many different scales, from deciding the arc of a full semester to setting activities for a single session.

In this final challenge, we explore how the creative abilities might help you develop and deliver great learning experiences.

Approach 1: Brainstorming

When sitting down to design a new class, it's easy to work with what is most familiar to us – e.g., to find the textbook that everyone uses, and then structure your lectures and assignments around that. But a creative problem-solving approach would encourage you to start by thinking divergently, coming up with a wide array of possible objectives, content, assignments, structures, grading approaches, etc., so you give yourself multiple options to choose from.

We encourage you to brainstorm in iterative stages. It's probably most straightforward to start with course learning objectives. Then, brainstorm content based on the objectives chosen. Brainstorm assignments based on the objectives and content. For each stage, try playing with different types of brainstorming constraints based on your needs and interests. For instance, when developing activities, you could narrow them to activities that can be done in ten minutes, or activities that require students to go outside, or activities that will teach them to use a particular software program. For grading, you could brainstorm ways to minimize your grading time, or ways for students to get feedback from one another.

Each step of the way, try to first generate ideas, then narrow down toward a coherent set of ideas and tools for your class. After you develop a broad array of ideas for each stage, you'll want to use specific criteria to select which ideas to carry forward. Criteria you might consider are: best for most/least advanced students; best for progression in the department's course sequence; best for my research program; best for my student evaluations; most fun; most/least in my comfort zone as a teacher; most likely to excite students; most likely to excite me. Or you could choose learning objectives based on which objectives give you lots of potential content to work with, or which content has the assignments you're most excited about.

Approach 2: Feedback

As you develop your syllabus, as well as the individual lectures, class sections, or assignments, find ways to get early and ongoing feedback.

It's easy to feel like once your syllabus is posted, you have no flexibility to deviate from the plan. In some institutions, the syllabus may be a legally binding document; in others, it still sets clear expectations for the students and you don't want to be that professor that keeps rescheduling exams or gets way off topic. In these cases, it's important to get feedback on the "fixed" things early enough that you can change them before the class starts. Alternatively, you can embrace the fact that it will be imperfect the first time through and know you can make changes the next time you teach the class. At the same time, remember that even within "the fixed syllabus" there's a lot that you can move around, especially if you set the expectation with students that you're going to change things based on their feedback. For instance, many teachers include the statement, "Readings may be updated to reflect student interest," and tell their students to look at the most recent version of the syllabus online because the readings will probably change.

You can also intentionally create space for ongoing feedback in your classes. For many teachers, the most familiar setting for this is in student evaluations. While these often come at the end of the class, you can probably also set up earlier evaluations (e.g., at midterm) in time to adjust the class. You might be able to have these arranged by your Center for Teaching and Learning (if you have one) or else you could make a short evaluation online using Google Forms or SurveyMonkey. Another approach is to ask a fellow instructor to sit in on your class and provide a peer review.

There are also many less formal ways you can get feedback. Some teachers like to end class with a short "minute paper," that asks students to list something they learned and something they're still unclear on as a way to gauge what might not have been clearly presented. Or you can break up a class with a short space for students to talk about the class content, assignments, and your teaching style. Try using some of the feedback formats in Exercise 8.5. Anja uses this approach regularly in her classes. She takes time after almost every class session and picks one piece of feedback to incorporate into the next session, essentially seeing each class (rather than each new semester) as a new chance to iterate. Students appreciate the responsiveness and become more candid and constructive in their feedback over time.

If you're feeling more adventurous, you may want to think about co-creating parts of the class with your students. For instance, you could have a set of modules/topics that you could teach, then let the students vote on which ones they're most interested in. Or you could let them create the prompt for a paper (or choose which prompt they like from a limited set of choices, if you'd like more control).

There are also many other people you can get feedback from. Ask your colleagues to look over your syllabus or read a draft essay prompt. Poll departmental alumni about what they liked best about their time in the program. Meet with the Center for Teaching and Learning on your campus, who will often provide consultations on your syllabus or assignments, observe or videotape your class, or arrange feedback sessions with your students.

No matter who you're getting feedback from, be sure that you're clear about what you want feedback on. Are you interested in how well a colleague thinks a proposed activity might work? Or on the order in which you're planning to cover different topics in class? Or on your lecturing style? If you know what you need, you'll be much better able to figure out whom to ask, what to share, and how to probe for feedback.

Approach 3: Language and Stories

Every teacher has unique experiences and narratives that shape how you approach your work as a teacher. Spend some time reflecting on the stories you hold about yourself. Who are you as a teacher? How does teaching fit into your identity as a scholar? Do you see it as a chore or as an opportunity? Is it a way to support your research, or does it get in the way of research? How do your stories about teaching influence your teaching and research practice?

You can also start to notice the narratives people around you have about teaching. How does your institution support teaching? What do your colleagues say about teaching (as a practice, or as a means to tenure, promotion, influencing students, etc.)? Which of these stories resonate with you? Why?

Finally, start to intentionally use these stories to shape your narrative and identity as an educator. Who do you want to be as a teacher? How can your courses support that emerging story? Are there ways you can you blend the different facets of your scholarly identity more effectively, for instance, by creating assignments that help move your research forward?

Other Ways to Use the Abilities to Teach a Class

Mindfulness: Practice bringing mindfulness into your classroom, whether it's noticing your reactions to student questions or interruptions or to your teaching evaluations. And notice how your students react to your teaching.

Emotions: Think about and acknowledge your emotions around teaching. Nerves, anger, worry, joy – explore what they are telling you. Notice when emotions arise around teaching, perhaps around grade disputes, for instance. You might also consider how emotions can be used to improve your students' learning outcomes; this is the subject of research covered in *The Spark of Learning*.[11]

(cont.)

Problem finding and framing: When you come up against a problem, don't rush to solutions or assume there's a single way forward. Take time to explore what the real problem is or frame the problem in a generative manner. If you're buried in grading, think big – not, "How might I grade these faster?" but, "How might my students get the feedback they need in a timely way?" This reframe helps you see that you may not need to be the one giving feedback. And next time you teach this class, can you revise the assignment or its timing so it doesn't happen again?

Prototyping: Treat every course and class as a prototype that you can experiment with and learn from. For instance, create a visual prototype of the lecture series overview to see how single lectures fit into the overall learning journey. If something doesn't work, reflect and adjust (next class or next year).

Energy: Consider: Does teaching give you energy or take energy? How does teaching influence your daily, weekly, and semesterly patterns of energy and time management as a researcher? Which aspects of your courses do you enjoy most? Least? How might you design courses to maximize the energy you get from teaching? How might you design courses to maximize your students' energy? How does the space where you teach affect your energy or your student's learning?

CONCLUSION

These examples are meant to give you a flavor of how the creative abilities can be integrated into the day-to-day practice of research, but these examples are only the beginning of what is possible. There are many ways to approach these and other challenges, and as we have done throughout the book, we encourage you to continue to explore and find the approach that resonates with you.

As you experiment, you will encounter an important question: How do you determine what the most relevant ability (or two) is to help you address a potential challenge you are facing? In Chapter 9, we discussed the design cycle, which provides one perspective on integrating different abilities. Thinking about the design cycle puts the abilities into a prearranged order that gives you a place to start and a path to follow when addressing a challenge. It starts with discovering your needs through mindfulness and emotional awareness and then moves through iterative problem finding, brainstorming, prototyping, and testing. Stanford's d.school, from which we adapted aspects of our curriculum, often teaches design initially using the idea of a cycle.[12] But it emphasizes that this linear depiction of the design process is a simplification that one eventually moves beyond.[13] These stages are not fixed, and real problem solving often requires that you cycle through in nonlinear steps or repeat stages you've already visited.[14]

What we found when we surveyed students who had taken our classes was that they rarely followed an exact cycle, and instead dove into a given problem-solving process by starting with the ability that felt most relevant.[15] One metaphor to help you think about how you might do this is to think of the abilities as different lenses you can look through and see what you might learn (Figure 10.1). So, if you're not sure where to start and feeling a bit paralyzed you can simply start with the first of the seven and try asking: What would happen if I approached this problem through a mindfulness lens? What would happen if I focused on emotions and human needs? Is there a way that the narrative I am telling is influencing the situation, and could I tell a new story? We have even had students in our classes play with this metaphorical idea in physical ways, making tangible reminders like a spinner that could sit on their desk and be spun to choose an ability to try at random.

Over time, the choice of lens to apply will feel less like a random spinner and more like something you know intuitively how to select. This comes about through deliberate practice. As we discussed in Chapter 1, mastery in any field takes months or years of intentional practice that challenges your brain (and body) to develop new pathways. By continuing to deliberately explore and apply the skills of a creative researcher, you'll cultivate the level of competency where you can quickly draw on the abilities to make your research flow.

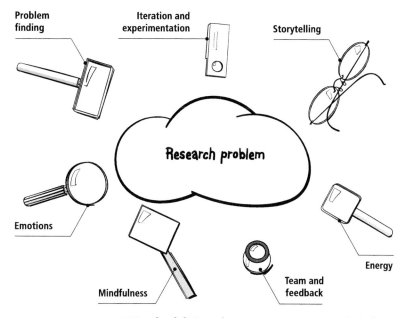

FIGURE 10.1 Using the abilities as lenses to view your research challenge

REFLECT

If you tried any of the challenges, we encourage you to reflect on the following questions:

10.1 What was different about the way you would have normally approached the problem? What did you like about that difference? What didn't you like?

10.2 How did you choose which ability to apply to your problem? How did you move between the abilities (if you selected more than one)?

10.3 How did the abilities fit together?

10.4 Did you feel confident in your process? Did you feel creative? Why or why not?

10.5 If you did more than one challenge, what was similar or different across each process?

11 Thirty-Day Creativity in Research Program for Individuals or Groups

INTRODUCTION

This chapter provides a suggested one-month learning progression for an individual or small group to experiment with the techniques in the book. Each week covers a particular topic or theme, which you will explore through reading the relevant chapters of the book, engaging in exercises to practice the topic, and then reflecting on what you did and what you learned. (At the end of the chapter, we also provide suggestions to faculty and administrators for adapting this material into a course or formal program.)

We provide detailed guidance for a thirty-day period, which is a sufficient length of time to experiment with all of the abilities covered in the book, but a short, finite enough period for your motivation and commitment to the exploration stay strong. The overall purpose of this progression is to develop your confidence using the creative abilities. You'll accomplish this by:

- practicing with each ability,
- understanding process versus content,
- learning how to decide what to do next,
- developing a habit of reflection for future growth,
- and hopefully, in the process, starting to develop more self-compassion and ease in your emotional relationship to your research.

Following the thirty-day immersion program, we also provide ideas for ways to continue your exploration by emphasizing more targeted learning outcomes, for instance, a focus on breakthrough research content or building a productive, efficient research process. While we have designed these as next steps, you could also choose to modify the thirty-day program using these suggestions. However, assuming you're interested in the holistic overview, buckle up, and join us for one month of experimenting with your research process!

HOW TO WORK THROUGH THIS PROGRAM

This book's curriculum emphasizes the importance of developing metacognitive awareness of your research process, including the behaviors and attitudes underlying creativity. In our experience, the best way to develop that awareness is to combine experiential activities (learning by doing) with reflection (conscious thinking about what you just did). Throughout, we will emphasize play and experimentation. Since the goal is to experiment with your research process, you may feel like there is less of a fixed outcome or goal than you are used to in a course focused on specific content. If you were in one of our classes, we'd be throwing you into the deep end of the pool, and then giving you the tools you might use to sew a life jacket or learn to swim. As a reader, we can't take away your chair and make you dive in wholeheartedly, but the more you embrace this spirit of messiness and not necessarily knowing what you are doing, the more radical your learning can become. Trust the process, keep a playful beginner's mind as much as possible, and have faith that you are likely growing in your creative research practice more than you realize.

You can work through this progression either as an individual or in a small group (e.g., a PhD cohort, a lab group, or a group of assistant professors). Both options have benefits and drawbacks.

Working as an individual simplifies the logistics considerably. You don't have to find a suitable group or schedule around other people. But even if you are working alone, we will still encourage you to seek feedback from other people. Thus, you may need to take extra initiative in identifying others in your life who can provide feedback at the points in the process where you need feedback – and these others may not understand what you are trying to do the same way a group working through the book with you would.

As with any group, working with a group to focus on your creative research practice will be as successful as the sum of the intentions of the group members. If you build a team committed to joint inquiry, you will have the benefits of feedback from people participating in the same learning and they will help keep you accountable. But the logistics of finding the right group members and scheduling time together can be challenging.

THE LEARNING PROGRESSION

Before You Begin

For everyone, whether you are working individually or in a group, the first steps to set yourself up for success are:

1 Schedule time into your calendar to read and do the recommended activities. You'll probably want to do the reading early in the week, and then schedule one or two additional dedicated sessions to experiment with the suggested exercises. You'll do other exercises in the course of your research, as we ask you to notice or try things in situ. (There are more detailed estimates of the time required in the overview for each week.)

2 Get a notebook where you can capture your ideas and reflections. The progression uses reflection through journaling, either in writing or drawing. Refer to the introduction to Section I for more guidance on how to use journaling and visual thinking to get the most out of your practice with the abilities. (If you're working as a group, you'll do additional reflection through group discussion.)

3 Make a commitment to yourself to do the readings and especially to engage in the exercises and reflection over the next thirty days.

If you are working in a small group, you'll obviously first need to find the members of that group. It helps if you can find like-minded people, specifically other people engaged in research who are also excited to learn this process. Beyond that, the sky's the limit in terms of who you might include. You could choose to work with people in very similar fields, or who are from across campus. With the former, you benefit from more shared experiences; with the latter, you benefit from new perspectives on the craft of research. While you could also work with people at diverse career stages, you might want to be conscious of power dynamics or habits that might get in the way of team learning. If you're an early PhD student, will you be comfortable sharing your struggles with the postdocs in your lab? And if you're a postdoc or professor, can you turn off "mentor/advice" mode to learn together with your lab group or advisees?

Once your group is formed, you'll want to schedule time for weekly check-ins. We recommend twenty to thirty minutes per participant, plus extra time for general socialization and getting coffee. You'll also want to find a convenient space to meet. Lastly, groups will probably find it useful to have a "week zero" meeting at which you discuss your expectations and develop norms or ground rules for working together.[1]

At the weekly check-ins, you should each share what you did, and what you learned, as well as share some of your responses to the reflection questions.

For everyone – working individually or in a group – you may want to play with positive and negative incentives to keep yourself committed to the process. For instance, if you're working in a team, maybe you agree to blast colleagues who miss a meeting with emails or throw a group party for everyone that stuck with it. As a note, it helps to match the rewards to the activity you're trying to achieve.[2] So, instead of rewarding yourself with an hour of TV if you do all of the recommended exercises each week, maybe reward yourself with a new book related to your work?

Overview

Once you've got yourself set up with time, a journal, and a commitment, it's time to dive in.

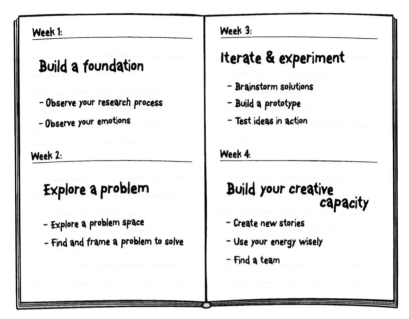

FIGURE 11.1 An overview of the thirty-day progression

In Week 1, you'll set the foundation for creativity (Figure 11.1). You'll experiment with becoming aware of how you currently do research. You'll start to become mindful of your thoughts and behaviors and to use emotional intelligence to uncover the role that emotions play in your research. You'll also build the habit of using reflection during your day-to-day work.

In Weeks 2 and 3, you'll practice solving a research-related problem using the creative abilities. You'll use the awareness you built in Week 1 to select a challenge and then practice finding and framing a tractable problem. Then, you'll use cycles of divergent and convergent thinking – brainstorming, prototyping, and testing – to rapidly experiment with and refine potential solutions.

Finally, in Week 4, you'll build the supports that underlie creative thinking. Specifically, you'll explore using language and stories, managing energy, and teaming to boost your creativity.

Week 1: The Foundation: Noticing Your Research Process

Readings	Exercises	Reflection prompts	Approximate time required (beyond reading)
Chapters 2, 3	2.2, 2.7 3.1, 3.5, 3.6	2.9 3.9, 3.10 Check in on what you've learned	• Daily observations of your current process • Brief reflection at end of each day • One session to reflect at end of the week

To build a more creative research process, you need to start from where you are. This week, you'll start noticing how you do research and take stock of what works and what you might change. Specifically, you'll (1) experiment with the ability of mindfulness, noticing your thoughts and behaviors, (2) use self-awareness and self-compassion to notice your emotions, and (3) apply these abilities to take stock of your current approach to research.

While you're using these abilities to explore your current approach to research, you'll receive further benefit because practicing these abilities and incorporating them into your daily work will also help you be more innovative and creative in the long run.

First, read Chapters 2 and 3. If you haven't yet, you will also want to read the introduction to Section I.

Second, do the exercises listed in the table above. (You're welcome to try all of the exercises listed in each chapter, but these are the most direct at helping you to notice your research process.) For each of these exercises, your goal is to notice what arises during your day-to-day work: What do you tend to do? What internal thoughts and thought patterns do you observe? What emotions do you feel? While you'll have lots of opportunities to try changing these things, for now, practice approaching what you see without judgment: Just notice what happens, without trying to change it. And when you do find yourself criticizing or judging what you do (which will arise naturally), try to notice when those judgments arise and use them as an opportunity to learn more about yourself and your process.

Third, be sure to do the reflection exercises. These help you look back beyond just this week to consider larger habits that you might have.

Fourth, at the end of the week, try freewriting about the current state of your research. What have you learned by observing how you work? What have you noticed that seems to be going well in your research practice, and what have you noticed that maybe could be improved?

Week 2: Finding and Framing a Research Challenge

Readings	Exercises	Reflection prompts	Approximate time required (beyond reading)
Chapter 4	Choose a research challenge	4.8	• 1.5–2 hours for exercises
Optional: 9 and 10 for ideas	4.1, 4.2, 4.4, 4.5	Check in on what you've learned	• One session to reflect at end of the week

You've now spent a week paying attention to how you do research. Hopefully, you've started to notice things about your research process that you might like to improve. Or maybe you have a content-related question that you want to move forward. Over the next two weeks, you'll practice solving a research-related challenge using the creative abilities. This week, you'll be choosing a specific challenge and then practicing the skills of problem finding and framing to frame that challenge as a tractable problem.

Read Chapter 4. You may also want to read Chapters 9 and 10 for examples of the types of problems you might want to address.

Next, select a challenge that you want to try solving. This could be a content-related challenge (maybe you're having trouble getting started on a new research project, or maybe you feel stuck on analyzing a dataset) or a process-related challenge (maybe you're struggling to find time to write, or maybe one of your collaborators is driving you nuts). As this is your first time experimenting with the new abilities, we encourage you to pick a real problem you're facing, but not something that's too close to home – if the challenge feels terrifying or paralyzing to even think about addressing, it's probably a sign that you should choose something less emotionally raw. You could use one of the challenges we describe in Chapter 9 or 10 (things like writing a paper or finding a dissertation topic); if you do select one of these, we encourage you to think bigger than what we suggest in the chapters. And lastly, remember that the primary goal of selecting this challenge is to use it to practice the abilities. If you don't pick the perfect one, you're just spending two weeks on it, and then you have all the time in the world to tackle the many other issues you might have picked!

For this challenge, start by exploring the problem space and experimenting with finding different problems within that space (Exercises 4.1 and 4.5). Also, take time to reflect on how you usually solve problems (Exercise 4.8).

Then, pick two or three specific problems you've identified within the problem space that seem particularly relevant. For each of these problems, practice framing the problem multiple ways (Exercises 4.2 and 4.4).

Finally, pick two or three specific framings of the problem, and try writing a How Might We statement for each one. To help you select a good framing, use the criteria and principles listed in Chapter 4 in the sections entitled, *How Do You Know You've Found the "Right" Problem?* and *What Do You Do with a Problem Once You've Found It?*

(You'll notice that for each of these steps we're asking you to work with multiple options. This helps you keep an open mind about possible directions for solutions.)

As a reminder, your deliberate exploration of the problem is partially about learning to lean into (rather than avoid) ambiguity.

Just as we told you not to rush to change your habits as you were becoming aware of them last week, try not to rush to solve the problem that you've chosen this week. Maybe you'll come up with an awesome solution right away through your prototyping and testing, but maybe you won't. Maybe your problem will take six months to solve. From the point of view of learning (though maybe not your challenge!), that's OK, as long as you're reflecting along the way.

After you've spent time exploring and framing your problem, reflect on what you learned. How did you develop your problem statements, and how did you select which framings to focus on? What was similar or different in your approach to the way you'd usually solve this problem? What worked well? What was challenging for you?

Week 3: Brainstorming, Prototyping, and Testing

Readings	Exercises	Reflection prompts	Approximate time required (beyond reading)
Chapter 5	5.1, select ideas for prototyping	5.8, 5.9	• 1.5–2 hours for exercises
Optional: 9 and 10 for ideas	5.6, 5.2 Test your prototype Decide what's next	Check in on what you've learned	• Ongoing testing of your prototype • One session to reflect at end of the week

Now that you've framed a tractable problem, you'll experiment with using cycles of divergent and convergent thinking to solve that problem. You'll first brainstorm potential solutions, then select one or more ideas to implement. You'll practice creating multiple types of prototypes of your potential solutions, and then test them out. Finally, you'll play with figuring out what to do next based on what you've learned.

Read Chapter 5. You may also want to read Chapters 9 and 10 for inspiration (paying special attention to the concluding portions) if you haven't read them yet.

Before you start iterating, take a moment to reflect on how you usually go about solving problems (Exercises 5.8 and 5.9).

Take one of the problem statements you generated last week, and brainstorm ways that you might solve that problem. Set a timer for four minutes and list as many ideas as possible. Then, set your timer to two minutes and apply one of the constraints from Exercise 5.1. Do two or three additional two-minute rounds with new constraints.

Come up with three different criteria to select possible solutions for prototyping. These might be (1) most exciting, (2) easiest to implement, and (3) most potential for transformation. Rank the ideas you generated using these criteria. Then, select one that you'll carry over into the prototyping phase.

Sketch out how you could build several types of prototypes for this idea (Exercise 5.6). At least one idea should be tactile (Exercise 5.2) and one should be a process (like a skit or a change in habit). Then, actually build or implement one of your ideas.

Now, test your prototype in action. Use it when you're doing whatever the challenge was that you were facing, and see how it might help you address that challenge.

After you've tested your prototype, reflect on what you learned. Ask the questions from Exercise 5.6. Then, look at Table 5.2 and think about what you would want to try next to keep refining your solution. Do you need to try another framing of the problem? Do you need to brainstorm more potential solutions? Do you want to refine your current prototype, or maybe try prototyping another solution that you generated in brainstorming?

Finally, reflect on what it was like to use an experimental, iterative approach to work toward an idea or solution. How was this similar or different to your current approach? What was it like being deliberate in using divergent and convergent thinking? What did you like, and what was challenging for you?

Week 4: Setting Yourself Up for Success

Readings	Exercises	Reflection prompts	Approximate time required (beyond reading)
Chapters 6, 7, 8	6.1 or 6.4, 6.6 7.1, 7.2 8.1, 8.6	6.8 7.7, 7.8 8.7 Check in on what you've learned	• Daily observation of energy and stories • 1.5–2 hours for exercises • One session to reflect at end of the week

In the final week, you'll experiment with the abilities that support overall creativity: using stories and managing your energy to motivate yourself to be creative. You'll also explore your support network and practice asking for early feedback.

First, read Chapters 6, 7, and 8.

Second, experiment with noticing and rewriting the stories you tell about your research. Do Exercise 6.1 and/or 6.4 to observe the current language you use when you talk or think about your research. If you want, you may want to reflect on whether this language changed at all as a result of your exploration with the creative abilities. Then, try Exercise 6.6 to practice updating your language to match who you want to be as a researcher.

Third, explore the ways that energy affects your working routines. Do Exercises 7.1 and 7.2 to notice your day-to-day patterns, and Reflections 7.7 and 7.8 to consider what works well and what doesn't about your current approach.

Fourth, experiment with getting early feedback (Exercise 8.1). Map your support network (Exercise 8.6), and then identify a gap. Find someone who can fill that gap and make a plan for reaching out to them. Also, think about when you usually tend to get feedback (Exercise 8.7).

Finally, reflect on what you learned. How do you usually go about getting feedback or working with other people, and what was it like to incorporate them into your research in new ways? What was noticing your energy levels like, and do you think you're using or managing them in effective ways?

Based on this exploration, you might want to make a plan to change your daily work habits or to get earlier feedback. That is definitely encouraged, but this might also be a great place to start a new cycle of problem finding, brainstorming, prototyping, and testing in order to get you to a solid plan.

WHERE TO NEXT?

Congratulations, you made it through a month of experimenting with your research process! Hopefully you feel more confident in using the abilities. But one month is just the start. Our author team has been playing with these exercises for years, and still sometimes feel novice when it comes to actually using them in our daily research.

If you are excited to try more, there are a number of different ways to continue to explore. First, you might want to spend more time on the topics covered in the thirty-day program. For instance, you could try additional problem-solving cycles (problem find/frame, brainstorm, prototype, test) on new problems. If you selected a process-related challenge, try one related to your research content, or vice versa. Try experimenting with different types of prototypes, or with getting more intentional feedback throughout the process (rather than just when you're testing the prototype).

Or you could pick up your original problem-solving challenge where you left off at the end of Week 3. Consider what you would still need to know to fully address your challenge and start there. You might want to reframe the problem based on your new knowledge, test your prototype in other settings, or perhaps try prototyping one of the other ideas you generated.

Or perhaps you want to spend more time really getting to know what you do now as a researcher and building in ways to be mindful of your research process, your emotions, your stories, your energy over time, and your space.

As we've emphasized throughout, there are no right answers – just keep exploring.

WAYS TO USE THIS LEARNING PROGRESSION IN A COURSE OR WORKSHOP

For faculty or administrators who are interested in turning this curriculum into a course or workshop, we wanted to share some of the lessons we have learned in the many iterations we have taught.

There are many different types of learning objectives you might want to emphasize. The progression we've provided focuses on a broad overview of the creative abilities. It is a general introduction to building creativity in research. However, by exploring certain dimensions of the curriculum more deeply, you could adapt the exercises to support additional goals.

First, to really develop creative research content, you might focus on the cognitive techniques that support iteration and experimentation. This model would focus on problem finding, brainstorming, prototyping, and feedback to rapidly develop and refine innovative research topics or approaches to doing that research. The foundational abilities – mindfulness and emotional intelligence – as well as the creative support structures would be taught as inputs for problem solving. This approach represents a more traditional design thinking curricular framing.[3]

Second, we have seen many PhD students transformed by the fact that our classes bring a human-centered perspective to research. Many students often feel alone, and the population struggles with high rates of depression.[4] With a slightly different emphasis, many elements of the book's curriculum could pivot to be about emotional well-being in research life. This model would focus on mindfulness, self-compassion, empathy, and storytelling, and would encourage teamwork as a way to not feel isolated during research.

Third, you could develop an explicitly process-oriented version, designed to build efficient, productive researchers. This model would focus on using mindfulness to observe one's research habits, and then using problem finding and iterative problem solving to refine one's process. It would also deeply explore how consciously managing energy and space can help researchers be more productive and creative.

Finally, you might emphasize what the d.school calls "radical collaboration."[5] In this model, you'd deliberately bring together inter-disciplinary teams of researchers and coach them to use the creative abilities to develop innovative research projects. One of our class alumni is now an administrator in her college's Office of Research; she has been using these techniques to help faculty in grant development.

There are also a variety of different formats you could use. We have taught many different versions of our course, from a two-hour taster workshop to a more formal class. One format we really like is having one or two full-day sessions for students to experience most of the abilities (i.e., go through a full cycle of problem finding, brain-storming, and prototyping at a fairly rapid speed), and then having one or several follow-up sessions for them to explore the additional abil-ities more deeply and/or conduct another iteration cycle with time to apply the abilities in their daily research activities. You also could expand the curriculum to fit a full semester, spending a week on each ability and then trying out the iteration cycle on multiple problems.

From a general pedagogical point of view, we prefer formats where you encourage the students to do exercises first, and then give them a chance to reflect (and maybe introduce some of the scientific rationale behind why they did what they did). We have also seen a lot of benefit from giving our students an "easy" challenge to work on first (something like developing a talk or optimizing their time man-agement strategies), and then – once they've had a chance to practice on a problem that isn't too emotionally raw – applying the abilities to one that is more pressing.

CONCLUSION

This chapter provided a guided progression to work through the many ideas presented in the book. For those of you who stuck with the program, you've now had a full taste of what creative problem solving might look like. For those of you who didn't, hopefully you got some inspiration for how you might practice the abilities in your research. Either way, there are numerous directions you can explore for your future learning. See what inspires you and try it out!

12 Mentoring Creativity

Learning to conduct original research is a complex process. As they gain competence in research practice, students gradually transition from a dependent phase where a professor provides ongoing feedback (e.g., through taking courses) to conducting independent research that results in an original thesis or dissertation project.[1] Research on this transition from advanced student to independent scholar emphasizes that it is challenging. Becoming a scholar requires a switch from solving predefined problems to learning to identify and solve one's own problems, as well as learning to manage the creativity required in independent research practice.[2] Indeed, in a study of factors contributing to graduate student success, Barbara Lovitts found that "creative intelligence" was a key distinguisher in determining how successful graduate students were at making the transition to being independent scholars.[3]

Advisors and supervisors play an important role in helping students become independent scholars, including developing content knowledge, analytical skills, and understanding of the research process.[4] In this chapter, we discuss the ways you might facilitate development of creative abilities in your students and other researchers. We focus specifically on the supervising of doctoral students, although you could also apply these ideas to advising undergraduate researchers, postdocs, or potentially to mentoring more established scholars. We first discuss the literature on mentoring in higher education. We then provide suggestions for using the creative abilities to explore your own mentoring practice. Finally, we suggest concrete ideas to model your creative research process for your students and to facilitate their use of the abilities. By way of terminology, we'll be using the terms *advisor* and *advisee* (commonly used in the USA), recognizing of course that these names along with the nature of the mentoring relationship or process vary substantially across countries. Advisors play multiple roles for their advisees, including that of collaborator, advocate, evaluator, and mentor.[5] A *mentor* is someone who "foster[s] critically supportive, nurturing relationships that actively support learning, socialization, and identity transformation" in their mentees.[6]

This chapter presents approaches that have application in a range of settings. We assume that mentoring is happening in a relatively unstructured setting, either one-on-one contact through meetings, email, etc., and/or through lab group meetings. A mentor who wants a formal approach (e.g., to use in a series of lab meetings over the course of a semester) may find it useful to combine these approaches with the progression described in Chapter 11. In order to simplify the chapter, we discuss the mentoring relationship as if a student or postdoc has one advisor, but recognize that in many (if not most) cases, multiple faculty are either co-advising or serving on a committee. We do not believe this makes a difference to the ideas presented here, except as complex personalities or diverse intellectual perspectives may complicate such relationships to pull a student in multiple directions.

MENTORING IN HIGHER EDUCATION

In higher education, a mentor is a "faculty person who establishes a working relationship with a student and shepherds him or her through the doctoral process to completion."[7] While mentoring is something that many faculty are expected to do, many researchers learn it on the job, picking up techniques from their PhD advisors or colleagues.[8] For many faculty, their mentoring approach is significantly influenced by their own experiences being mentored during the PhD.[9]

Effective mentoring in higher education generally aligns with the principles of adult learning. Research students come to their graduate work with existing experiences and understandings of their academic disciplines and how research functions. The mentor's role is to provide the means to continually examine the students' existing understanding as students have new research experiences.[10] Besides facilitating critical reflection, mentors serve a vital role in transmitting formal and informal norms, ensuring that graduate students understand "how things work" in academic culture.[11] At its best, the mentoring relationship is reciprocal: Mentors provide feedback and guidance about the mentee's work, but can also learn through the relationship, for instance, by working on a new research topic.[12] Most significantly for creative research practice, mentors provide "learning experiences that will build [mentees'] self-confidence," including helping them develop creative confidence.[13]

Michael Galbraith and Waynne James developed a framework that outlines six overlapping functions performed by effective mentors.[14] Two of these are particularly relevant to mentoring creative research practice. In acting as a model, the mentor "draws on personal experiences ... to share thoughts and genuine feelings that emphasize the value of learning from unsuccessful or difficult experiences"; this is especially effective in encouraging "mentees to take necessary risks, make decisions without certainty of successful results, and continue to overcome difficulties."[15] In acting as a facilitator, the mentor works to help the student "expand individual views, uncovers the underlying experiential and information basis for assumptions, and presents multiple viewpoints to generate a more in-depth analysis of decisions and actions."[16] We explore these two functions as they relate to mentoring creativity later in the chapter.

ASSESS YOUR CURRENT MENTORING PRACTICE

Before you can effectively model or facilitate creative research practice, it helps to possess a conscious understanding of your own creative research practice. Thus, the more a mentor is mindful of their own choices about what they do in their own research, why they do it, and how, the more likely they will be to clearly and transparently translate the logic behind those choices in a form that mentees may absorb. At the same time, the effort to consciously translate and model the research process for mentees can also increase your understanding, as the mentoring relationship becomes a place to practice being conscious of how you use the creative abilities. Mentoring creative research practice illustrates the old adage that you don't fully know what you know until you teach it to someone else. We thus encourage you to pause and spend some time exploring your current approach to mentoring your students.

Use Mindfulness to Become Aware of Your Current Mentoring Practice

Like many challenges we have presented so far, mindfulness provides a foundation for considering your creativity mentoring practice. It's difficult to design a path forward if you don't understand where you are starting from.

In our study of the creative practice of scholars at Stanford, we found that each of the researchers we interviewed had an internal logic to their mentoring approach, but some of them were not conscious of it themselves.[17] Mindfulness can help you become more aware of your approach, your assumptions, and even your overall mentoring framework – essentially making your logic of mentoring more explicit. As we suggested in the mindfulness chapter (Chapter 2), you might aim to become aware of your behaviors, thoughts, and emotions as you mentor.

The next time you meet with a student, notice your behaviors: how you interact and what you do as a mentor. How do you prepare for the meeting? What do you talk about? When does the student drive the conversation, and when do you drive the conversation?

You might also pay attention to how your thinking works when you relate to your students. How do you answer their questions: with a direct answer, or with another question that encourages them to reflect and try to solve the issue on their own first? What instructions do you give to the student for follow-up and how do you decide what to say? How much direction or control do you give to the student in these instructions?

Mindfulness can also help you become aware of how emotions might be affecting your approach to mentoring. You can use the skills of self-awareness and self-compassion to notice what emotions arise when you engage in mentoring: When do you feel excited? When do you feel anxious? When do you feel frustrated? Why? Also, notice to what extent you engage with your students' emotions. If a student came to you in tears, how would you react?

Finally, as you explore, you can also investigate the stories you hold about yourself as a mentor. What is your identity as a mentor? Are you conscious of having one? Are you a good mentor, a reluctant mentor, a mentor who experiences imposter syndrome? Are you a nurturing or strict mentor?

To continue exploring your approach as a mentor, we encourage you to reflect on the following sorts of questions:

- When and how did you start mentoring?
- What are your emotions about mentoring?
- What is your most and least favorite part of the mentoring process?
- How do you interact with a new student? How do you set them up to do excellent work?
- What do you do when your students get stuck? How do you advise them to overcome their difficulties? How is this advice similar to or different from how you work on your own projects?
- What kinds of mentoring situations do you end up in most often? Do your students tend to come to you for content advice? Process advice? Practical advice? Are there particular questions or situations that arise frequently?
- How do you interact with students in individual versus group settings? Do you have a lab group or other regular meeting for all your advisees? What is your vision for your lab group?
- What explicit or implicit stories about research might you be conveying through your mentoring?
- How do you manage the emotional aspects of PhD students' lives?

- What qualities do you appreciate in mentors you've had? Do you see any of those qualities in yourself as a mentor?
- How do you talk about the PhD journey with your students? What are the stories you share about being a researcher?

Create a Feedback Network for Mentoring

After your initial assessment, a way to continually assess your mentoring practice is to explicitly seek out feedback about your mentoring. Unlike research, which gives feedback at least in the form of papers accepted or rejected and grants funded or declined, feedback about mentoring can be scarce unless you seek it out.[18] At some institutions, it might be limited to teaching evaluations on formal courses. This means that if you want to understand how those most impacted by your mentoring practice (your research students) experience it, you have to deliberately look for opportunities to receive feedback.

Like the other types of feedback discussed in Chapter 8, there is a spectrum of ways you could go about getting feedback on mentoring. On the more informal side, at the end of a lab meeting or a one-on-one meeting, you could ask students to say one thing they like and one thing they'd change about your mentoring style. Or you can ask your colleagues for advice on how you mentor. When one of our colleagues was writing his first comprehensive exam questions, for instance, he asked a weekly writing group for feedback on his draft questions. For a more formal approach, you could develop an annual survey for your students to fill out, with targeted questions about your mentoring, about their development as researchers, and about persistent challenges or questions about research they have.

HELP YOUR STUDENTS BUILD CREATIVE CONFIDENCE

Once you've assessed your current mentoring approach, you can start developing ways to better mentor your students' use of the creative abilities, thereby encouraging the attitudes and behaviors that through practice lead to the development of creative confidence.

As research students learn how to do independent research, they typically progress along a continuum from more supervised to more independent. Many students' first foray into research is by observing others: reading research papers, attending research talks, hearing about older students' projects, and seeing you do research. As they do this exploration, they start to see how a project is conceptualized, what makes "good" research in your field, and what types of methods are commonly used. Many early students also have the opportunity to "get their feet wet" on an ongoing research project. By serving as a research assistant or lab tech, students get to practice applying research methods, analyzing data, and solving problems when things don't work as planned. Students ultimately do their own research on an entire project, from developing a dissertation proposal, to collecting and analyzing the data, to writing it up. For the student's own research, the advisor's role is to scaffold the student's learning and provide feedback, but the decision making is primarily in the student's hands. For many scholars, postdoctoral training provides a further step in the transition to independent researcher. In some fields having control of the entire project (from conceptualization to writing) might not come until a postdoc or even later.

In this section, we provide ideas of ways you can help students at all of these stages develop through modeling and facilitation. These ideas are meant to be suggestive, not exhaustive, of the approaches you might take. Try these out, or develop others; over time, you'll discover and refine the mentoring approaches that work for you.

Model Creative Practice: Make the Research Process Explicit

One of the key roles of a mentor is to demystify the process of doing research.[19] A lot of the things researchers do are not immediately obvious to students. As a mentor, you can uncover and unpack this tacit knowledge, essentially by making the things that are clear in your head transparent. In this way, you help students start to see research as a process and start to convey how the creative abilities shape researchers' decisions about how to move through this process. More specifically, making the research process explicit for your students helps them create the habit of being mindful of their creative practice (and of the research process in general). Once they start noticing how research happens and why, they start building a mental framework to organize new knowledge.[20]

Making the process of doing research explicit may also address student anxieties that arise from human intolerance for ambiguity. What feels like a simple research task for you may be a very ambiguous situation for a graduate student. It is almost like looking behind the scenes of a theater production and becoming familiar with how all the pieces come together. It could be scary to have attended plays as an audience member and then suddenly be tasked with the director's role, but by spending time backstage seeing how a play is produced it becomes easier to imagine creating a performance on your own.

One way to make the research process explicit for your students is to find places to talk about the process behind research, not just its content. After your students read a research paper, attend research seminars or talks, or hear about more advanced students' projects, take time to reflect on the process of research that it demonstrated. Ask your students: Why do you think the author chose to use this method over that one? Why did they choose to work on this case or in that setting? What steps and decisions in the research process do you think are missing from the final published version, and why? How do you think the researcher was affected by serendipity or other things that were out of their control?

When possible, try to create opportunities for your students to ask these questions of the authors directly. You could invite other scholars to talk and ask them to tell the whole story (not the polished final version) of a research project. Encourage your students to take a beginner's mindset and ask "why?" for every decision made along the way. For example, as PhD students, Nicola and Amanda both took a research methods class where every week a senior scholar would present the "unabridged" story behind a published paper. This seminar was where we started developing some of our ideas about creativity in research, hearing how many of the scholars embraced the role of serendipity and iteration in their work – an idea that was very empowering to students trying to make the "right" decisions at every stage.

You can also find occasions to talk about the steps that you take as you move through your own research process, intentionally modeling your metacognitive process for your students. For instance, describe to your students why you decided to use a particular methodology, and what other options you considered. How did you decide when data analysis was complete enough to start writing a paper? How did you choose which journal or publisher to target? Moreover, be explicit about when and why you're using different thinking modes or drawing on a particular creative ability. When are you in a more divergent, brainstorming mode, and when are you narrowing down your options? What emotions might you be feeling as you make these decisions, and how do they affect what you're doing, or why? Did you ever get stuck in the course of this project, or did things not work out as planned? What did you do then?

Facilitate Creative Practice: Nudge Your Students to Use the Creative Abilities

Once students are working on their own project, you can structure your feedback to encourage them to use the creative abilities. From a learning theory perspective, this is a way of scaffolding their abilities – providing supports for your students to practice with, and then gradually removing these supports as students gain mastery.[21] By modeling your own process, you helped provide them with a framework about how the research process works and what the creative abilities are. Now, you'll provide targeted questions that guide them to practice with the creative abilities. With practice, these abilities will become more habitual for your students, so you'll hopefully need to provide fewer nudges over time.

Mindfulness of Process

Mindfulness of process is essentially about helping your students be more aware of what they are doing, thinking, and feeling. In your role as facilitator, you build on the framework you helped your students develop by learning about other people's research process, but now you can encourage them to reflect on their own process and develop their own metacognitive abilities. To do this, you might experiment with framing your mentoring to be about both process and content. When you meet with students, ask them for updates that include both their process – how they're deciding what to do – and the outcomes of those decisions. It can also be helpful to encourage their use of practices that preserve time for reflection, like academic freewriting.[22]

Emotional Intelligence

To build your students' emotional self-awareness and self-compassion, you might ask them to notice and discuss their emotions as they do research. This could be as part of your inquiries about their research process (e.g., "Did you notice any emotional responses while you were deciding whether you'd gathered enough data?"). You may also notice evidence of your students' emotional state when you meet with them – maybe they seem particularly enthusiastic or are shaking their pen nervously. Take this as an opportunity to build the students' awareness of their feelings and help them use these emotions to inform their research: "You seem tense. Is it related to choosing a dissertation topic? Or something else?" As a note, some students can understandably be hesitant to appear vulnerable with a perceived superior, so it will help if you are willing to talk explicitly about your own vulnerabilities as a scholar.[23]

Finding and Framing Problems

To help your students become more comfortable in ambiguous situations, you may want to nudge them to slow down when they are solving a problem. For instance, when they are developing a research question, you might ask them to write multiple framings of the question (perhaps from different perspectives or at several scales). Or when a student comes in with a solution already selected or a problem already solved, ask them to reflect on how they chose that one. Did they consider any alternative approaches? Why or why not? How did they test out or select from among the alternatives?

When you discuss problem framing, you might also talk more generally about the ambiguity that comes with any creative and innovative work. How does it feel for the student to be in an ambiguous situation and not know the right answer? Why is it important to slow down and not jump to a conclusion? Even emphasizing that there is no right answer can be helpful for students to hear. Martin Schwartz made this point eloquently in an essay in *Cell* called "The Importance of Stupidity in Scientific Research." Our students have appreciated this particular essay.[24]

Iterating and Experimenting

There are a number of ways you might develop your students' ability to learn through incremental small failures and experimentation. You can consciously use language that helps your students see research as an iterative process. For instance, you can talk about paper drafts, abstracts, or conference presentations as "prototypes," helping students see them as works in progress and not get too attached to any particular version. Or you can frame aspects of research iteration – such as generating preliminary data from pilot experiments to write a successful proposal, or conducting exploratory interviews to develop a credible survey instrument – that might already be common in your discipline as "adaptive research management," so students understand how these early stage activities fit into a larger learning cycle.

You can also encourage your students to use divergent or convergent thinking at the appropriate moments. When a student comes to you with a question, instead of telling them what you would do, ask them to brainstorm with you about possible next steps and multiple paths to the same goal. When a student comes in with a surprising result, ask them to brainstorm possible explanations for that result. When a student is deciding which journal to send their paper to or which conference to attend, help them use a deliberate selection process. Work with them to generate selection criteria (e.g., previous research the journal has published, cost, potential visibility) and then apply those criteria, perhaps visually with voting dots or by writing the potential options in a matrix.

You could even make your use of convergent and divergent thinking more formal: Whenever your student comes to you with an idea (e.g., a research question or conference abstract), you could ask them to come in with three potential options and a rationale for selecting one. This has the added benefits of allowing you to make course corrections easily, which can be especially valuable for early stage students, and of helping students not become too attached to any one idea too soon.

Encourage Your Students to Use the Supporting Abilities

In your role as a facilitator, you can work with students to use the creative support structures to enhance their learning and research.

Encourage your students to notice how they use language and to become aware of the stories they've internalized about their research. When you hear a student using a particular phrase or telling a story about their research – about getting stuck, about problem solving, etc. – ask them to reflect on their words. You could ask where they developed that story, whether they believe it on further reflection, and whether they think it supports their identity as a creative scholar. You could also have them deliberately articulate and reflect on the stories they believe, for instance, about why they want to do research or about their strengths and weaknesses as a scholar. Then, ask them to craft their ideal story of who they are as a scholar.

You may also want to think about the stories that your students hear about what research is or should be, whether told in your group or the broader department. These are subtle, but important. Whether you are in a lab (where you have more control) or just a department, what are the collective stories you tell about research, about mentoring, about feedback, and about creativity? How can you build on those with your students?

Talk to your students about energy. Help them explore how their energy fluctuates over time and how that relates to what they're working on. You can also try to give your students some autonomy over when and where they work. Obviously, in some fields there are particular things that need to happen at particular times (like caring for samples), or your space might be constrained by institutional rules or safety requirements. But, to the extent possible, let students use their time as they'd like so they can optimize their energy, rather than conforming to a strict single standard. And try to let the students shape the space where they work to enhance their energy. This could be through decorating student offices, or by setting expectations that students spend some time in the department but otherwise are free to work where they please.

Finally, create opportunities for students to get feedback early on their projects. Help students think about what types of feedback they might need at any given time and encourage them to explicitly express those needs when they ask for input. Then, try to match your feedback with their needs. (It can be hard, but try to resist the urge to edit typos when they give you the first draft of an abstract or outline.) By giving them the feedback they need when they are ready for it, you'll encourage them to continue seeking input early and often. When you provide suggestions on where to go next, make sure to discuss both their content and their research process. You might find it helpful to encourage your students to think about how they can expand their feedback network beyond you as their advisor in order to take advantage of diverse perspectives. You can also create opportunities for students to practice giving feedback to other people. This can be to their peers (e.g., in a group meeting or by encouraging them to form or join a writing group) or even to you (when you're trying to figure out what to do next on some aspect of a project, tell the students what you've done so far and ask them to reflect with you on your process). Learning to both give and get feedback is an important part of research practice.

CONCLUSION

Creativity is essential to doing independent research. By modeling your research process and facilitating your students' use of the creative abilities, you contribute to their eventual development of creative confidence and increase the probability that they will become successful, innovative researchers. The ideas we've provided in this chapter are just a starting point to open up the conversation about creative research practice with your mentees. As we've done throughout the book, we encourage you to take these suggestions as a springboard from which to experiment: Try them out, come up with others, and over time you'll find the creativity mentoring approaches that feel the most natural for you and your students.

A NOTE FOR PHD STUDENTS

If you're reading this chapter and thinking, "I wish my advisor would do this!" there are ways that you might start "managing up." First, you could give them the book, and say that you just read this mentoring chapter and would appreciate some advice on approaching creativity in research. Or you could ask directly for input on specific abilities. For instance, when you're talking about a research talk you just watched, ask your advisor to help you fill in the steps of the research process that the presenter didn't cover. Or when you're facing a new challenge or problem, ask your advisor for several different perspectives on the problem or how you might solve it.

13 Conclusion

Congratulations! By reading this far, you have made an investment into your creativity and innovation as a researcher and hopefully have already noticed differences in your research practice.

One year, eight chapters, and a signed contract into writing this book, Amanda and Nicola looked at one another and realized that maybe the book needed a conclusion. So, we opened up a new Google Doc and titled it "Benediction," the placeholder file for a final piece of text that would actually be written to tie everything into a nice bow and send you out into the world. This is iteration and prototyping at its finest.

For the author team, each stage of this project has been an experience of living the ideas presented in the text. The book itself represents one of the longest continuous learning, experimentation, and iteration cycles that any of us has ever engaged in. Throughout, each stage has been a prototype for the next stage. In the early days, back when we thought we were probably joking about writing a book, there was a running OneNote file on Amanda's computer that helped capture team ideas "to go into the book." These were ideas that came up as we went about the teaching we were committed to, but the book was still a figment, maybe to be written in ten years. Then the book proposal became a prototype presented in formal form, providing us both with feedback from reviewers and the confidence of a signed contract. In the manuscript writing stage, the iteration continued, from color-coded maps of the table of contents that helped us recognize that maybe there were two different types of abilities, to our process for getting stories, chapters, and exercises from seed to fruit. And we're sure that even the version of the published book you now hold in your hand is missing the dozen great ideas for exercises or stories to include that we've had since we turned it in. (Check out the website!)[1]

As what we've just said makes clear, the project has felt messy and uncomfortable at times. When we first started working on this project in 2010, we said, "Gee, this really should be someone's dissertation." But there was no someone around who needed a project and our team was passionate about the idea. So, we gingerly committed to reaching the first small milestone with the people we had: "Let's run a pilot workshop teaching design thinking but tailored for research students." And then we committed to the next workshop. And a full class, and the first conference, and the study of innovative scholars at Stanford.[2] And then more classes, and a paper evaluating the curriculum.[3] And eventually, the joke about the book became less funny and more of a "What if?" At various points, the momentum that we've just summarized tidily stalled or stopped, competing for energy with the need to finish PhD projects, paid teaching loads, family commitments, and the parts of our respective research agendas that count the most for tenure. But our team continually focused only one step ahead, doing the best we could on the current step and then pausing to ask: What would happen if we kept working on this for one more step? By staying mindful of how we were working and aware of what everyone on the team needed, we arrived somewhere we did not dare to dream when we began.

We believe this project looks like a lot of research – accumulated knowledge and collaboration and ideas that eventually find their way into a coherent theory in a published manuscript. That is one of the core ideas of this book: Doing research is often messy and the path forward is rarely certain. Thus, the better equipped you are to dive into that mess and be deliberate in your navigation, the more likely it is that you'll emerge with a useful (and dare we say innovative?) idea. Conversely, the more you hold tightly to one outcome or aim for too much control, the more likely you are to struggle along the way. In other words, process matters. Like moving through a crowded room, it's much more likely that you'll get where you intended if you watch where you're going but also respond fluidly to how others move.

Throughout this book, we've given you concrete strategies for navigating your own research more creatively. First, we explored four foundational abilities for conducting creative research: mindfulness (Chapter 2), emotional intelligence (Chapter 3), problem finding and framing (Chapter 4), and experimentation and iteration (Chapter 5). By paying attention to what you're doing and thinking, and by paying attention to your emotions and empathizing with the people around you, you started to gain insight into how you do research and the nature of the problems you are facing. By slowing down to explore a problem space, find the right problem to solve, and frame it in a tractable way, you set yourself up to move efficiently toward a solution. And by moving consciously through phases of divergent and convergent thinking, you learned how to rapidly iterate and experiment with the content and process of your research.

Second, we explored three additional abilities that support your creativity: storytelling (Chapter 6), managing energy (Chapter 7), and using teams for feedback (Chapter 8). By reflecting on the stories you tell, consciously shaping your space and energy to boost motivation, and building a team of people to help your research journey, you amplified your use of each of the creative abilities. Each of these abilities played a dual role: it simultaneously reflected your creative identity and can be used to craft a new way of working in the world (thus, contributing toward building a new identity).

Third, we introduced a number of examples of how these creative abilities interact in the day-to-day practice of research to allow you to bring it all into your own research life or lab. Chapters 9 and 10 showed how you might apply the abilities to common challenges faced by early career and senior scholars, respectively. Chapter 11 provided a guided curriculum for you to apply the abilities to a particular challenge that you're facing, and Chapter 12 discussed the ways you might mentor these abilities in other people. These chapters also introduced two different ways of understanding how the abilities interact. In Chapter 9, we depicted the abilities as a cycle: You start by using mindfulness and emotional intelligence to explore the roots of a problem, then use techniques of problem finding and framing to select and frame a tractable problem statement, and then use successive cycles of divergent and convergent thinking to iterate toward a solution. Along the way, the creative support structures boost your use of the other abilities. This cycle also reflects the sequence of readings and exercises we used in the thirty-day progression in Chapter 11. In contrast, Chapters 10 and 12 presented the abilities as lenses through which you could view a particular research challenge: How does your thinking about a problem and its potential solutions change if you (or your students) actively think about it as a prototype or seek ways to get diverse feedback?

Along the way, we've encouraged you to experiment with the techniques and ideas presented. Wherever your exploration has taken you, we hope you've learned something new about yourself and your research practice.

LESSONS LEARNED FOR A CREATIVE RESEARCH PRACTICE

Across the book, we have focused on the abilities used by creative researchers (Figure 13.1) and the conditions that support their use. Here, we summarize key messages that draw primarily on the ability chapters, but which are reinforced throughout the book. Applying these lessons will make your research more productive and fun, we hope.

Lesson 1: Be Aware of Your Research Process

Knowing what you're doing at any given time in your research enables you to choose intentionally where to go next. Instead of operating on autopilot, being aware of your process helps you understand what challenges you're facing at any time and select the appropriate tools or path to move forward. Creativity relies on a combination of

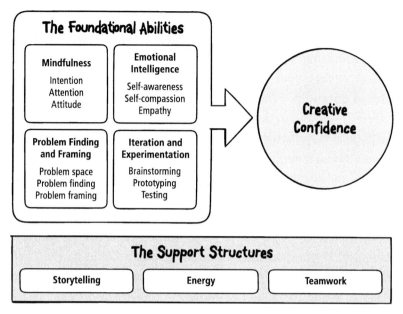

FIGURE 13.1 The creative abilities

divergent and convergent thinking: generating lots of ideas and then purposefully selecting and implementing some of those ideas. To be creative, you need to know when to zoom out and consider the big picture, and when to narrow your focus. Choosing the best path forward also entails knowing what's happening at any given moment, understanding what your goals are (both short- and long-term), and spending time to investigate your assumptions about the nature of problems you're facing.

To be aware of your research process, you draw on the skills of mindful awareness (Chapter 2), moving between divergent and convergent thinking (Chapter 5), observing the language you use and stories that you tell (Chapter 6), and knowing your energy cycles (Chapter 7). Through these skills, you develop a habit of thinking about your research as a process and being intentional in what you are doing in that process.

Lesson 2: Recognize Your Emotional Intuition

While researchers are typically adept at relying on reason to guide decision making, your emotions are another invaluable resource in navigating the process and content of your research. Humans have evolved numerous internal guides to help us make good decisions, both split-second reactions and long-term planning. Instead of ignoring (or burying) emotions as irrelevant, becoming conscious of your emotional reactions provides a way to tap into these evolved guidance systems and connect with your gut instincts. You can use emotions both to understand why you are stuck and to proactively avoid problems before they arise.

When you make use of your emotional intuition, you are obviously relying on the abilities of self-awareness and self-compassion (which we introduced in Chapter 3). But mindfulness (Chapter 2) and the ability to recognize the emotional dimensions when you find and frame problems (Chapter 4) also contribute to your facility with emotions.

Lesson 3: Tolerate Ambiguity

As discussed in Chapter 4, ambiguity refers to a situation or statement that is unclear because it can be understood in more than one way. When faced with a messy problem or an elusive goal, humans naturally feel discomfort. Often this discomfort can lead you to latch onto an answer too quickly, settling with the existing paradigm or solution just because it removes the discomfort. However, this exact discomfort has been motivating inventors and scientists to find the answer for centuries and led to many important innovations. When you are in an ambiguous situation, you have more possible solutions available to you, meaning that you have many more options from which to innovate and find that breakthrough solution.

You practiced ambiguity tolerance by mindfully recognizing when you are facing an ambiguous situation (Chapter 2) and slowing down to explore a problem space, rather than jumping to the first solution that came to mind (Chapter 4). However, ambiguity tolerance also benefits from observing and managing your emotions, specifically the discomfort that comes with not knowing (Chapter 3).

Lesson 4: Learn through Iteration

Whether you are faced with a challenge of too many ideas or no idea where to start, pairing cycles of divergent and convergent thinking can help you iterate toward a solution. Taking small risks and getting input on them provides an opportunity for iterative learning, but it also requires you to become comfortable presenting work that is less than finished to others. While presenting unpolished work can be uncomfortable, it is also an efficient way to gradually improve your messy ideas through incremental learning.

Learning through experimentation and iteration relates most directly to the process of brainstorming and prototyping (Chapter 5), but also draws heavily on self-compassion (Chapter 3) and seeking early feedback (Chapter 8). The stories you tell about failure, perfection, and success also shape your willingness to take risks and learn from them (Chapter 6).

Lesson 5: Bring Other People into Your Research

Finally, drawing on other people can boost your individual creativity. Different academic disciplines have differing expectations for collaboration in the conduct of research, but even the most independent of researchers can benefit from seeking and incorporating diverse perspectives. Bringing other people into your research can help you see things in a new light, generate surprising ideas, identify limitations before they become a problem, and provide necessary emotional support.

To effectively make use of others' insights and perspectives, you need the skills of empathy (Chapter 3), the ability to test prototypes with others (Chapter 5), and an orientation toward teaming and feedback (Chapter 8).

CONTINUE TO PRACTICE CREATIVITY IN RESEARCH

In the introduction, we discussed the idea of deliberate practice, wherein you work toward mastery by continually challenging yourself.[4] There is a lot of material in this book, both explicit exercises and ideas of things that you can try. Going forward, we encourage you to continue exploring new ways to practice the skills we've covered and explore the ideas we've presented. If your use of the abilities starts to feel familiar or habitual, that's great – it means it's going to be more automatic for you to use – but if you want to keep progressing toward mastery, you'll need to continue being deliberate in your use of the skills. Find new domains to apply them in or try teaching them to someone else. Our author team has been teaching these abilities for a decade, yet we each always need reminders that we have to intentionally practice these skills in our own work and continually find new ways to apply them.

As you continue to practice deliberately, you may want to think more explicitly about your identity as a researcher and what role creativity plays in your self-conception. As we discussed in the chapter on using language and stories (Chapter 6), the more you believe a narrative to be true, the more it will actualize in your day-to-day life. There are infinite ways that you can actively claim your creativity in research, but here are a few ideas to get you started:

1 Tell process stories often. When you talk to others, be explicit about what stage your ideas are at. Emphasize that there is more than one problem and more than one possible approach to solving that problem.
2 Talk about risk and your feelings about it, especially within your teams or with your students. Be vocal about the potential for any one idea to fail. Be aware of feelings or fears and be compassionate with yourself and your teammates.
3 Portray your work as a continual learning experience. Think and talk about the iteration process and the value of feedback. Be someone who learns by doing and trying as well as thinking.
4 Be explicit about your excitement. Share your triumphs.

5 Claim your wild ideas. Be the person in the meeting who throws out the wild idea (and names it as such): "This might be crazy but what if ... ?"

6 Give yourself permission to imagine and tell stories of multiple futures. Play with where your research or career might take you.

7 Tell people you are creative or that you have innovative ways of solving problems. Explicitly mention creativity or innovation in self-promotional writing, such as cover letters or on public-facing websites. Talk about your creative practice in job interviews, performance evaluations, and other occasions when you need to reflect on your strengths and challenges as a scholar.

By living this identity (even if it doesn't feel genuine at first), you create the brain connections that link together your self-conception, your understanding of creativity, and your day-to-day actions. And maybe some of your energy will rub off on those around you!

OUR HOPE FOR YOUR CREATIVE FUTURE

At this point, how you embrace creativity in your research is up to you. Wherever you started this journey – whether as a generally creative person looking for some new ideas or someone more analytically minded who wanted a shot of creativity – we hope you've found some skills and ideas that resonate with you. Now, it really is a choose-your-own adventure. Decide what areas of your research process or content you'd like to improve or what abilities you'd like to continue to practice, and use some of the ideas from the book to tackle them. In any case, we'd love to hear how you're using the text or any other reactions you have.

And remember that you don't just design once. Things change and you have to keep being mindful, keep noticing your changing emotions, keep framing and reframing the problem you are solving, and keep iterating. You might get to a place you never anticipated – like setting out to design a workshop at your own university and ten years later writing the conclusion to a book.

Research matters. And creativity matters for research. So have fun out there.

APPENDIX Comparing Creative Practice Frameworks

In this book, we present seven creative abilities, inspired by empirical research about how to be creative and our own experience teaching and revising the Research as Design curriculum over a decade. However, there are many other frameworks in the literature, and here we provide a brief discussion of similarities and differences between the ideas we present in this book and those of other scholars. We present these to enable you to explore a range of other ideas about cultivating creativity. And for those of you who have previously read one or more of these other books, we offer these thoughts regarding ways the different abilities and frameworks are related.

As a caveat, this short summary is by no means a comprehensive survey of creativity frameworks. Here, we focus on three works that can be considered peers to this book: Shelley Carson's *Your Creative Brain* (2010), *Keith* Sawyer's *Zig Zag* (2013), and Matthew Cronin and Jeffrey Loewenstein's *The Craft of Creativity* (2018). Each of these is a recent, research-based exploration of how to be more creative, though all three are focused on creativity in general rather than creativity in scholarly settings. Our work and its contemporaries are descended from a long line of earlier frameworks, like James Adams' *Conceptual Blockbusting*,[1] Robert Epstein's Generativity Theory,[2] and Roger von Oech's *A Whack on the Side of the Head*.[3] We have opted not to explicitly address these older frameworks; while they continue to be relevant (and great reads), many of the concepts they contain have been incorporated into newer work. We also discuss the design thinking framework, as it provided the genesis for many of our ideas.

YOUR CREATIVE BRAIN (2010)

Shelley Carson's *Your Creative Brain* explores the neuroscience underlying creativity in everyday life.[4] She discusses seven "brain-sets" (brain activation patterns) of creativity: Absorb, Envision, Connect, Reason, Evaluate, Transform, and Stream. "Absorb" refers to accessing "externally and internally generated information with an uncritical eye," much like the beginner's mind approach we discuss in Chapter 4.[5] "Envision" is about using visual thinking to imagine new ideas; this is a tool that we introduce in the Section I introduction, but don't explicitly call out as a separate ability. "Connect" is a divergent thinking phase wherein you "associate novel information to produce a multitude of ideas,"[6] and "Stream" is using "skill-appropriate improvisation."[7] "Reason" and "Evaluate" are both types of convergent thinking. In Reason, you purposefully work through a problem with planning and goal setting; in Evaluate, you judge your ideas to winnow down the multitude you've accumulated. Neither of these skills seemed necessary to emphasize for scholarly creativity, as they are core items of the analytic toolkit with which most researchers are highly skilled. Finally, in "Transform" you "put your negative emotions to work for you," actively using emotional intelligence and awareness of uncomfortable, distressing moods to generate creative ideas, echoing the way we suggest using emotions as a diagnostic tool.[8]

ZIG ZAG (2013)

Keith Sawyer's *Zig Zag* presents eight steps for creativity: Ask, Learn, Look, Play, Think, Fuse, Choose, and Make.[9] "Ask" is essentially the ability we term problem finding and framing; it entails the art of asking a tractable, generative question, including searching a problem space and transforming (what we call framing) the problem. "Learn" focuses on developing mastery through deliberate practice. While we didn't call out deliberate practice as a key ability, we have emphasized its importance throughout the text through our use of reflection and exercises that ask you to practice concepts actively. "Look" focuses on mindfulness and awareness: being aware of your surroundings, exploring other people's assumptions through empathy, and seeking out new experiences. Another way to think about Look is as an encouragement to cultivate a beginner's mind.

Sawyer's remaining five steps all highlight different dimensions of iteration and experimentation. "Play" and "Think" are the divergent stage. In Play, you use imagination to explore how things might be and cultivate divergent thinking. In Think, you actively generate lots of ideas, similar to brainstorming. "Fuse" is about combining ideas in new and interesting ways through the power of combined divergent and convergent thinking. "Choose" is a convergent thinking step: using critique and editing to select the best ideas or combinations of ideas. Finally, "Make" is an approach to prototyping that highlights the creation of tangible artifacts, actively building or doing something in the world rather than letting yourself sit in idea mode forever.

As we have in this text, Sawyer emphasizes that creativity is not a linear process; while there's a somewhat natural progression through each of the eight steps in the order presented in the book, creative people often "zigzag" between them depending on the problem: "Each step feeds the other seven."[10]

THE CRAFT OF CREATIVITY (2018)

Matthew Cronin and Jeffrey Loewenstein's *The Craft of Creativity* draws on interviews with diverse creative individuals to develop a theory of how humans innovate.[11] Like ours, this book espouses a shift from focusing on outcomes to an emphasis on process: "If our aim is to learn to generate creative products, then our task is to improve our ability to navigate the creative process."[12] As we have in this text, the authors also emphasize that creativity is a skill you can develop.

The first several chapters each highlight a different cognitive process for creativity. "Gaining Insight" is about ways of thinking to generate new ideas, specifically by changing your perspectives on a situation and changing the stories that you tell (echoing our ideas about problem framing and storytelling). "Turning Potential into Inventions" focuses on acting, building, and learning through an iterative process, testing your ideas concretely in the world to refine them. The second half of the book focuses on concrete tools to help you be more creative. These include specific ways to explore new perspectives (including generating ideas and combining ideas in novel ways) and using cues to remind yourself to do so. The authors also discuss the challenging but generative power of uncertainty (much like our take on tolerating ambiguity).

DESIGN THINKING

Finally, since our curriculum was heavily inspired by design thinking, it's worth considering how the design mindsets we've adapted match the scientific literature above and the abilities we've presented. There are many variations on what the exact design thinking process entails. Here, we present a version from Stanford's d.school,[13] along with one from the design consultancy IDEO,[14] as these map most closely to the roots of this project. It's worth noting that unlike the frameworks above, which derive from research, design thinking derives from professional practice, particularly in the realm of product design.

The Hasso Plattner Institute of Design at Stanford emphasizes eight core abilities of skilled designers. They organize these abilities into two categories: tangible and intangible. Four tangible abilities describe "distinct ways of understanding or modifying" information, either "diverging to new possibilities [or] converging towards clarity."[15] "Synthesize Information" is the ability to gather information from diverse sources and find new problems and insights into those problems using that information. "Learn from Others (People and Contexts)" melds building awareness of your context through mindfulness and using empathy to understand challenges in a deeper way. "Experiment Rapidly" refers to using quick iteration to generate ideas, test them out, and learn. "Build and Craft Intentionally" relates to (1) creating useful prototypes and (2) matching the way that you share your prototype with your audience and the type of feedback that you need. The four intangible abilities do not refer to specific actions one takes, but instead "[require] the brain to move among and across modes of thinking and making."[16] First is "Navigate Ambiguity," the process of consciously staying in uncertain situations that we discussed in Chapter 4. Second is "Move between Concrete and Abstract," which refers to the process of moving intentionally between divergent or convergent thinking and considering both abstract ideas as well as concrete instances where those ideas play out. "Communicate Deliberately" is about communicating effectively with your audience, whether in the process of soliciting feedback or sharing a more polished project; it focuses on the use of stories as a communication tool. Finally, "Design Your Design Work" is a meta-ability; designers need the metacognition to deliberately shape their approaches to solving problems using design. According to the d.school's pedagogy, someone fluent in design thinking knows how to use each ability and nimbly transitions between abilities depending on the context.

IDEO, a design and innovation company, describes design thinking as a combination of seven mindsets. Four of these are essentially identical to the Stanford abilities: "Make It"; "Empathy"; "Embrace Ambiguity"; and "Iterate, Iterate, Iterate." This is not surprising as the two organizations have worked closely together. However, with its focus on mindsets (which are a higher-order cognitive process than abilities), IDEO's perspective on designers' creativity highlights a few additional ideas.[17] The fifth mindset is "Optimism," the belief that progress is possible on even the most intractable challenge. This overall positive orientation appears in our work in the focus on viewing challenges as sources of opportunity, for instance, viewing negative emotions as diagnostic tools or viewing small failures as a source of learning.

IDEO also makes "Learning from Failure" a core mindset (paralleling our emphasis on becoming comfortable with sharing less than polished work to others in Chapter 5). The seventh IDEO mindset is "Creative Confidence," or the general belief that you can enhance your creative abilities, an idea we introduced in the introduction and have highlighted throughout as an important outcome of intentional creative practice.

LOOKING ACROSS THE FRAMEWORKS

Looking across the frameworks presented, we see a number of similarities and a number of differences emerge. First, all frameworks suggest that creative practice is a multidimensional thing. Even though different frameworks emphasize different elements of creativity, you generally need to mix and match different skills or thinking patterns to generate truly novel ideas. Secondly, all frameworks treat idea generation and analysis as two sides of the same coin. To be creative, you need to come up with interesting, novel perspectives, and then use an evaluative approach to select the most promising ones. And as we discussed in Chapter 1, you have to actually implement your ideas, which requires trying them out in the world. Lastly, all frameworks treat creativity as something that you can learn through practice, not as a trait that is inherent (the "creative genius" stereotype) or associated with particular personality types. These are all stances that we have taken in this text.

There are also differences, both between the individual frameworks and between the frameworks and our treatment of creativity. As shown in Table A.1, each of the frameworks has substantial overlap with our core abilities, particularly problem finding along with iteration and experimentation. Each framework approaches these core creative abilities with a slightly different emphasis, providing an opportunity to go deeper to understand the different types of cognition and behavior that comprise each of these abilities. Like us, both Carson and Sawyer emphasize the role of mindful awareness – gathering information by noticing what is happening – as a starting point for developing new ideas. However, only Carson mentions the use of one's own emotions (self-awareness) as a tool for enhancing creativity. Design thinking also emphasizes emotions as a source of creative insight, though generally with a focus on empathy rather than one's own emotions. There is also much less discussion of the supporting abilities in the other frameworks. Cronin and Loewenstein provide a nuanced discussion on the role of stories in shaping one's perceptions of problems and their solutions, dovetailing nicely with our work on consciously crafting new language and stories. The design thinking framework emphasizes many different components of teaming and feedback, from the value of learning from others to the need to be intentional in how you share information to seek feedback.[18] None of the frameworks discusses the role of energy in a substantial fashion.

There are key parts of each framework that we do not cover. We don't talk about Carson's "Stream" (deliberate improvisation), although it could be used as a tool for prototyping, nor do we delve too substantially into "Reason" (planning and setting goals) as we considered this to be a skill that most researchers already use. Sawyer emphasizes the role of deliberately seeking new experiences to expand your creativity, a topic which we do not address but that researchers might find useful, especially given the need for sustained creativity on multiyear projects. Cronin and Loewenstein have a great discussion of finding cues in your everyday life to remind you to step back and change perspective. We use cues in a couple of the mindfulness exercises, but you probably could find many more ways to build upon cues as reminders for each of the abilities. Finally, the design thinking framework has a meta-ability, "Design Your Design Work," related to the deliberate design of the problem-solving process you use. Throughout the book, we've encouraged you to approach your creative research practice this way and given you the skills to do so (e.g., be aware of where in your process you are, consciously use the supporting abilities to enhance the type of thinking you need to do, etc.), but do not call it out as a separate ability.

What we take away from this comparison echoes what we have emphasized about creativity throughout the book: While there are core abilities that cross settings, there is also a rich diversity of possible techniques that any individual researcher might draw upon. As you continue your deliberate practice and discovery about how to optimize your own creativity, we hope these frameworks (and others) might inspire you to go deeper, perhaps looking to one of these authors for fresh inspiration about the abilities we discuss and/or experimenting with the topics and strategies that we don't cover (or don't cover in as much detail).

Table A.1 *Comparing creativity frameworks*

Abilities from *Cultivating Creative Research Practice*	Abilities from *Your Creative Brain*	Abilities from *Zig Zag*	Abilities from *The Craft of Creativity*	Abilities from Design Thinking
Mindfulness	Absorb	Learn; Look		
Emotional Intelligence	Transform			Learn from Others
Problem Finding	Absorb	Ask; Play	Gaining Insight: the value of persistence	Navigate Ambiguity
Iteration and Experimentation	Envision; Connect; Reason; Evaluate; Stream	Play; Think; Fuse; Choose; Make	Turning Potential into Inventions; various thinking tools	Synthesize Information; Experiment Rapidly; Move between Concrete and Abstract; Build and Craft Intentionally
Storytelling and Narrative Energy			Gaining Insight	

Table A.1 (cont.)

Abilities from _Cultivating Creative Research Practice_	Abilities from _Your Creative Brain_	Abilities from _Zig Zag_	Abilities from _The Craft of Creativity_	Abilities from Design Thinking
Teaming and Feedback				Learn from Others; Build and Craft Intentionally; Communicate Deliberately
Background: deliberate practice, journaling, visual thinking	Envision	Learn		
Not covered in our framework	Reason; Stream	Look: seek new experiences	Cues as Clues	Design Your Design Work

Notes

I THE CREATIVITY AT THE HEART OF YOUR RESEARCH

1. Ulla Johansson-Sköldberg, Jill Woodilla, and Mehves Çetinkaya, "Design Thinking: Past, Present and Possible Futures," *Creativity and Innovation Management* 22, no. 2 (2013): 121–146; Hasso Plattner, Christoph Meinel, and Larry J. Leifer, *Design Thinking: Understand – Improve – Apply* (Heidelberg; New York: Springer, 2011).

2. Teresa M. Amabile et al., "Assessing the Work Environment for Creativity," *The Academy of Management Journal* 39, no. 5 (October 1, 1996): 1154–1184, https://doi.org/10.5465/256995; Mark A. Runco and Robert S. Albert, "Creativity Research: A Historical View," in *The Cambridge Handbook of Creativity*, ed. James C. Kaufman and Robert J. Sternberg (New York: Cambridge University Press, 2010), 78–94; Robert J. Sternberg and Todd I. Lubart, "The Concept of Creativity: Prospects and Paradigms," in *Handbook of Creativity*, ed. Robert J. Sternberg (New York: Cambridge University Press, 1999), 3–15; Robert J. Sternberg and James C. Kaufman, eds., Preface, in *The Nature of Human Creativity* (Cambridge: Cambridge University Press, 2018), xviii–xxiv, https://doi.org/10.1017/9781108185936.002.

3. Teresa M. Amabile, "A Model of Creativity and Innovation in Organizations," *Research in Organizational Behavior* 10, no. 1 (1988): 123–167; Sherry Phelan and Angela M. Young, "Understanding Creativity in the Workplace: An Examination of Individual Styles and Training in Relation to Creative Confidence and Creative Self-Leadership," *The Journal of Creative Behavior* 37, no. 4 (December 1, 2003): 266–281, https://doi.org/10.1002/j.2162-6057.2003.tb00994.x.

4. Robert L. DeHaan, "Teaching Creative Science Thinking," *Science* 334, no. 6062 (December 16, 2011): 1499–1500, https://doi.org/10.1126/science.1207918.

5. Richard E. Mayer, "Problem Solving," in *The Oxford Handbook of Cognitive Psychology*, ed. Daniel Reisberg, Oxford Handbooks Online (Oxford: Oxford

University Press, 2013), www.oxfordhandbooks.com/view/10.1093/oxfor dhb/9780195376746.001.0001/oxfordhb-9780195376746-e-48.

6. R. B. Freeman, *Charles Darwin: A Companion* (Dawson: Folkestone, 1978). For more daily routines of scientists, artists, and writers, see Mason Currey, *Daily Rituals: How Artists Work* (New York: Alfred A. Knopf, 2013) or "Daily Routines," http://dailyroutines.typepad.com/ daily_routines.

7. Shelley Carson, *Your Creative Brain: Seven Steps to Maximize Imagination, Productivity, and Innovation in Your Life* (Hoboken, NJ: John Wiley & Sons, 2010).

8. Rebecca McMillan, Scott Barry Kaufman, and Jerome L. Singer, "Ode to Positive Constructive Daydreaming," *Frontiers in Psychology* 4 (2013), http s://doi.org/10.3389/fpsyg.2013.00626; Marily Oppezzo and Daniel L. Schwartz, "Give Your Ideas Some Legs: The Positive Effect of Walking on Creative Thinking," *Journal of Experimental Psychology: Learning, Memory, and Cognition* 40, no. 4 (2014): 1142–1152, https://doi.org/10.1037/a0036577.

9. J. Watts and N. Robertson, "Burnout in University Teaching Staff: A Systematic Literature Review," *Educational Research* 53, no. 1 (2011): 33–50, https://doi.org/10.1080/00131881.2011.552235; see also C. Mitchell Adrian et al., "Issues Causing Stress among Business Faculty Members," *Journal of Academic Administration in Higher Education* 10, no. 1 (2014): 41–46; Gail Kinman, "Work Stressors, Health and Sense of Coherence in UK Academic Employees," *Educational Psychology* 28, no. 7 (2008): 823–835, https://doi.org/10.1080/01443410802366298; Kevin Eagan et al., "Undergraduate Teaching Faculty: The 2013–2014 HERI Faculty Survey" (Los Angeles: Los Angeles Higher Education Research Institute, UCLA, 2014).

10. National Science Foundation, "2016 Doctorate Recipients from U.S. Universities" (Washington, DC: National Center for Science and Engineering Statistics, Directorate for Social, Behavioral and Economic Sciences, March 2018).

11. Martin A. Schwartz, "The Importance of Stupidity in Scientific Research," *Journal of Cell Science* 121, no. 11 (June 1, 2008): 1771, https:// doi.org/10.1242/jcs.033340.

12. Jerrell D. Coggburn and Stephen R. Neely, "Publish or Perish? Examining Academic Tenure Standards in Public Affairs and Administration Programs," *Journal of Public Affairs Education* 21, no. 2 (June 1, 2015):

199–214, https://doi.org/10.1080/15236803.2015.12001828; Clark G. Ross, "Toward a New Consensus for Tenure in the Twenty-First Century," *Academe*, 2015, www.aaup.org/article/toward-new-consen sus-tenure-twenty-first-century#.W3Rsvy3MwYF.

13. Arthur G. Bedeian, Shannon G. Taylor, and Alan N. Miller, "Publish or Perish: Academic Life as Management Faculty Live It," *Career Development International* 16, no. 5 (September 20, 2011): 422–445, https://doi.org/10.1108/13620431111167751.

14. We know of two exceptions. *The Slow Professor* by Maggie Berg and Barbara Seeber stresses the importance of building unstructured time into research, but the authors' focus is on stress reduction, not creativity. The edited volume *Cultivating Creativity in Methodology and Research: In Praise of Detours* similarly argues about the importance of creative process by telling narrative stories of scholars' practices, but does not provide concrete guidance for those seeking to develop these skills. Maggie Berg and Barbara K. Seeber, *The Slow Professor: Challenging the Culture of Speed in the Academy* (Toronto: University of Toronto Press, 2016); Charlotte Wegener, Ninna Meier, and Elina Maslo, eds., *Cultivating Creativity in Methodology and Research: In Praise of Detours* (Cham, Switzerland: Palgrave Macmillan, 2018).

15. Ray Bradbury, *Zen in the Art of Writing: Releasing the Creative Genius Within You*, Later Printing edn. (New York: Bantam, 1992); Joe Fassler, ed., *Light the Dark: Writers on Creativity, Inspiration, and the Artistic Process* (New York: Penguin Books, 2017); Myron Howard Nadel and Marc Raymond Strauss, *The Dance Experience: Insights into History, Culture and Creativity*, 3rd edn. (Hightstown, NJ: Princeton Book Company, 2014); Edwin E. Catmull and Amy Wallace, *Creativity, Inc.: Overcoming the Unseen Forces That Stand in the Way of True Inspiration* (London: Transworld Publishers Limited, 2014); Julia Cameron, *The Artist's Way: A Spiritual Path to Higher Creativity*, 25th anniversary edn. (New York: Tarcher Perigee, 2016); Bernard Roth, *The Achievement Habit: Stop Wishing, Start Doing, and Take Command of Your Life* (New York, NY: HarperBusiness, 2015); Mihaly Csikszentmihalyi, *Creativity: Flow and the Psychology of Discovery and Invention*, reprint (New York: Harper Perennial, 2013).

16. Amabile et al., "Assessing the Work Environment for Creativity"; Runco and Albert, "Creativity Research"; Sternberg and Lubart, "The Concept of Creativity: Prospects and Paradigms"; Carson, *Your Creative Brain*; Sternberg and Kaufman, Preface.

17. R. Keith Sawyer, *Explaining Creativity: The Science of Human Innovation*, 2nd edn. (Oxford, New York: Oxford University Press, 2012); Howard Gardner and Emily Weinstein, "Creativity," in *The Nature of Human Creativity*, ed. Robert J. Sternberg and James C. Kaufman (Cambridge: Cambridge University Press, 2018), 94–109, https://doi.org/10.1017/9781108185936.002.

18. Sawyer, *Explaining Creativity*, 8.

19. Phelan and Young, "Understanding Creativity in the Workplace," 269; see also Ben Grossman-Kahn, "Defining Creative Confidence," *Children's Creativity Museum Education Blog* (blog), December 27, 2011, http://childrenscreativity.wordpress.com/2011/12/27/defining-creative-confidence/; Tom Kelley and David Kelley, *Creative Confidence: Unleashing the Creative Potential Within Us All* (New York: Drown Business, 2013).

20. Michael L. A. Hsu, Sheng-Tsung Hou, and Hsueh-Liang Fan, "Creative Self-Efficacy and Innovative Behavior in a Service Setting: Optimism as a Moderator," *The Journal of Creative Behavior* 45, no. 4 (December 1, 2011): 258–272, https://doi.org/10.1002/j.2162-6057.2011.tb01430.x; Pamela Tierney and Steven M. Farmer, "Creative Self-Efficacy Development and Creative Performance over Time," *Journal of Applied Psychology* 96, no. 2 (2011): 277–293, https://doi.org/10.1037/a0020952; Shung J. Shinand Jing Zhou, "When Is Educational Specialization Heterogeneity Related to Creativity in Research and Development Teams? Transformational Leadership as a Moderator," *The Journal of Applied Psychology* 92, no. 6 (November 2007): 1709–1721, https://doi.org/10.1037/0021-9010.92.6.1709.

21. Albert Bandura, "Self-Efficacy," in *Encyclopedia of Human Behavior*, ed. V. S. Ramachaudran, vol. 4 (New York: Academic Press, 1994), 71.

22. Carol S. Dweck, *Mindset: The New Psychology of Success* (New York: Random House, 2006).

23. Aaron Hochanadel and Dora Finamore, "Fixed and Growth Mindset in Education and How Grit Helps Students Persist in the Face of Adversity," *Journal of International Education Research* 11, no. 1 (2015): 47–50; Susan A O'Neill, "Developing a Young Musician's Growth Mindset: The Role of Motivation, Self-Theories, and Resiliency," in *Music and the Mind: Essays in Honour of John Sloboda*, ed. Irène Deliège and Jane Davidson (New York: Oxford University Press, 2011), 31–46.

24. Maciej Karwowski, "Creative Mindsets: Measurement, Correlates, Consequences," *Psychology of Aesthetics, Creativity, and the Arts* 8, no. 1 (2014): 62–70, https://doi.org/10.1037/a0034898; Maciej Karwowski et al., "Big Five Personality Traits as the Predictors of Creative Self-Efficacy and Creative Personal Identity: Does Gender Matter?," *The Journal of Creative Behavior* 47, no. 3 (September 1, 2013): 215–232, https://doi.org/10.1002/jocb.32.

25. Peter Medawar, *Pluto's Republic: Incorporating The Art of the Soluble and Induction and Intuition in Scientific Thought*, Later Printing edn. (Oxford: Oxford University Press, 1984), 31.

26. Amanda E. Cravens et al., "Reflecting, Iterating, and Tolerating Ambiguity: Highlighting the Creative Process of Scientific and Scholarly Research for Doctoral Education," *International Journal of Doctoral Studies* 9 (2014): 229–247.

27. Naama Mayseless, Ayelet Eran, and Simone G. Shamay-Tsoory, "Generating Original Ideas: The Neural Underpinning of Originality," *NeuroImage* 116 (August 1, 2015): 232–239, https://doi.org/10.1016/j.neuroimage.2015.05.030; Rex Eugene Jung et al., "The Structure of Creative Cognition in the Human Brain," *Frontiers in Human Neuroscience* 7 (2013), https://doi.org/10.3389/fnhum.2013.00330.

28. Rob Pope, *Creativity: Theory, History, Practice* (London: Routledge, 2005), 63.

29. Plattner, Meinel, and Leifer, *Design Thinking: Understand – Improve – Apply*; Johansson-Sköldberg, Woodilla, and Çetinkaya, "Design Thinking: Past, Present and Possible Futures."

30. Eliza Kienitz et al., "Targeted Intervention to Increase Creative Capacity and Performance: A Randomized Controlled Pilot Study," *Thinking Skills and Creativity* 13 (September 1, 2014): 57–66, https://doi.org/10.1016/j.tsc.2014.03.002; Shelley Goldman et al., "Assessing d.Learning: Capturing the Journey of Becoming a Design Thinker," in *Design Thinking Research: Measuring Performance in Context*, Hasso Plattner, Christoph Meinel, and Larry Leifer, eds., *Understanding Innovation* (Berlin, Heidelberg: Springer Berlin Heidelberg, 2012), 13–33, https://doi.org/10.1007/978-3-642-31991-4_2; Sara L. Beckman and Michael Barry, "Innovation as a Learning Process: Embedding Design Thinking," *California Management Review* 50, no. 1 (October 1, 2007): 25–56, https://doi.org/10.2307/41166415.

31. Maureen Carroll et al., "Destination, Imagination and the Fires Within: Design Thinking in a Middle School Classroom," *International Journal of Art & Design Education* 29, no. 1 (2010): 37–53, https://doi.org/10.1111/j.1476-8070.2010.01632.x.

32. Deana McDonagh and Joyce Thomas, "Rethinking Design Thinking: Empathy Supporting Innovation," *Australasian Medical Journal* 3, no. 8 (2010): 458–464.

33. Joshua Cohen, "Harnessing Mobile Tech and Students to Promote Development in Kenya," March 19, 2012, www.gsb.stanford.edu/news/headlines/cohen-mobile-kenya.html.

34. Terry Anderson and Julie Shattuck, "Design-Based Research A Decade of Progress in Education Research?," *Educational Researcher* 41, no. 1 (January 1, 2012): 16–25, https://doi.org/10.3102/0013189X11428813; Arthur Bakker and Dolly van Eerde, "An Introduction to Design-Based Research with an Example From Statistics Education," in *Approaches to Qualitative Research in Mathematics Education: Examples of Methodology and Methods*, Angelika Bikner-Ahsbahs, Christine Knipping, and Norma Presmeg, eds., *Advances in Mathematics Education* (Dordrecht: Springer Netherlands, 2015), 429–466; Allan Collins, Diana Joseph, and Katerine Bielaczyc, "Design Research: Theoretical and Methodological Issues," *Journal of the Learning Sciences* 13, no. 1 (January 1, 2004): 15–42, https://doi.org/10.1207/s15327809jls1301_2; Feng Wang and Michael J. Hannafin, "Design-Based Research and Technology-Enhanced Learning Environments," *Educational Technology Research and Development* 53, no. 4 (December 1, 2005): 5–23, https://doi.org/10.1007/BF02504682.

35. Nicola Ulibarri et al., "Research as Design: Developing Creative Confidence in Doctoral Students Through Design Thinking," *International Journal of Doctoral Studies* 9 (2014): 249–270.

36. David A. Kolb, *Experiential Learning: Experience as the Source of Learning and Development* (Upper Saddle River, NJ: Pearson Education, 2015).

37. Christopher Johns, *Guided Reflection: Advancing Practice* (Oxford: Blackwell, 2002).

38. K. Anders Ericsson, Ralf T. Krampe, and Clemens Tesch-Römer, "The Role of Deliberate Practice in the Acquisition of Expert Performance," *Psychological Review* 100, no. 3 (1993): 363; K. Anders Ericsson et al., eds.,

The Cambridge Handbook of Expertise and Expert Performance, 2nd edn. (Cambridge: Cambridge University Press, 2018).

39. John Dewey, *Experience and Education* (New York: Collier Books, Macmillan, 1938), 6.

40. Donald A. Schön, *Educating the Reflective Practitioner* (San Francisco: Jossey-Bass, 1990).

41. Jennifer A. Livingston, "Metacognition: An Overview," 2003, https://eric .ed.gov/?id=ED474273; Barbara White and John Frederiksen, "A Theoretical Framework and Approach for Fostering Metacognitive Development," *Educational Psychologist* 40, no. 4 (December 1, 2005): 211–223, https://doi.org/10.1207/s15326985ep4004_3.

42. David Boud, Rosemary Keogh, and David Walker, eds., *Reflection: Turning Experience into Learning* (London: Routledge, 2013).

SECTION I   DEVELOP YOUR CREATIVE ABILITIES

1. *OED Online* (Oxford University Press), www.oed.com.

2. Karin H. James and Laura Engelhardt, "The Effects of Handwriting Experience on Functional Brain Development in Pre-Literate Children," *Trends in Neuroscience and Education* 1, no. 1 (December 1, 2012): 32–42, https://doi.org/10.1016/j.tine.2012.08.001.

3. Dannelle D. Stevens and Joanne E. Cooper, *Journal Keeping: How to Use Reflective Writing for Learning, Teaching, Professional Insight and Positive Change* (Sterling, VA: Stylus Publishing, 2009), 7–8.

4. Stevens and Cooper, *Journal Keeping*, 13.

5. Saleh Mohammad Abu Jado, "The Effect of Using Learning Journals on Developing Self-Regulated Learning and Reflective Thinking among Pre-Service Teachers in Jordan," *Journal of Education and Practice* 6, no. 5 (2015): 89.

6. Leona M. English and Marie A. Gillen, eds., *Promoting Journal Writing in Adult Education: New Directions for Adult and Continuing Education, Number 90* (San Francisco: Jossey-Bass, 2001); Jennifer A. Moon, *Learning Journals* (London: Routledge, 1999).

7. Jado, "The Effect of Using Learning Journals on Developing Self-Regulated Learning and Reflective Thinking among Pre-Service Teachers in Jordan"; Taleb Durgahee, "Reflective Practice: Nursing Ethics through Story Telling," *Nursing Ethics* 4, no. 2 (March 1, 1997): 135–146, https://doi.org/ 10.1177/096973309700400205.

8. Stevens and Cooper, *Journal Keeping*, 5.

9. Stevens and Cooper, *Journal Keeping*, Appendix A.

10. Jado, "The Effect of Using Learning Journals on Developing Self-Regulated Learning and Reflective Thinking among Pre-Service Teachers in Jordan," 89.

11. Joan Bolker, *Writing Your Dissertation in Fifteen Minutes a Day: A Guide to Starting, Revising, and Finishing Your Doctoral Thesis* (New York: Owl Books, 1998), 5.

12. Stuart K. Card, Jock Mackinlay, and Ben Shneiderman, eds., *Readings in Information Visualization: Using Vision to Think* (San Francisco, CA: Morgan Kaufmann, 1999), 6.

13. Lars Björklund, "The Repertory Grid Technique: Making Tacit Knowledge Explicit: Assessing Creative Work and Problem Solving Skills," in *Researching Technology Education: Methods and Techniques*, ed. Howard Middleton (Rotterdam: Sense Publishers, 2008), 46–69, http:// urn.kb.se/resolve?urn=urn:nbn:se:liu:diva-69231.

14. I. Stigliani and D. Ravasi, "Combining Qualitative Methods to Study Collective Cognition in Organizations," in *Handbook of Qualitative Organizational Research: Innovative Pathways and Methods*, ed. E. Elsbach and R. M. Kramer (New York: Routledge, 2016), 445, https://doi .org/10.4324/9781315849072; see also Andy Clark, *Supersizing the Mind: Embodiment, Action, and Cognitive Extension* (Oxford: Oxford University Press, 2010); Andy Clark and David Chalmers, "The Extended Mind," *Analysis* 58, no. 1 (1998): 7–19.

15. Carson, *Your Creative Brain*.

16. Edward R. Tufte, *The Visual Display of Quantitative Information*, 2nd edn. (Cheshire, CT: Graphics Press, 2001).

17. B. Shneiderman, "The Eyes Have It: A Task by Data Type Taxonomy for Information Visualizations," in *Proceedings 1996 IEEE Symposium on Visual Languages*, 1996, 336–343, https://doi.org/10.1109/ VL.1996.545307.

2 MIND YOUR PROCESS AND BE INTENTIONAL

1. Matthew A. Killingsworth and Daniel T. Gilbert, "A Wandering Mind Is an Unhappy Mind," *Science* 330, no. 6006 (November 12, 2010): 932, https:// doi.org/10.1126/science.1192439.

2. Katherine A. MacLean et al., "Intensive Meditation Training Improves Perceptual Discrimination and Sustained Attention," *Psychological*

Science 21, no. 6 (June 2010): 829–839, https://doi.org/10.1177/0956797610371339.

3. Andrew C. Hafenbrack, Zoe Kinias, and Sigal G. Barsade, "Debiasing the Mind Through Meditation: Mindfulness and the Sunk-Cost Bias," *Psychological Science* 25, no. 2 (February 1, 2014): 369–376, https://doi.org/10.1177/0956797613503853.

4. Jonathan Greenberg, Keren Reiner, and Nachshon Meiran, "'Mind the Trap': Mindfulness Practice Reduces Cognitive Rigidity," *PLOS ONE* 7, no. 5 (May 15, 2012): e36206, https://doi.org/10.1371/journal.pone.0036206.

5. Viviana Capurso, Franco Fabbro, and Cristiano Crescentini, "Mindful Creativity: The Influence of Mindfulness Meditation on Creative Thinking," *Frontiers in Psychology* 4 (2014), https://doi.org/10.3389/fpsyg.2013.01020; Lorenza S. Colzato et al., "Prior Meditation Practice Modulates Performance and Strategy Use in Convergent- and Divergent-Thinking Problems," *Mindfulness* 8, no. 1 (February 1, 2017): 10–16, https://doi.org/10.1007/s12671-014-0352-9.

6. J. David Creswell and Emily K. Lindsay, "How Does Mindfulness Training Affect Health? A Mindfulness Stress Buffering Account," *Current Directions in Psychological Science* 23, no. 6 (December 1, 2014): 401–407, https://doi.org/10.1177/0963721414547415; Jenny Gu et al., "How Do Mindfulness-Based Cognitive Therapy and Mindfulness-Based Stress Reduction Improve Mental Health and Wellbeing? A Systematic Review and Meta-Analysis of Mediation Studies," *Clinical Psychology Review* 37, Supplement C (April 1, 2015): 1–12, https://doi.org/10.1016/j.cpr.2015.01.006; Richard J. Davidson et al., "Alterations in Brain and Immune Function Produced by Mindfulness Meditation," *Psychosomatic Medicine* 65, no. 4 (August 2003): 564–570; Lisa Flook et al., "Mindfulness for Teachers: A Pilot Study to Assess Effects on Stress, Burnout, and Teaching Efficacy," *Mind, Brain, and Education* 7, no. 3 (September 1, 2013): 182–195, https://doi.org/10.1111/mbe.12026.

7. Watts and Robertson, "Burnout in University Teaching Staff: A Systematic Literature Review."

8. Baba Shiv, "How Do You Find Breakthrough Ideas? What Neuroscience Tells Us about Getting the Best out of Yourself, Your Colleagues, and the Boss," *Insights by Stanford Business* (blog), October 15, 2013, www.gsb.stanford.edu/insights/baba-shiv-how-do-you-find-breakthrough-ideas.

9. Esther I. de Bruin, Renée Meppelink, and Susan M. Bögels, "Mindfulness in Higher Education: Awareness and Attention in University Students Increase During and After Participation in a Mindfulness Curriculum Course," *Mindfulness* 6 (October 2015): 1137–1142.

10. Delany Dean, "Meditation: Intention, Attention, and Attitude," *KC Mindfulness* (blog), May 11, 2008, https://kcmindfulness.wordpress.com/meditation-intention-attention-and-attitude/.

11. Kristin Neff, *Self-Compassion: The Proven Power of Being Kind to Yourself*, reprint (New York: William Morrow Paperbacks, 2015).

12. Mark Bertin, "Emotional Rescue: Using Mindfulness to Reset Your Reactions," *Mindful: Healthy Mind, Healthy Life* (blog), April 12, 2016, www.mindful.org/emotional-rescue-using-mindfulness-to-reset-your-reactions/; Sharon Salzberg, "Mindfulness and Difficult Emotions," *Tricycle: The Buddhist Review*, Spring 2013, https://tricycle.org/magazine/mindfulness-and-difficult-emotions/.

13. "Guided Meditation and Mindfulness – The Headspace App," Headspace, www.headspace.com, accessed December 5, 2018; "Experience Calm," www.calm.com, accessed December 5, 2018.

14. Jon Kabat-Zinn and Thich Nhat Hanh, *Full Catastrophe Living: Using the Wisdom of Your Body and Mind to Face Stress, Pain, and Illness*, 2nd edn. (New York: Bantam, 2013).

15. Jeremy Adam Smith et al., "The State of Mindfulness Science," *Greater Good Magazine*, December 5, 2017, https://greatergood.berkeley.edu/article/item/the_state_of_mindfulness_science.

16. Jared R. Lindahl et al., "The Varieties of Contemplative Experience: A Mixed-Methods Study of Meditation-Related Challenges in Western Buddhists," *PLOS ONE* 12, no. 5 (May 24, 2017): e0176239, https://doi.org/10.1371/journal.pone.0176239.

17. This exercise was inspired by the Mindfulness-Based Stress Reduction program, which uses a version of this exercise for eating a raisin; for an online script see "Mindfully Eating a Raisin," MBSR Training Online, October 9, 2013, https://mbsrtraining.com/mindfully-eating-a-raisin-exercise/.

18. Exercise adapted from Kelly McGonigal, *The Willpower Instinct: How Self-Control Works, Why It Matters, and What You Can Do to Get More of It* (New York: Avery, 2013).

3   USE EMOTIONS TO DIAGNOSE PROBLEMS AND MOVE FORWARD

1. Medawar, *Pluto's Republic*, 28–41.
2. Laith Al-Shawaf et al., "Human Emotions: An Evolutionary Psychological Perspective," *Emotion Review* 8, no. 2 (April 1, 2016): 173–186, https://doi.org/10.1177/1754073914565518; Joseph E. LeDoux, "Evolution of Human Emotion," *Progress in Brain Research* 195 (2012): 431–442, https://doi.org/10.1016/B978-0-444-53860-4.00021-0.
3. Daniel Kahneman, *Thinking, Fast and Slow* (New York: Farrar, Straus and Giroux, 2011).
4. Gerald L. Clore and Jeffrey R. Huntsinger, "How Emotions Inform Judgment and Regulate Thought," *Trends in Cognitive Science* 11, no. 9 (2007): 393–399, https://doi.org/10.1016/j.tics.2007.08.005.
5. Kahneman, *Thinking, Fast and Slow*; Lily A. Gutnik et al., "The Role of Emotion in Decision-Making: A Cognitive Neuroeconomic Approach towards Understanding Sexual Risk Behavior," *Journal of Biomedical Informatics* 39 (April 7, 2006), https://doi.org/10.1016/j.jbi.2006.03.002.
6. John T. Cacioppo and William Patrick, *Loneliness: Human Nature and the Need for Social Connection* (New York: W. W. Norton & Company, 2008); Matthew D. Lieberman, *Social: Why Our Brains Are Wired to Connect* (New York: Crown, 2013).
7. John A. Bargh, "Our Unconscious Mind: Unconscious Impulses and Desires Impel What We Think and Do in Ways Freud Never Dreamed Of," *Scientific American* 310 (January 2014); Lieberman, *Social*.
8. Daniel Goleman, *Emotional Intelligence* (New York: Bantam Books, 2005).
9. Bessel van der Kolk, *The Body Keeps the Score: Brain, Mind, and Body in the Healing of Trauma*, reprint (New York, NY: Penguin Books, 2015).
10. Iris van de Pavert et al., "The General Relationship between Internalizing Psychopathology and Chronic Physical Health Conditions: A Population-Based Study," *Social Psychiatry and Psychiatric Epidemiology* 52 (2017): 1257–1265, https://doi.org/doi:10.1007/s00127-017-1422-9; see also Nicola S. Schutte et al., "A Meta-Analytic Investigation of the Relationship between Emotional Intelligence and Health," *Personality and Individual Differences* 42 (2007): 921–923, https://doi.org/doi:10.1016/j.paid.2006.09.003.

11. "Mental Health: Degree and Depression," *Nature* 544, no. 7650 (April 20, 2017): 383, https://doi.org/10.1038/nj7650-383a; see also Teresa M Evans et al., "Evidence for a Mental Health Crisis in Graduate Education," *Nature Biotechnology* 36, no. 3 (2018).

12. John D. Mayer and Peter Salovey, "The Intelligence of Emotional Intelligence," *Intelligence* 17, no. 4 (October 1, 1993): 433–442, https://doi.org/10.1016/0160-2896(93)90010-3.

13. Goleman, *Emotional Intelligence.*

14. Rimma Teper, Chen-Bo Zhong, and Michael Inzlicht, "How Emotions Shape Moral Behavior: Some Answers (and Questions) for the Field of Moral Psychology," *Social and Personality Psychology Compass*, September 1, 2015, 1–14, https://doi.org/10.1111/spc3.12154.

15. Neff, *Self-Compassion.*

16. Kristin D. Neff and Roos Vonk, "Self-Compassion Versus Global Self-Esteem: Two Different Ways of Relating to Oneself," *Journal of Personality* 77, no. 1 (2009), https://doi.org/10.1111/j.1467-6494.2008.00537.x.

17. Cacioppo and Patrick, *Loneliness*, 52–72.

18. Schutte et al., "A Meta-Analytic Investigation of the Relationship between Emotional Intelligence and Health."

19. Howe Chern Wan, Luke A. Downey, and Con Stough, "Understanding Non-Work Presenteeism: Relationships between Emotional Intelligence, Boredom, Procrastination and Job Stress," *Personality and Individual Differences* 65 (July 2014): 86–90, https://doi.org/10.1016/j.paid.2014.01.018.

20. Dana L. Joseph et al., "Why Does Self-Reported Emotional Intelligence Predict Job Performance? A Meta-Analytic Investigation of Mixed EI," *Journal of Applied Psychology* 100, no. 2 (2015): 298–342, http://dx.doi.org/10.1037/a0037681.

21. Bill George et al., "Discovering Your Authentic Leadership," *Harvard Business Review* (February 1, 2007), https://hbr.org/2007/02/discovering-your-authentic-leadership.

22. Neff and Vonk, "Self-Compassion Versus Global Self-Esteem: Two Different Ways of Relating to Oneself."

23. Glenn Geher, Kian Betancourt, and Olivia Jewell, "The Link between Emotional Intelligence and Creativity," *Imagination, Cognition and Personality* 37, no. 1 (September 1, 2017): 5–22, https://doi.org/10.1177/0276236617710029.

24. Gloria Barczak, Felicia Lassk, and Jay Mulki, "Antecedents of Team Creativity: An Examination of Team Emotional Intelligence, Team Trust and Collaborative Culture," *Creativity and Innovation Management* 19, no. 4 (December 1, 2010): 332–345, https://doi.org/10.1111/j.1467-8691.2010.00574.x.

25. Jeanne Nakamura and Mihaly Csikszentmihalyi, "The Concept of Flow," in *Oxford Handbook of Positive Psychology*, ed. C.R. Snyder and S.J. Lopez (Oxford: Oxford University Press, 2009).

26. James Clifford and George E. Marcus, eds., *Writing Culture: The Poetics and Politics of Ethnography: A School of American Research, Advanced Seminar* (Berkeley: University of California Press, 1986).

27. Stephen M. Fiore, "Interdisciplinarity as Teamwork: How the Science of Teams Can Inform Team Science," *Small Group Research* 39, no. 3 (June 1, 2008): 251–277, https://doi.org/10.1177/1046496408317797.

28. Robert I. Sutton, *The No Asshole Rule: Building a Civilized Workplace and Surviving One That Isn't*, reprint (New York: Business Plus, 2010).

29. Sheila Jasanoff, *States of Knowledge: The Co-Production of Science and the Social Order* (London; New York: Routledge, 2004); Alan Irwin, *Citizen Science: A Study of People, Expertise and Sustainable Development* (London; New York: Routledge, 2002), https://doi.org/10.4324/9780203202395; Alison M. Meadow et al., "Moving toward the Deliberate Coproduction of Climate Science Knowledge," *Weather, Climate, and Society* 7, no. 2 (April 1, 2015): 179–191, https://doi.org/10.1175/WCAS-D-14-00050.1; Barbara A. Israel et al., "Review of Community-Based Research: Assessing Partnership Approaches to Improve Public Health," *Annual Review of Public Health* 19, no. 1 (1998): 173–202, https://doi.org/10.1146/annurev.publhealth.19.1.173.

30. "About the Great Backyard Bird Count," Audubon, January 21, 2015, www.audubon.org/conservation/about-great-backyard-bird-count.

31. Meredith Gibbs, "Toward a Strategy for Undertaking Cross-Cultural Collaborative Research," *Society & Natural Resources* 14, no. 8 (September 1, 2001): 673–687, https://doi.org/10.1080/08941920120547; Jenny Cameron et al., "Navigating Dilemmas of Community Development: Practitioner Reflections on Working with Aboriginal Communities," *Community Development* 47, no. 4 (July 8, 2016): 546–561, https://doi.org/10.1080/15575330.2016.1205116.

32. Norman K. Denzin and Yvonna S. Lincoln, *The SAGE Handbook of Qualitative Research* (Thousand Oaks, CA: SAGE, 2011).

33. "Bioengineering Students Develop Better Cystic Fibrosis Treatment for Patients On-the-Go," Stanford Byers Center for Biodesign, 2018, http://b iodesign.stanford.edu/our-impact/stories/bioengineering-students-devel op-better-cystic-fibrosis-treatment.html.

34. J. David Creswell et al., "Neural Correlates of Dispositional Mindfulness during Affect Labeling," *Psychosomatic Medicine* 69, no. 6 (August 2007): 560–565, https://doi.org/10.1097/PSY.0b013e3180f6171f; Matthew D. Lieberman et al., "Putting Feelings Into Words," *Psychological Science* 18, no. 5 (May 1, 2007): 421–428, https://doi.org/10.1111/j.1467-9280.20 07.01916.x; Matthew D. Lieberman et al., "Subjective Responses to Emotional Stimuli during Labeling, Reappraisal, and Distraction," *Emotion* 11, no. 3 (June 2011): 468–480, https://doi.org/10.1037/a0023503.

35. Neff, *Self-Compassion*.

36. Rachael E. Jack et al., "Four Not Six: Revealing Culturally Common Facial Expressions of Emotion," *Journal of Experimental Psychology. General* 145, no. 6 (2016): 708–730, https://doi.org/10.1037/xge0000162.

37. Kirsten Weir, "A Complex Emotion," *Monitor on Psychology* 43, no. 10 (November 2012), www.apa.org/monitor/2012/11/emotion.aspx.

38. One caveat: For people dealing with certain mental illnesses or past trauma, there may be actual differences in brain structure or function that influence how events and circumstances are perceived and experienced emotionally (see Kolk, *The Body Keeps the Score*). We are talking here about people who fall into the range of variation generally regarded as normal.

39. William Burnett and David John Evans, *Designing Your Life: How to Build a Well-Lived, Joyful Life* (New York: Alfred A. Knopf, 2016).

40. Adrienne Abramowitz and Howard Berenbaum, "Emotional Triggers and Their Relation to Impulsive and Compulsive Psychopathology," *Personality and Individual Differences* 43, no. 6 (October 1, 2007): 1356–1365, https://doi.org/10.1016/j.paid.2007.04.004; Robert B. Wall, "Tai Chi and Mindfulness-Based Stress Reduction in a Boston Public Middle School," *Journal of Pediatric Health Care* 19, no. 4 (July 1, 2005): 230–237, https://doi.org/10.1016/j.pedhc.2005.02.006.

41. Anne Lamott, *Bird by Bird: Some Instructions on Writing and Life* (New York: Anchor Books, 1995), 25.

42. "Active Listening," U.S. Department of State, www.state.gov/m/a/os/65
759.htm, accessed December 5, 2018; "Active Listening," The University
of Adelaide, www.adelaide.edu.au/writingcentre/sites/default/files/docs/
learningguide-activelistening.pdf.

43. Exercise adapted from Neff, *Self-Compassion*.

44. Original credit for the *Five why's* methodology probably belongs to
Sakichi Toyoda, founder of Toyota Industries. Our team's use of this tool
has been influenced by the Stanford d.school. See also: Warren Berger, *A
More Beautiful Question: The Power of Inquiry to Spark Breakthrough
Ideas* (New York, NY: Bloomsbury USA, 2014), 93; "Design Thinking
Bootleg" (Hasso Plattner Institute of Design at Stanford University, 2017),
https://dschool.stanford.edu/resources/design-thinking-bootleg.

4   SOLVE THE RIGHT PROBLEM

1. Mark A. Runco, *Problem Finding, Problem Solving, and Creativity*
(Norwood, NJ: Ablex Publishing Corporation, 1994).

2. "What Is Problem? Definition and Meaning," BusinessDictionary, www
.businessdictionary.com/definition/problem.html, accessed December 6,
2018.

3. Lisa V. Bardwell, "Problem-Framing: A Perspective on Environmental
Problem-Solving," *Environmental Management* 15, no. 5 (September 1,
1991): 603–612, https://doi.org/10.1007/BF02589620.

4. For more on how problems shape the solutions you might consider, see
Michael Mintrom and Joannah Luetjens, "Policy Entrepreneurs and
Problem Framing: The Case of Climate Change," *Environment and
Planning C: Politics and Space* 35, no. 8 (2017): 1362–1377, https://doi.org/
10.1177/2399654417708440.

5. Kitty Klein and Devon Barnes, "The Relationship of Life Stress to Problem
Solving: Task Complexity and Individual Differences," *Social Cognition*
12, no. 3 (September 1, 1994): 187–204, https://doi.org/10.1521/
soco.1994.12.3.187.

6. Bharat Kumar, Balavenkatesh Kanna, and Suresh Kumar, "The Pitfalls of
Premature Closure: Clinical Decision-Making in a Case of Aortic Dissection,"
BMJ Case Reports (October 7, 2011), https://doi.org/10.1136/bcr.08.2011.4594;
Francesc Borrell-Carrió and Ronald M. Epstein, "Preventing Errors in Clinical
Practice: A Call for Self-Awareness," *The Annals of Family Medicine* 2, no. 4
(July 1, 2004): 310–316, https://doi.org/10.1370/afm.80.

7. Adrian Furnham and Tracy Ribchester, "Tolerance of Ambiguity: A Review of the Concept, Its Measurement and Applications," *Current Psychology* 14, no. 3 (September 1, 1995): 179–199, https://doi.org/10.10 07/BF02686907.

8. David L. McLain, Efstathios Kefallonitis, and Kimberly Armani, "Ambiguity Tolerance in Organizations: Definitional Clarification and Perspectives on Future Research," *Frontiers in Psychology* 6, no. 344 (2015), https://doi.org/10.3389/fpsyg.2015.00344.

9. Furnham and Ribchester, "Tolerance of Ambiguity," 179.

10. Jeffrey L. Herman et al., "The Tolerance for Ambiguity Scale: Towards a More Refined Measure for International Management Research," *International Journal of Intercultural Relations* 34, no. 1 (January 1, 2010): 58–65, https://doi.org/10.1016/j.ijintrel.2009.09.004.

11. Deborah Tegano, "Relationship of Tolerance of Ambiguity and Playfulness to Creativity," *Psychological Reports* 66 (1990): 1047–1056; For a dissenting view, see Peter Merrotsy, "Tolerance of Ambiguity: A Trait of the Creative Personality?," *Creativity Research Journal* 25, no. 2 (2013): 232–237, https://doi.org/10.1080/10400419.2013.783762.

12. Katya Stoycheva, "Tolerance for Ambiguity, Creativity, and Personality," *Bulgarian Journal of Psychology* 1–4 (2010): 178–188; Franck Zenasni, Maud Besançon, and Todd Lubart, "Creativity and Tolerance of Ambiguity: An Empirical Study," *Journal of Creative Behavior* 42, no. 1 (2008): 61–73.

13. Megan L. Endres, Richaurd Camp, and Morgan Milner, "Is Ambiguity Tolerance Malleable? Experimental Evidence with Potential Implications for Future Research," *Frontiers in Psychology* 20, no. 1 (2008): 67–71, https://doi.org/10.1080/10400410701842029.

14. R. Reiter-Palmon, "Problem Finding," in *Encyclopedia of Creativity*, ed. Mark A. Runco and Steven R. Pritzker, 2nd edn. (San Diego: Academic Press, 2011), 258, https://doi.org/10.1016/B978-0-12-375038-9.00180-1.

15. Reiter-Palmon, "Problem Finding."

16. Allen Newell and Herbert Alexander Simon, *Human Problem Solving* (Englewood Cliffs, NJ: Prentice Hall, 1972).

17. Reiter-Palmon, "Problem Finding," 250.

18. Berger, *A More Beautiful Question*, 8.

19. "Embrace: Design for Extreme Affordability," Extreme, https://extreme. stanford.edu/projects/embrace, accessed August 21, 2018; "Home,"

Embrace Innovations, www.embraceinnovations.com, accessed August 21, 2018.

20. Pamela A. Matson, Rosamond Naylor, and Ivan Ortiz-Monasterio, "Integration of Environmental, Agronomic, and Economic Aspects of Fertilizer Management," *Science* 280, no. 5360 (April 3, 1998): 112–115, https://doi.org/10.1126/science.280.5360.112; Pamela A. Matson, ed., *Seeds of Sustainability: Lessons from the Birthplace of the Green Revolution in Agriculture* (Washington: Island Press, 2012).

21. Berger, *A More Beautiful Question.*

22. Carolyn de la Peña, "The Tomato Harvester," Boom California, June 24, 2013, https://boomcalifornia.com/2013/06/24/thinking-through-the-tomato-harvester.

23. Amanda E. Cravens, "Negotiation and Decision Making with Collaborative Software: How MarineMap 'Changed the Game' in California's Marine Life Protected Act Initiative," *Environmental Management* 57, no. 2 (February 2016): 474–497, https://doi.org/10.1007/s00267-015-0615-9.

24. Berger, *A More Beautiful Question,* 71–134.

25. Burnett and Evans, *Designing Your Life,* 74–82.

26. "Design Thinking Bootleg."

27. Eugene Bardach and Eric M. Patashnik, *A Practical Guide for Policy Analysis: The Eightfold Path to More Effective Problem Solving,* 5th edn. (Los Angeles: CQ Press, 2015).

28. Original credit for the Five Why's methodology probably belongs to Sakichi Toyoda, founder of Toyota Industries. Our team's use of this tool has been influenced by the Stanford d.school. See also Berger, *A More Beautiful Question;* "Design Thinking Bootleg."

29. "Powers of Ten and the Relative Size of Things in the Universe," Eames Office, October 9, 2013, www.eamesoffice.com/the-work/powers-of-ten.

30. "Thinking in Powers of Ten," Eames Office, March 25, 2014, www.eamesoffice.com/education/powers-of-ten-2; "Design Thinking Bootleg."

31. "Design Thinking Bootleg."

32. Heath Umbach, "Design Sprint Shorts: Episode 4 – Assumption Storming," Fresh Tilled Soil, April 12, 2017, www.freshtilledsoil.com/design-sprint-shorts-episode-4-assumption-storming.

5 ITERATE AND EXPERIMENT

1. Kelly McGonigal, *The Upside of Stress: Why Stress Is Good for You, and How to Get Good at It* (New York: Avery, 2015).

2. Kris Byron and Shalini Khazanchi, "A Meta-Analytic Investigation of the Relationship of State and Trait Anxiety to Performance on Figural and Verbal Creative Tasks," *Personality and Social Psychology Bulletin* 37, no. 2 (February 1, 2011): 269–283, https://doi.org/10.1177/0146167210392788; Andrew Steptoe, "Negative Emotions in Music Making: The Problem of Performance Anxiety," in *Music and Emotion: Theory and Research*, ed. P. N. Juslin and J. A. Sloboda, Series in Affective Science (New York: Oxford University Press, 2001), 291–307; Karen L. R. Smith, William B. Michael, and Dennis Hocevar, "Performance on Creativity Measures with Examination-taking Instructions Intended to Induce High or Low Levels of Test Anxiety," *Creativity Research Journal* 3, no. 4 (January 1, 1990): 265–280, https://doi.org/10.1080/10400419009534360.

3. "Anxiety and Perfectionism in Academia | PLOS ECR Community," *The Student Blog* (blog), May 17, 2016, https://blogs.plos.org/thestudentblog/2016/05/17/academiaanxiety; Kerry Ann Rockquemore, "Start of Series of Essays about Dealing with Academic Perfectionism," Inside Higher Ed, November 7, 2012, www.insidehighered.com/advice/2012/11/07/start-series-essays-about-dealing-academic-perfectionism.

4. Shulamit Mor et al., "Perfectionism, Control, and Components of Performance Anxiety in Professional Artists," *Cognitive Therapy and Research* 19, no. 2 (April 1, 1995): 207–225, https://doi.org/10.1007/BF02229695.

5. Gary A Davis, "Barriers to Creativity and Creative Attitudes," in *Encyclopedia of Creativity*, ed. Mark A Runco and Steven R. Pritzker, vol. 1 (San Diego: Academic Press, 1999), 165–174; Roger von Oech, *A Whack on the Side of the Head: How You Can Be More Creative*, 2nd edn. (New York: Grand Central Publishing, 2008); James L. Adams, *Conceptual Blockbusting: A Guide to Better Ideas*, 4th edn. (Cambridge, MS: Basic Books, 2001).

6. Amber Simpson and Adam Maltese, "'Failure Is a Major Component of Learning Anything': The Role of Failure in the Development of STEM Professionals," *Journal of Science Education and Technology* 26, no. 2 (April 1, 2017): 223–237, https://doi.org/10.1007/s10956-016-9674-9.

7. Amy Hackney Blackwell and Elizabeth Manar, eds., "Prototype," in *UXL Encyclopedia of Science*, 3rd edn. (Farmington Hills, MI: UXL, 2015), https://bit.ly/2C2zakS; Assistant Secretary for Public Affairs, "Prototyping," Usability.gov, February 19, 2014, www.usability.gov/how-to-and-tools/methods/prototyping.html.

8. William F. McComas, Michael P. Clough, and Hiya Almazroa, "The Role and Character of the Nature of Science in Science Education," in *The Nature of Science in Science Education: Rationales and Strategies*, ed. William F. McComas, Science and Technology Education Library (Dordrecht: Springer Netherlands, 2002), 3–39, https://doi.org/10.1007/0-306-47215-5_1.

9. Claire E. Ashton-James and Tanya L. Chartrand, "Social Cues for Creativity: The Impact of Behavioral Mimicry on Convergent and Divergent Thinking," *Journal of Experimental Social Psychology* 45 (2009): 1036, https://doi.org/10.1016/j.jesp.2009.04.030.

10. Aaron Kozbelt, Ronald A. Beghetto, and Mark A. Runco, "Theories of Creativity," in *The Cambridge Handbook of Creativity*, ed. James C. Kaufman and Robert J. Sternberg (New York: Cambridge University Press, 2010), 20–47.

11. Ashton-James and Chartrand, "Social Cues for Creativity: The Impact of Behavioral Mimicry on Convergent and Divergent Thinking," 1036.

12. Kozbelt, Beghetto, and Runco, "Creativity Research," 32.

13. Arthur Cropley, "In Praise of Convergent Thinking," *Creativity Research Journal* 18, no. 3 (July 1, 2006): 391–404, https://doi.org/10.1207/s15326934crj1803_13; Dean Keith Simonton, "On Praising Convergent Thinking: Creativity as Blind Variation and Selective Retention," *Creativity Research Journal* 27, no. 3 (July 3, 2015): 262–270, https://doi.org/10.1080/10400419.2015.1063877.

14. Joy Paul Guilford, "Creativity," *American Psychologist* 5, no. 9 (1950): 444–454, https://doi.org/10.1037/h0063487; Joy Paul Guilford, *Intelligence, Creativity and Their Educational Implications* (Robert R. Knapp, 1968).

15. Mark A. Runco and Selcuk Acar, "Divergent Thinking as an Indicator of Creative Potential," *Creativity Research Journal* 24, no. 1 (January 1, 2012): 66–75, https://doi.org/10.1080/10400419.2012.652929.

16. Mayseless, Eran, and Shamay-Tsoory, "Generating Original Ideas."

17. Runco and Acar, "Divergent Thinking as an Indicator of Creative Potential"; Joy Paul Guilford and Ralph Hoepfner, *The Analysis of Intelligence* (New York: McGraw-Hill, 1971).

18. Runco and Acar, "Divergent Thinking as an Indicator of Creative Potential."

19. Rex E. Jung et al., "Quantity Yields Quality When It Comes to Creativity: A Brain and Behavioral Test of the Equal-Odds Rule," *Frontiers in Psychology* 6 (2015): 864, https://doi.org/10.3389/fpsyg.2015.00864; Alfredo M. Choperena, "Fast Cycle Time—Driver of Innovation and Quality," *Research-Technology Management* 39, no. 3 (May 1, 1996): 36–40, https://doi.org/10.1080/08956308.1996.11671062.

20. Runco and Acar, "Divergent Thinking as an Indicator of Creative Potential."

21. Steven P. Dow et al., "Prototyping Dynamics: Sharing Multiple Designs Improves Exploration, Group Rapport, and Results," in *Session: Innovation & Design* (Vancouver: CHI 2011, 2011); Rikke Dam and Teo Siang, "Design Thinking: Get Started with Prototyping," The Interaction Design Foundation, www.interaction-design.org/literature/article/design-thinking-get-started-with-prototyping, accessed December 15, 2018.

22. Mark A. Runco and Min Basadur, "Assessing Ideational and Evaluative Skills and Creative Styles and Attitudes," *Creativity and Innovation Management* 2, no. 3 (September 1, 1993): 166–173, https://doi.org/10.1111/j.1467-8691.1993.tb00088.x.

23. Cropley, "In Praise of Convergent Thinking."

24. John F. Feldhusen, "Creativity: A Knowledge Base, Metacognitive Skills, and Personality Factors," *The Journal of Creative Behavior* 29, no. 4 (December 1, 1995): 255–268, https://doi.org/10.1002/j.2162-6057.1995.tb01399.x.

25. Cropley, "In Praise of Convergent Thinking," 399.

26. Cropley, "In Praise of Convergent Thinking," 391.

27. Pradip N. Khandwalla, "An Exploratory Investigation of Divergent Thinking through Protocol Analysis," *Creativity Research Journal* 6, no. 3 (January 1, 1993): 241–259, https://doi.org/10.1080/10400419309534481.

28. Cropley, "In Praise of Convergent Thinking"; Runco and Acar, "Divergent Thinking as an Indicator of Creative Potential."

29. George H. Stankey, Roger N. Clark, and Bernard T. Bormann, "Adaptive Management of Natural Resources: Theory, Concepts, and Management

Institutions," US Department of Agriculture, Forest Service, Pacific Northwest Research Station, 2005, www.fs.fed.us/pnw/pubs/pnw_gtr654 .pdf.

30. Cravens, "Negotiation and Decision Making with Collaborative Software."

31. For instance, Nicole Ardoin and colleagues developed an experimental protocol with a pilot study at a local California beach, then conducted a revised version of the experiment in the Galapagos. See Mele Wheaton et al., "Using Web and Mobile Technology to Motivate Pro-Environmental Action after a Nature-Based Tourism Experience," *Journal of Sustainable Tourism* 24, no. 4 (April 2, 2016): 594–615, https://doi.org/10.1080/0966 9582.2015.1081600; Nicole M. Ardoin et al., "Post-Trip Philanthropic Intentions of Nature-Based Tourists in Galapagos," *Journal of Ecotourism* 15, no. 1 (January 2, 2016): 21–35, https://doi.org/10.1080/ 14724049.2016.1142555.

32. Warren Berger, "The Secret Phrase Top Innovators Use," *Harvard Business Review*, September 17, 2012, https://hbr.org/2012/09/the-secre t-phrase-top-innovato.

33. Michael Marinello, "In Search Of Better Brainstorming Through A Two Step Process" (Masters Thesis, Arizona State University, 2013), https://repository .asu.edu/attachments/110638/content/Marinello_asu_0010N_12917.pdf.

34. Burnett and Evans, *Designing Your Life*, 63–86.

35. Mark S. Beasley and J. Gregory Jenkins, "A Primer for Brainstorming Fraud Risks," *Journal of Accountancy*, December 1, 2003, www.journalofac countancy.com/issues/2003/dec/aprimerforbrainstormingfraudrisks. html.

36. Alex F. Osborn, *Applied Imagination: Principles and Procedures of Creative Thinking* (New York: Charles Scribner's Sons, 1953), 300–301.

37. Jonah Lehrer, "Groupthink," *The New Yorker*, January 23, 2012, www.n ewyorker.com/magazine/2012/01/30/groupthink.

38. Scott G. Isaksen, *A Review of Brainstorming Research: Six Critical Issues for Inquiry* (Buffalo, NY: Creative Problem Solving Group – Buffalo, June 1998), https://pdfs.semanticscholar.org/4abc/961cb62e8b230 f9683125e984eec3550caa4.pdf.

39. Eric F. Rietzschel, Bernard A. Nijstad, and Wolfgang Stroebe, "Productivity Is Not Enough: A Comparison of Interactive and Nominal Brainstorming Groups on Idea Generation and Selection," *Journal of*

Experimental Social Psychology 42 (2006): 244–251, https://doi.org/10.1 016/j.jesp.2005.04.005.

40. Michael Diehl and Wolfgang Stroebe, "Productivity Loss in Brainstorming Groups: Toward the Solution of a Riddle," *Journal of Personality and Social Psychology* 53, no. 3 (1987): 497–509, https://doi.org/10.1037/0022- 3514.53.3.497; Beasley and Jenkins, "A Primer for Brainstorming Fraud Risks"; Nicholas Kohn and Steven Smith, "Collaborative Fixation: Effects of Others' Ideas on Brainstorming," *Applied Cognitive Psychology* 25 (2010): 359–371, https://doi.org/10.1002/acp.1699.

41. Robert I. Sutton and Andrew Hargadon, "Brainstorming Groups in Context: Effectiveness in a Product Design Firm," *Administrative Science Quarterly* 41, no. 4 (1996): 685–718, https://doi.org/10.2307/2393872.

42. Bob Sutton, "Why The New Yorker's Claim That Brainstorming 'Doesn't Work' Is An Overstatement And Possibly Wrong," *Bob Sutton* (blog), January 26, 2012, https://bit.ly/2TbGAg9.

43. Joseph F. Brazel, Tina D. Carpenter, and J. Gregory Jenkins, "Auditors' Use of Brainstorming in the Consideration of Fraud: Reports from the Field," *The Accounting Review* 85, no. 4 (2010): 1273–1301.

44. Paul Paulus and Vincent Brown, "Toward More Creative and Innovative Group Idea Generation: A Cognitive-Social-Motivational Perspective of Brainstorming," *Social and Personality Psychology Compass* 1, no. 1 (2007): 248–265, https://doi.org/10.1111/j.1751-9004.2007.00006.x.

45. Beasley and Jenkins, "A Primer for Brainstorming Fraud Risks."

46. Matthew Feinberg and Charlan Nemeth, "The 'Rules' of Brainstorming: An Impediment to Creativity?" (Berkeley, CA: UC Berkeley: Institute for Research on Labor and Employment, July 28, 2008), https://escholarship .org/uc/item/69j9g0cg.

47. Kelly Leonard and Tom Yorton, *Yes, And: How Improvisation Reverses "No, But" Thinking and Improves Creativity and Collaboration – Lessons from The Second City* (HarperBusiness, 2015).

48. Barry Schwartz, *The Paradox of Choice: Why More Is Less*, 2nd edn. (New York: Ecco, 2016).

49. Blackwell and Manar, "Prototype"; Assistant Secretary for Public Affairs, "Prototyping."

50. Stanford University Medical Center, "Unexpected Brain Structures Tied to Creativity, and to Stifling It," ScienceDaily, May 28, 2015, www.scien cedaily.com/releases/2015/05/150528084158.htm.

51. Roth, *The Achievement Habit*.

52. Kyra Bobinet, *Well Designed Life: 10 Lessons in Brain Science & Design Thinking for a Mindful, Healthy, & Purposeful Life* (Walnut Creek, CA: engagedIN Press, 2015).

53. McGonigal, *The Willpower Instinct*.

54. Bobinet, *Well Designed Life*.

55. Dow et al., "Prototyping Dynamics: Sharing Multiple Designs Improves Exploration, Group Rapport, and Results."

56. Simpson and Maltese, "Failure Is a Major Component of Learning Anything."

57. Mark D. Cannon and Amy C. Edmondson, "Failing to Learn and Learning to Fail (Intelligently): How Great Organizations Put Failure to Work to Innovate and Improve," *Long Range Planning* 38 (2005): 301, https://doi.org/10.1016/j.lrp.2005.04.005.

58. Cannon and Edmondson, "Failing to Learn and Learning to Fail (Intelligently): How Great Organizations Put Failure to Work to Innovate and Improve."

59. Cannon and Edmondson, "Failing to Learn and Learning to Fail (Intelligently): How Great Organizations Put Failure to Work to Innovate and Improve," 302.

60. Cannon and Edmondson, "Failing to Learn and Learning to Fail (Intelligently): How Great Organizations Put Failure to Work to Innovate and Improve"; Daniel Goleman, *Vital Lies, Simple Truths: The Psychology of Self-Deception* (New York: Touchstone, 1996); Shelley E. Taylor, *Positive Illusions* (New York: Basic Books, 1991).

61. Schwartz, "The Importance of Stupidity in Scientific Research."

62. Catherine Brady, *Elizabeth Blackburn and the Story of Telomeres: Deciphering the Ends of DNA* (Cambridge, MA: The MIT Press, 2009).

63. "Andrew Wiles: What Does It Feel Like to Do Maths?" plus.maths.org, December 1, 2016, https://plus.maths.org/content/andrew-wiles-what-does-if-feel-do-maths.

64. Dweck, *Mindset*.

65. Noelle Nelson, Selin A. Malkoc, and Baba Shiv, "Emotions Know Best: The Advantage of Emotional versus Cognitive Responses to Failure," *Journal of Behavioral Decision Making* 31, no. 1 (January 1, 2018): 40–51, https://doi.org/10.1002/bdm.2042.

66. Melanie Stefan, "A CV of Failures," *Nature* 468, no. 7322 (November 17, 2010): 467–467, https://doi.org/10.1038/nj7322-467a.

67. Dow et al., "Prototyping Dynamics: Sharing Multiple Designs Improves Exploration, Group Rapport, and Results."

SECTION II CULTIVATE CONDITIONS THAT SUPPORT CREATIVITY

1. Csikszentmihalyi, *Creativity*, 1.

6 CHOOSE YOUR LANGUAGE AND STORIES

1. Penelope Eckert, *Linguistic Variation as Social Practice* (Malden, Mass: Wiley-Blackwell, 2000); Deborah Schiffrin, *Approaches to Discourse* (Oxford, UK: Wiley-Blackwell, 1994); W. Peter Robinson and Howard Giles, eds., *The New Handbook of Language and Social Psychology* (Chichester, England: Wiley, 2001).

2. Lynda D. McNeil, "Homo Inventans: The Evolution of Narrativity," *Language & Communication* 16, no. 4 (October 1, 1996): 331–360, https://doi.org/10.1016/S0271-5309(96)00025-0.

3. John E. Joseph, *Language and Identity – National, Ethnic, Religious* (London: Palgrave Macmillan UK, 2004), 15.

4. Julie Goldstein, Jules Davidoff, and Debi Roberson, "Knowing Color Terms Enhances Recognition: Further Evidence from English and Himba," *Journal of Experimental Child Psychology* 102, no. 2 (February 1, 2009): 219–238, https://doi.org/10.1016/j.jecp.2008.06.002.

5. Guillaume Thierry et al., "Unconscious Effects of Language-Specific Terminology on Preattentive Color Perception," *Proceedings of the National Academy of Sciences* 106, no. 11 (March 17, 2009): 4567–4570, https://doi.org/10.1073/pnas.0811155106.

6. Anthony J. Sanford and Catherine Emmott, *Mind, Brain and Narrative* (Cambridge University Press, 2012).

7. McNeil, "Homo Inventans"; David Herman, "Narratology as a Cognitive Science," *Image & Narrative: Online Magazine of the Visual Narrative*, no. 1 (September 2000): 1.

8. H. Porter Abbott, *The Cambridge Introduction to Narrative*, 2nd edn. (Cambridge; New York: Cambridge University Press, 2008), 3; Ann R. Eisenberg, "Learning to Describe Past Experiences in Conversation,"

Discourse Processes 8, no. 2 (April 1, 1985): 177–204, https://doi.org/10
.1080/01638538509544613.

9. Abbott, *The Cambridge Introduction to Narrative*, 2–3.

10. Peter Baldock, *The Place of Narrative in the Early Years Curriculum: How the Tale Unfolds* (London; New York: Routledge, 2006), 17–38.

11. Ronald J. Berger and Richard Quinney, eds., *Storytelling Sociology: Narrative as Social Inquiry* (Boulder, CO: Lynne Rienner Pub, 2004), 4.

12. "Story | Definition of Story in English by Oxford Dictionaries," Oxford Dictionaries | English, https://en.oxforddictionaries.com/definition/stor y, accessed December 12, 2018.

13. A phrase is simply a statement – several words joined together. A narrative is a sequence of events, generally conveying some causal linkages. A frame is a particular way of representing an event, highlighting certain components while obscuring others. And a script is a story that a person has been socialized to believe. See Sanford and Emmott, *Mind, Brain and Narrative*, 2; Robert M. Entman, *Projections of Power: Framing News, Public Opinion, and U.S. Foreign Policy* (Chicago: University of Chicago Press, 2004), 26; Keith V. Bletzer and Mary P. Koss, "Narrative Constructions of Sexual Violence as Told by Female Rape Survivors in Three Populations of the Southwestern United States: Scripts of Coercion, Scripts of Consent," *Medical Anthropology* 23, no. 2 (April 1, 2004): 113–156, https://doi.org/10.1080/01459740490448911.

14. Sanford and Emmott, *Mind, Brain and Narrative*.

15. Randy Olson, *Houston, We Have a Narrative: Why Science Needs Story*, reprint (Chicago: University of Chicago Press, 2015); Joshua Schimel, *Writing Science: How to Write Papers That Get Cited and Proposals That Get Funded* (Oxford; New York: Oxford University Press, 2011); Michael F. Dahlstrom, "Using Narratives and Storytelling to Communicate Science with Nonexpert Audiences," *Proceedings of the National Academy of Sciences* 111, no. Supplement 4 (September 16, 2014): 13614–13620, https://doi.org/10.1073/pnas.1320645111.

16. Aaron T. Beck et al., *Cognitive Therapy of Depression* (New York: The Guilford Press, 1987), 4; Michelle G. Craske, *Cognitive-Behavioral Therapy*, 2nd edn. (Washington, DC: American Psychological Association, 2017).

17. Michael White and David Epston, *Narrative Means to Therapeutic Ends* (New York: W. W. Norton & Company, 1990); Catrina Brown and Tod

Augusta-Scott, *Narrative Therapy: Making Meaning, Making Lives* (Thousand Oaks, CA: SAGE Publications, Inc, 2006).

18. Steven M. Herman, "The Relationship Between Therapist–Client Modality Similarity and Psychotherapy Outcome," *The Journal of Psychotherapy Practice and Research*, no. 1 (1998): 56–64.

19. Lisa Feldman Barrett, Kristen A. Lindquist, and Maria Gendron, "Language as Context for the Perception of Emotion," *Trends in Cognitive Sciences* 11, no. 8 (August 1, 2007): 330, https://doi.org/10.101 6/j.tics.2007.06.003.

20. Andrea M. Moore and Gina G. Barker, "Confused or Multicultural: Third Culture Individuals' Cultural Identity," *International Journal of Intercultural Relations* 36, no. 4 (July 1, 2012): 553–562, https://doi.org/ 10.1016/j.ijintrel.2011.11.002.

21. Sara Speybroeck et al., "The Role of Teachers' Expectations in the Association between Children's SES and Performance in Kindergarten: A Moderated Mediation Analysis," *PLoS ONE* 7, no. 4 (April 10, 2012), htt ps://doi.org/10.1371/journal.pone.0034502.

22. Anna P. Goddu et al., "Do Words Matter? Stigmatizing Language and the Transmission of Bias in the Medical Record," *Journal of General Internal Medicine* 33, no. 5 (May 1, 2018): 685–691, https://doi.org/10.1007/s1160 6-017-4289-2.

23. A possible exception is instances of the deepest, earliest, or most traumatic stories that become encoded in the body and emotional memories. See Kolk, *The Body Keeps the Score.*

24. Alvaro Pascual-Leone et al., "The Plastic Human Brain Cortex," *Annual Review of Neuroscience* 28, no. 1 (2005): 377–401, https://doi.org/10.114 6/annurev.neuro.27.070203.144216.

25. Rick Hanson, *Hardwiring Happiness: The New Brain Science of Contentment, Calm, and Confidence* (New York: Harmony, 2013); Rick Hanson and Richard Mendius, *Buddha's Brain: The Practical Neuroscience of Happiness, Love & Wisdom* (Oakland: New Harbinger Publications, 2009); Linda Graham, *Bouncing Back: Rewiring Your Brain for Maximum Resilience and Well-Being* (Novato, California: New World Library, 2013).

26. Pascual-Leone et al., "The Plastic Human Brain Cortex."

27. Graham, *Bouncing Back*, 91–92.

28. Andrew J. Reagan et al., "The Emotional Arcs of Stories Are Dominated by Six Basic Shapes," *EPJ Data Science* 5, no. 1 (December 2016): 31, https://doi.org/10.1140/epjds/s13688-016-0093-1.

29. Salman Rushdie, "Excerpts From Rushdie's Address: 1,000 Days 'Trapped Inside a Metaphor,'" *The New York Times*, December 12, 1991, http://movies2.nytimes.com/books/99/04/18/specials/rushdie-address.html.

30. Renee Liang, ed., *New Beginnings: New Kiwi Women Write Their Stories* (Auckland, New Zealand: Monster Fish Publishing, 2013).

31. Kolk, *The Body Keeps the Score*, 240–244.

32. Dominique Morisano et al., "Setting, Elaborating, and Reflecting on Personal Goals Improves Academic Performance," *The Journal of Applied Psychology* 95, no. 2 (March 2010): 255–264, https://doi.org/10.1037/a0018478.

33. Timothy D. Wilson, *Redirect: Changing the Stories We Live By*, reprint (New York, NY: Back Bay Books, 2015); Kirsten Weir, "Revising Your Story," *Monitor on Psychology* 43, no. 3 (March 2012): 28.

34. Cited in Tara Parker-Pope, "Writing Your Way to Happiness," *Well: The New York TImes* (blog), January 19, 2015, https://well.blogs.nytimes.com/2015/01/19/writing-your-way-to-happiness.

35. David Edwards, *Art Therapy* (London; Thousand Oaks: SAGE Publications Ltd, 2004); Michael Franklin, "Art Therapy and Self-Esteem," *Art Therapy* 9, no. 2 (April 1, 1992): 78–84, https://doi.org/10.1080/07421656.1992.10758941; Sarah C. Slayton, Jeanne D'Archer, and Frances Kaplan, "Outcome Studies on the Efficacy of Art Therapy: A Review of Findings," *Art Therapy* 27, no. 3 (January 1, 2010): 108–118, https://doi.org/10.1080/07421656.2010.10129660; Deirdre Heenan, "Art as Therapy: An Effective Way of Promoting Positive Mental Health?," *Disability & Society* 21, no. 2 (March 1, 2006): 179–191, https://doi.org/10.1080/09687590500498143.

36. Edwards, *Art Therapy*, 9.

37. Eckert, *Linguistic Variation as Social Practice*.

38. Christopher J. Bryan et al., "Motivating Voter Turnout by Invoking the Self," *Proceedings of the National Academy of Sciences* 108, no. 31 (August 2, 2011): 12653–12656, https://doi.org/10.1073/pnas.1103343108.

39. Livingston, "Metacognition"; White and Frederiksen, "A Theoretical Framework and Approach for Fostering Metacognitive Development."

40. Cravens et al., "Reflecting, Iterating, and Tolerating Ambiguity: Highlighting the Creative Process of Scientific and Scholarly Research for Doctoral Education," 238.

41. Pauline Rose Clance and Suzanne Ament Imes, "The Imposter Phenomenon in High Achieving Women: Dynamics and Therapeutic Intervention," *Psychotherapy: Theory, Research & Practice* 15, no. 3 (1978): 241–247, https://doi.org/10.1037/h0086006; Rachel Herrmann, "Impostor Syndrome Is Definitely a Thing," *The Chronicle of Higher Education*, November 16, 2016, www.chronicle.com/article/Impostor-S yndrome-Is/238418.

42. Leah Cannon, "How Many PhD Graduates Become Professors?" Life Science Network, September 15, 2016, www.nsf.gov/statistics/srvydocto rates; "Doctoral Students' Career Expectations: Principles and Responsibilities" (The Royal Society, December 18, 2014), https://doi.org/ 10.1098/report.2014.0001.

7 MANAGE YOUR ENERGY

1. "Definition of Energy in English by Oxford Dictionaries," Oxford Dictionaries | English, accessed September 28, 2018, https://en.oxforddic tionaries.com/definition/energy.

2. Melissa S. Cardon et al., "The Nature and Experience of Entrepreneurial Passion," *Academy of Management Review* 34, no. 3 (July 1, 2009): 511– 532, https://doi.org/10.5465/amr.2009.40633190; Xiao-Ping Chen, Xin Yao, and Suresh Kotha, "Entrepreneur Passion And Preparedness In Business Plan Presentations: A Persuasion Analysis of Venture Capitalists' Funding Decisions," *Academy of Management Journal* 52, no. 1 (February 1, 2009): 199–214, https://doi.org/10.5465/amj.2009.36462018.

3. Christine Porath et al., "Thriving at Work: Toward Its Measurement, Construct Validation, and Theoretical Refinement," *Journal of Organizational Behavior* 33, no. 2 (February 1, 2012): 250–275, https://doi .org/10.1002/job.756.

4. Ronit Kark and Abraham Carmeli, "Alive and Creating: The Mediating Role of Vitality and Aliveness in the Relationship between Psychological Safety and Creative Work Involvement," *Journal of Organizational Behavior* 30, no. 6 (August 1, 2009): 785–804, https://doi.org/10.1002/jo b.571; Leanne Atwater and Abraham Carmeli, "Leader–Member Exchange, Feelings of Energy, and Involvement in Creative Work," *The Leadership Quarterly* 20, no. 3 (June 1, 2009): 264–275, https://doi.org/10.1016/j.lea qua.2007.07.009; Carsten K. W. De Dreu, Matthijs Baas, and Bernard A. Nijstad, "Hedonic Tone and Activation Level in the Mood-Creativity Link:

Toward a Dual Pathway to Creativity Model," *Journal of Personality and Social Psychology* 94, no. 5 (May 2008): 739–756, https://doi.org/10.1037/0022-3514.94.5.739.

5. Charlotte Fritz, Chak Fu Lam, and Gretchen M. Spreitzer, "It's the Little Things That Matter: An Examination of Knowledge Workers' Energy Management," *Academy of Management Perspectives* 25, no. 3 (August 1, 2011): 28–39, https://doi.org/10.5465/amp.25.3.zol28.

6. Gretchen M. Spreitzer, Chak Fu Lam, and Ryan W. Quinn, "Human Energy in Organizations," in *The Oxford Handbook of Positive Organizational Scholarship*, ed. Gretchen M. Spreitzer and Kim S. Cameron (Oxford, UK: Oxford University Press, 2011), https://doi.org/10.1093/oxfordhb/9780199734610.013.0012.

7. Stephen Kaplan, "Meditation, Restoration, and the Management of Mental Fatigue," *Environment and Behavior* 33, no. 4 (July 1, 2001): 480–506, https://doi.org/10.1177/00139160121973106; M. Muraven and R. F. Baumeister, "Self-Regulation and Depletion of Limited Resources: Does Self-Control Resemble a Muscle?," *Psychological Bulletin* 126, no. 2 (March 2000): 247–259.

8. Spreitzer, Lam, and Quinn, "Human Energy in Organizations."

9. Robert E. Thayer, "Energy, Tiredness, and Tension Effects of a Sugar Snack versus Moderate Exercise," *Journal of Personality and Social Psychology* 52, no. 1 (January 1987): 119–125.

10. These categories follow common trends in the literature, although different scholars use different terminology. For instance, Cole et al. (2012) use the terms behavioral, cognitive, and affective energy. For our purposes, we follow Shraga and Shirom (2009) and Spreitzer et al. (2011). Michael S. Cole, Heike Bruch, and Bernd Vogel, "Energy at Work: A Measurement Validation and Linkage to Unit Effectiveness," *Journal of Organizational Behavior* 33, no. 4 (May 1, 2012): 445–467, https://doi.org/10.1002/job.759; Ofira Shraga and Arie Shirom, "The Construct Validity of Vigor and Its Antecedents: A Qualitative Study," *Human Relations* 62, no. 2 (February 1, 2009): 271–291, https://doi.org/10.1177/0018726708100360; Spreitzer, Lam, and Quinn, "Human Energy in Organizations."

11. Spreitzer, Lam, and Quinn, "Human Energy in Organizations."

12. Robert E. Thayer, *The Biopsychology of Mood and Arousal* (Oxford, New York: Oxford University Press, 1990).

13. Robert E. Thayer, *Calm Energy: How People Regulate Mood with Food and Exercise* (Oxford, New York: Oxford University Press, 2003).

14. Thayer, *Calm Energy*.

15. Verena Steiner, *Energiekompetenz: Produktiver denken, wirkungsvoller arbeiten, entspannter leben* (München: Pendo, 2005).

16. Rosa Levandovski, Etianne Sasso, and Maria Paz Hidalgo, "Chronotype: A Review of the Advances, Limits and Applicability of the Main Instruments Used in the Literature to Assess Human Phenotype," *Trends in Psychiatry and Psychotherapy* 35, no. 1 (2013): 3–11; J. A. Horne and O. Ostberg, "A Self-Assessment Questionnaire to Determine Morningness-Eveningness in Human Circadian Rhythms," *International Journal of Chronobiology* 4, no. 2 (1976): 97–110.

17. Horne and Ostberg, "A Self-Assessment Questionnaire to Determine Morningness-Eveningness in Human Circadian Rhythms."

18. O. Östberg, "Zur Typologie der circadianen Phasenlage," in *Biologische Rhythmen und Arbeit: Bausteine zur Chronobiologie und Chronohygiene der Arbeitsgestaltung*, ed. Gunther Hildebrandt (Vienna: Springer Vienna, 1976), 117–137, https://doi.org/10.1007/978-3-7091-844 2-4_13.

19. Horne and Ostberg, "A Self-Assessment Questionnaire to Determine Morningness-Eveningness in Human Circadian Rhythms"; Michael Breus and Mehmet C. Oz, *The Power of When: Discover Your Chronotype – and the Best Time to Eat Lunch, Ask for a Raise, Have Sex, Write a Novel, Take Your Meds, and More* (New York: Little, Brown and Company, 2016).

20. McGonigal, *The Willpower Instinct*.

21. D. F. Dinges et al., "Temporal Placement of a Nap for Alertness: Contributions of Circadian Phase and Prior Wakefulness," *Sleep* 10, no. 4 (August 1987): 313–329.

22. Ned Herrmann, *The Creative Brain*, 2nd edn. (Lake Lure, N.C.: Brain Books, 1989).

23. Drake Baer, "How Dali, Einstein, And Aristotle Perfected The Power Nap," Fast Company, December 10, 2013, www.fastcompany.com/3023 078/how-dali-einstein-and-aristotle-perfected-the-power-nap.

24. Spreitzer, Lam, and Quinn, "Human Energy in Organizations."

25. Robert L. Cross, Andrew Parker, and Rob Cross, *The Hidden Power of Social Networks: Understanding How Work Really Gets Done in*

Organizations (Boston, MA: Harvard Business Review Press, 2004); Rob Cross, Wayne Baker, and Andrew Parker, "What Creates Energy in Organizations?" *MIT Sloan Management Review*, July 15, 2003, https://sloanreview.mit.edu/article/what-creates-energy-in-organizations.

26. Elaine Hatfield, John T. Cacioppo, and Richard L. Rapson, *Emotional Contagion* (Cambridge: Cambridge University Press, 1993); Sigal G. Barsade, "The Ripple Effect: Emotional Contagion and Its Influence on Group Behavior," *Administrative Science Quarterly* 47, no. 4 (December 1, 2002): 644–675, https://doi.org/10.2307/3094912.

27. Bradley P. Owens et al., "Relational Energy at Work: Implications for Job Engagement and Job Performance," *The Journal of Applied Psychology* 101, no. 1 (January 2016): 35–49, https://doi.org/10.1037/apl0000032.

28. Randall Collins, "Emotional Energy as the Common Denominator of Rational Action," *Rationality and Society* 5, no. 2 (April 1, 1993): 203–230, https://doi.org/10.1177/1043463193005002005.

29. Glen A. Nix et al., "Revitalization through Self-Regulation: The Effects of Autonomous and Controlled Motivation on Happiness and Vitality," *Journal of Experimental Social Psychology* 35, no. 3 (May 1, 1999): 266–284, https://doi.org/10.1006/jesp.1999.1382; Spreitzer, Lam, and Quinn, "Human Energy in Organizations."

30. Jacqueline C. Vischer, "Towards an Environmental Psychology of Workspace: How People Are Affected by Environments for Work," *Architectural Science Review* 51, no. 2 (June 1, 2008): 97–108, https://doi.org/10.3763/asre.2008.5114; Jungsoo Kim and Richard de Dear, "Nonlinear Relationships between Individual IEQ Factors and Overall Workspace Satisfaction," *Building and Environment* 49 (March 1, 2012): 33–40, https://doi.org/10.1016/j.buildenv.2011.09.022.

31. Jan Dul and Canan Ceylan, "The Impact of a Creativity-Supporting Work Environment on a Firm's Product Innovation Performance," *Journal of Product Innovation Management* 31, no. 6 (November 1, 2014): 1254–1267, https://doi.org/10.1111/jpim.12149.

32. Scott Doorley and Scott Witthoft, *Make Space: How to Set the Stage for Creative Collaboration* (Hoboken, NJ: John Wiley & Sons, 2012).

33. Rebecca Solnit, *Wanderlust: A History of Walking* (New York: Penguin Books, 2001).

8 MAKE YOUR RESEARCH A TEAM SPORT

1. Amy C. Edmondson, Vanessa Hart, and Edgar H. Schein, *Teaming: How Organizations Learn, Innovate, and Compete in the Knowledge Economy* (San Francisco: Jossey-Bass, 2012).

2. Sawyer, *Explaining Creativity*.

3. Paul B. Paulus, "Groups, Teams, and Creativity: The Creative Potential of Idea-Generating Groups," *Applied Psychology* 49, no. 2 (April 1, 2000): 237–262, https://doi.org/10.1111/1464-0597.00013; Carmit T. Tadmor et al., "Beyond Individual Creativity: The Superadditive Benefits of Multicultural Experience for Collective Creativity in Culturally Diverse Teams," *Journal of Cross-Cultural Psychology* 43, no. 3 (April 1, 2012): 384–392, https://doi.org/10.1177/0022022111435259.

4. You-Na Lee, John P. Walsh, and Jian Wang, "Creativity in Scientific Teams: Unpacking Novelty and Impact," *Research Policy* 44, no. 3 (April 1, 2015): 684–697, https://doi.org/10.1016/j.respol.2014.10.007.

5. Liz Mineo, "Over Nearly 80 Years, Harvard Study Has Been Showing How to Live a Healthy and Happy Life," *Harvard Gazette* (blog), April 11, 2017, https://bit.ly/2eGEsqq.

6. Clance and Imes, "The Imposter Phenomenon in High Achieving Women."

7. Richard Osbaldiston and John Paul Schott, "Environmental Sustainability and Behavioral Science: Meta-Analysis of Proenvironmental Behavior Experiments," *Environment and Behavior* 44, no. 2 (March 1, 2012): 257–299, https://doi.org/10.1177/0013916511402673.

8. Sohui Lee and Chris Golde, "Starting an Effective Dissertation Writing Group," Hume Writing Center, Stanford University, n.d., https://unmgrc.u nm.edu/writing-groups/documents/starting-an-effective-group.pdf; Bolker, *Writing Your Dissertation in Fifteen Minutes a Day*; Noreen B. Garman and Maria Piantanida, *The Authority to Imagine: The Struggle Toward Representation in Dissertation Writing* (New York: Peter Lang, 2006).

9. Jill E. Perry-Smith and Pier Vittorio Mannucci, "From Creativity to Innovation: The Social Network Drivers of the Four Phases of the Idea Journey," *Academy of Management Review* 42, no. 1 (2015), https://doi .org/10.5465/amr.2014.0462.

10. Baba Shiv, The Sanwa Bank, Ltd, Professor of Marketing, Stanford Graduate School of Business, personal communication.

11. Robert D. Putnam, *Bowling Alone: The Collapse and Revival of American Community* (New York, NY: Simon & Schuster, 2000); Seok-Woo Kwon

and Paul S. Adler, "Social Capital: Maturation of a Field of Research," *Academy of Management Review* 39, no. 4 (October 1, 2014): 412–422, https://doi.org/10.5465/amr.2014.0210.

12. Lee and Golde, "Starting an Effective Dissertation Writing Group"; Bolker, *Writing Your Dissertation in Fifteen Minutes a Day.*

13. Katleen E. M. de Stobbeleir, Susan J. Ashford, and Dirk Buyens, "Self-Regulation of Creativity at Work: The Role of Feedback-Seeking Behavior in Creative Performance," *Academy of Management Journal* 54, no. 4 (August 1, 2011): 811–831, https://doi.org/10.5465/amj.2011.64870144.

14. Lee, Walsh, and Wang, "Creativity in Scientific Teams."

15. "Design Thinking Bootleg."

16. "Design Thinking Bootleg."

17. Russ Schoen, "PPCO: Why It Is a Great Creative Power Tool to Take out for a Spin This Summer," *Innovation Bound* (blog), August 2, 2012, http://innovationbound.tumblr.com/post/28560980922/ppco-why-it-is-a-great-creative-power-tool-to.

18. Inspired by the NCFDD mentoring map, "National Center for Faculty Development and Diversity," https://www.facultydiversity.org, accessed December 12, 2018.

9   INTEGRATE THE CREATIVE ABILITIES, PART I

1. Marshall B. Rosenberg and Deepak Chopra, *Nonviolent Communication: A Language of Life*, 3rd edn. (Encinitas, CA: PuddleDancer Press, 2015).

2. If you find yourself in this situation, you can find resources online at Isaiah Hankel, "What To Do When Your Academic Advisor Mistreats You," Cheeky Scientist, November 18, 2014, https://cheekyscientist.com/academic-advisor; Stanford Office of the Vice Provost for Graduate Education, "Advising and Mentoring," https://vpge.stanford.edu/academic-guidance/advising-mentoring, accessed September 10, 2018; Kathryn R. Wedemeyer-Strombel, "Graduate School Should Be Challenging, Not Traumatic," *The Chronicle of Higher Education*, November 14, 2018, www.chronicle.com/article/Graduate-School-Should-Be/245028.

3. See "Student–Advisor Expectation Scales" PDF, Stanford Office of the Vice Provost for Graduate Education, "Advising Practices and Resources," https://vpge.stanford.edu/academic-guidance/advising-mentoring/advising-0, accessed August 23, 2018.

4. Roger Fisher, William L. Ury, and Bruce Patton, *Getting to Yes: Negotiating Agreement Without Giving In*, revised (New York: Penguin Books, 2011), 58–81.

5. However, it is worth noting that the burdens of taking on extra advising work are not distributed fairly among faculty. Research shows that women tend to pick up the slack for absentee or ineffective advisors far more often than men, and they do not receive any additional compensation for it. See Katrin Schultheiss, "Ghost Advising," *The Chronicle of Higher Education*, March 4, 2018, www.chronicle.com/article/Ghost-Advising/242729.

6. John P. Robinson and Ann Bostrom, "The Overestimated Workweek? What Time Diary Measures Suggest," *Monthly Labor Review* 117, no. 8 (1994): 11–23.

7. John Robinson and Geoffrey Godbey, *Time for Life: The Surprising Ways Americans Use Their Time* (University Park: Penn State University Press, 2008); Robinson and Bostrom, "The Overestimated Workweek?"

8. Tony Schwartz and Catherine McCarthy, "Manage Your Energy, Not Your Time," *Harvard Business Review*, October 1, 2007, https://hbr.org/2007/10/manage-your-energy-not-your-time.

9. Matthew Walker, *Why We Sleep: Unlocking the Power of Sleep and Dreams* (New York: Scribner, 2017).

10. Harvard Health Publishing, "Eating to Boost Energy," Harvard Health, www.health.harvard.edu/healthbeat/eating-to-boost-energy, accessed December 12, 2018.

11. Rachel Dresdale, "Work–Life Balance Vs. Work–Life Integration, Is There Really A Difference?" Forbes, December 18, 2016, https://bit.ly/2kaTbyR; "Work/Life Integration," Human Resources, Berkeley-Haas, www.haas.berkeley.edu/human-resources/life-integration, accessed December 12, 2018.

12. Bobinet, *Well Designed Life*.

13. McGonigal, *The Willpower Instinct*.

14. "Design Thinking Bootleg."

10 INTEGRATE THE CREATIVE ABILITIES, PART II

1. Our favorites include Paul J. Silva, *How to Write a Lot: A Practical Guide to Productive Academic Writing* (Washington, DC: American Psychological Association, 2007); Schimel, *Writing Science*.

2. For guidance, see Bolker, *Writing Your Dissertation in Fifteen Minutes a Day*.

3. Scott A. Bollens, *Trajectories of Conflict and Peace: Jerusalem and Belfast Since 1994* (Oxford: Routledge, 2018).

4. Lauren E. Oakes, *In Search of the Canary Tree: The Story of a Scientist, a Cypress, and a Changing World* (New York: Basic Books, 2018).

5. Myra Strober, *Interdisciplinary Conversations: Challenging Habits of Thought* (Stanford, CA: Stanford University Press, 2010).

6. Amy Edmondson, "Psychological Safety and Learning Behavior in Work Teams," *Administrative Science Quarterly* 44, no. 2 (June 1, 1999): 350–383, https://doi.org/10.2307/2666999.

7. Amy C. Edmondson, "Psychological Safety, Trust, and Learning in Organizations: A Group-Level Lens," in *Trust and Distrust in Organizations: Dilemmas and Approaches*, ed. Roderick M. Kramer and Karen S. Cook, The Russell Sage Foundation Series on Trust (New York: Russell Sage Foundation, 2004), 239–272.

8. National Cancer Institute, "NIH 'Partner Agreement' – Collaboration 'Prenup' Questionnaire," Team Science Toolkit, October 15, 2012, https://teamsciencetoolkit.cancer.gov/Public/TSResourceTool.aspx?tid=1&rid=776.

9. National Cancer Institute, "Team Diagnostic Survey – Based on Hackman's Model of Effective Teams," October 25, 2010, https://teamsciencetoolkit.cancer.gov/Public/TSResourceTool.aspx?tid=1&rid=60; Ruth Wageman, J. Richard Hackman, and Erin Lehman, "Team Diagnostic Survey: Development of an Instrument," *The Journal of Applied Behavioral Science* 41, no. 4 (December 1, 2005): 373–398, https://doi.org/10.1177/0021886305281984.

10. National Cancer Institute, "Team Science Toolkit," www.teamsciencetoolkit.cancer.gov/Public/Home.aspx, accessed August 26, 2018.

11. Sarah Rose Cavanagh, *The Spark of Learning: Energizing the College Classroom with the Science of Emotion* (Morgantown, West Virginia: West Virginia University Press, 2016).

12. "Design Thinking Bootleg."

13. Carissa Carter and Scott Doorley, "2018 Is the Year of the Intangibles," BRIGHT Magazine, January 3, 2018, https://brightthemag.com/education-design-thinking-intangible-ambiguity-stanford-cd09f959a83c.

14. Mark A. Runco and Gayle Dow, "Problem Finding," in *Encyclopedia of Creativity*, ed. Mark A. Runco and Steven R. Pritzker, vol. 2 (San Diego: Academic Press, 1999), 433–435.

15. Ulibarri et al., "Research as Design: Developing Creative Confidence in Doctoral Students Through Design Thinking."

11   THIRTY-DAY CREATIVITY IN RESEARCH PROGRAM FOR INDIVIDUALS OR GROUPS

1. For ideas on how to set group norms and ground rules, see "Tool: Creating Norms," *Learning Forward* (blog), https://bit.ly/2aJgGeJ, accessed September 14, 2018; Roger Schwarz, "8 Ground Rules for Great Meetings," *Harvard Business Review*, June 15, 2016, https://hbr.org/2016/06/8-groun d-rules-for-great-meetings.
2. Gretchen Rubin, *Better Than Before: What I Learned About Making and Breaking Habits – to Sleep More, Quit Sugar, Procrastinate Less, and Generally Build a Happier Life*, reprint (New York: Broadway Books, 2015).
3. "Design Thinking Bootleg."
4. Katia Levecque et al., "Work Organization and Mental Health Problems in PhD Students," *Research Policy* 46, no. 4 (May 1, 2017): 868–879, https:// doi.org/10.1016/j.respol.2017.02.008; Evans et al., "Evidence for a Mental Health Crisis in Graduate Education."
5. "About," Stanford d.school, https://dschool.stanford.edu/about, accessed December 12, 2018.

12   MENTORING CREATIVITY

1. Barbara E. Lovitts, "Being a Good Course-taker Is Not Enough: A Theoretical Perspective on the Transition to Independent Research," *Studies in Higher Education* 30, no. 2 (2005): 137–154, https://doi.org/10 .1080/03075070500043093; Barbara E. Lovitts, "The Transition to Independent Research: Who Makes It, Who Doesn't, and Why," *The Journal of Higher Education* 79, no. 3 (2008): 296–325, https://doi.org/10.1353/jhe.0.0006.
2. Susan K. Gardner, "'What's Too Much and What's Too Little?': The Process of Becoming an Independent Researcher in Doctoral Education," *The Journal of Higher Education* 79, no. 3 (2008): 326–350, https://doi.org/10.1 353/jhe.0.0007; Lucinda S Spaulding and Amanda J Rockinson-Szapkiw, "Hearing Their Voices: Factors Doctoral Candidates Attribute to Their Persistence," *International Journal of Doctoral Studies* 7 (2012): 199–219; Lovitts, "Being a Good Course-taker Is Not Enough."
3. Lovitts, "The Transition to Independent Research," 304–305.

4. Anne Lee, "How Are Doctoral Students Supervised? Concepts of Doctoral Research Supervision," *Studies in Higher Education* 33, no. 3 (June 1, 2008): 267–281, https://doi.org/10.1080/03075070802049202; Sarah J. Fletcher and Carol A. Mullen, eds., *SAGE Handbook of Mentoring and Coaching in Education* (Los Angeles: SAGE Publications, 2012).

5. Benita J. Barnes and Ann E. Austin, "The Role of Doctoral Advisors: A Look at Advising from the Advisor's Perspective," *Innovative Higher Education* 33, no. 5 (March 1, 2009): 297–315, https://doi.org/10.1007/s10755-008-90 84-x; Michael W. Galbraith and Waynne B. James, "Mentoring by the Community College Professor: One Role Among Many," *Community College Journal of Research and Practice* 28, no. 8 (September 1, 2004): 689–701, https://doi.org/10.1080/10668920390277073.

6. Carol A. Mullen, "Mentoring: An Overview," in *SAGE Handbook of Mentoring and Coaching in Education*, ed. Sarah J. Fletcher and Carol A. Mullen (Los Angeles: SAGE Publications, 2012), 7.

7. Michael T. Nettles and Catherine M. Millett, *Three Magic Letters: Getting to Ph.D.* (Baltimore: Johns Hopkins University Press, 2006), 98.

8. Virginia Gewin, "Learning to Mentor," *Nature* 436, no. 7049 (July 20, 2005): 436–437, https://doi.org/10.1038/nj7049-436a.

9. Lee, "How Are Doctoral Students Supervised?"; Gill Turner, "Learning to Supervise: Four Journeys," *Innovations in Education and Teaching International* 52, no. 1 (January 2, 2015): 86–98, https://doi.org/10.1080/14703297.2014.981840.

10. Ken Young and Sandra Harris, "Mentoring Doctoral Students in Educational Leadership Programs," in *SAGE Handbook of Mentoring and Coaching in Education*, ed. Sarah J. Fletcher and Carol A. Mullen (Los Angeles: SAGE Publications, 2012), 339–353.

11. Catherine A. Hansman, "Empowerment in the Faculty-Student Mentoring Relationship," in *SAGE Handbook of Mentoring and Coaching in Education*, ed. Sarah J. Fletcher and Carol A. Mullen (Los Angeles: SAGE Publications, 2012), 369; Benita J. Barnes, Elizabeth A. Williams, and Martha L. A. Stassen, "Dissecting Doctoral Advising: A Comparison of Students' Experiences across Disciplines," *Journal of Further and Higher Education* 36, no. 3 (August 1, 2012): 309–331, https://doi.org/10.1080/0309877X.2011.614933; Laura Lunsford, "Doctoral Advising or Mentoring? Effects on Student Outcomes," *Mentoring and*

Tutoring: Partnership in Learning 20, no. 2 (May 1, 2012): 251–270, https://doi.org/10.1080/13611267.2012.678974.

12. Hansman, "Empowerment in the Faculty-Student Mentoring Relationship," 373.

13. Hansman, 373.

14. Galbraith and James, "Mentoring by the Community College Professor."

15. Galbraith and James, 696.

16. Galbraith and James, 695.

17. Cravens et al., "Reflecting, Iterating, and Tolerating Ambiguity: Highlighting the Creative Process of Scientific and Scholarly Research for Doctoral Education."

18. Duncan Nulty, Margaret Kiley, and Noel Meyers, "Promoting and Recognising Excellence in the Supervision of Research Students: An Evidence-based Framework," *Assessment and Evaluation in Higher Education* 34, no. 6 (December 1, 2009): 693–707, https://doi.org/10.1080/02602930802474193.

19. Barnes, Williams, and Stassen, "Dissecting Doctoral Advising"; Lunsford, "Doctoral Advising or Mentoring?"; Antoinette McCallin and Shoba Nayar, "Postgraduate Research Supervision: A Critical Review of Current Practice," *Teaching in Higher Education* 17, no. 1 (February 1, 2012): 63–74, https://doi.org/10.1080/13562517.2011.590979.

20. Susan A. Ambrose et al., *How Learning Works: Seven Research-Based Principles for Smart Teaching* (San Francisco, CA: Jossey-Bass, 2010).

21. Ambrose et al.

22. Bolker, *Writing Your Dissertation in Fifteen Minutes a Day.*

23. Brené Brown, *Daring Greatly: How the Courage to Be Vulnerable Transforms the Way We Live, Love, Parent, and Lead* (New York: Avery, 2012).

24. Schwartz, "The Importance of Stupidity in Scientific Research."

13 CONCLUSION

1. www.creativityinresearch.org.

2. Cravens et al., "Reflecting, Iterating, and Tolerating Ambiguity: Highlighting the Creative Process of Scientific and Scholarly Research for Doctoral Education."

3. Ulibarri et al., "Research as Design: Developing Creative Confidence in Doctoral Students Through Design Thinking."

4. Ericsson, Krampe, and Tesch-Römer, "The Role of Deliberate Practice in the Acquisition of Expert Performance"; Ericsson et al., *The Cambridge Handbook of Expertise and Expert Performance.*

APPENDIX COMPARING CREATIVE PRACTICE
        FRAMEWORKS

1. Adams, *Conceptual Blockbusting.*
2. Robert Epstein, *Cognition, Creativity, and Behavior: Selected Essays* (Westport, Conn: Praeger, 1996).
3. Oech, *A Whack on the Side of the Head.*
4. Carson, *Your Creative Brain.*
5. Carson, 17.
6. Carson, 16.
7. Carson, 18.
8. Carson, 17.
9. Keith Sawyer, *Zig Zag: The Surprising Path to Greater Creativity* (San Francisco: Jossey-Bass, 2013).
10. Sawyer, 9.
11. Matthew A. Cronin and Jeffrey Loewenstein, *The Craft of Creativity* (Stanford, CA: Stanford Business Books, 2018).
12. Cronin and Loewenstein, 19.
13. Carissa Carter, "Let's Stop Talking about THE Design Process," *Stanford d.School* (blog), October 6, 2016, https://medium.com/stanford-d-school/lets-stop-talking-about-the-design-process-7446e52c13e8; Carter and Doorley, "2018 Is the Year of the Intangibles."
14. IDEO.ORG, "Mindsets," Design Kit, accessed October 15, 2018, http://www.designkit.org/mindsets.
15. Carter and Doorley, "2018 Is the Year of the Intangibles."
16. Carter and Doorley.
17. Fiona Kennedy, Brigid Carroll, and Joline Francoeur, "Mindset Not Skill Set: Evaluating in New Paradigms of Leadership Development," *Advances in Developing Human Resources* 15, no. 1 (February 1, 2013): 10–26, https://doi.org/10.1177/1523422312466835.
18. Interestingly, Sawyer's earlier book *Explaining Creativity* is all about teams and collaboration. He argues that creativity is fundamentally social, and that "everyday creativity emerges unpredictably from a group of people." However, none of these ideas is emphasized in *Zig Zag*; he mentions collaboration only briefly as part of Make. Sawyer, *Explaining Creativity.*

List of Exercises

Index